C000125605

. JENN

Jenny Landreth is a writer and script editor. She has written two guide books, *Great London Trees* and *Swimming London*, and her book *Swell: A Waterbiography* was shortlisted for the William Hill Sports Book of the Year and was a *Sunday Times* Book of the Year in 2017. Jenny comes from a family of am-dram devotees, and lives in London.

JENNY LANDRETH

Break a Leg

A memoir, manifesto and celebration
of amateur theatre

VINTAGE

1 3 5 7 9 10 8 6 4 2

Vintage is part of the Penguin Random House group of companies
whose addresses can be found at global.penguinrandomhouse.com

Penguin
Random House
UK

Copyright © Jenny Landreth 2020

Jenny Landreth has asserted her right to be identified as the
author of this Work in accordance with the Copyright,
Designs and Patents Act 1988

First published in Vintage in 2021
First published in hardback by Chatto & Windus in 2020

penguin.co.uk/vintage

A CIP catalogue record for this book is available
from the British Library

ISBN 9781529110524

Printed and bound in Great Britain by Clays Ltd, Elcograf S.p.A.

The authorised representative in the EEA is Penguin Random House
Ireland, Morrison Chambers, 32 Nassau Street, Dublin D02 YH68.

Penguin Random House is committed to a sustainable future
for our business, our readers and our planet. This book is
made from Forest Stewardship Council® certified paper.

MIX
Paper from
responsible sources
FSC® C018179

For my mum

My mum in 1966, doing her best 'furious on the phone acting'. (She had four small children at this point, so the 'furious' part came easily.)

BREAK A LEG

Contents

CONTENTS

Prologue

Many people have an idea of what they think amateur theatre is. Some of those ideas are based on preconceptions, some are based on snobbery, and some are gleaned from how amateur theatre is portrayed in other media, including plays. If you are one of the many thousands of people who partake in am-dram in the UK, you may well be familiar with some of the assumptions, and I'm pretty certain they won't reflect your experience. If you are outside this world, you might approach it with a whole heap of prejudices. But amateur theatre might not be what you think it is. So, though it's a risk to start a book with a cliché, I am going to go on a journey. I'm going on a journey to discover amateur theatre, as if I were some kind of Christopher Columbus in brutally heavy stage make-up. Actually, it's more of a rediscovery, because I'm going back to my roots.

If you are hoping for a book that laughs at am-dram's shonky sets and home-made costumes, you've come to the wrong place. There will certainly be some taking the piss, because who doesn't love to poke fun at pretensions and luvvies? Who doesn't get a vicarious thrill when things go wrong? Celebrating things going wrong is practically a national sport, we almost like it better than when things go right. If I do mock, amateur theatre is certainly mature and resilient enough to take it. But mocking is not the purpose I'm setting out with; one of the things this book will do is take amateur theatre seriously. Why? Because amateurs are really serious about their work, even though they are mostly doing it for fun. This has got to be a laugh, hasn't it, otherwise what on earth is the point?

As I started my research, a friend said to me, 'I hope this isn't going to be all froth and light.' Oh no, no, no, I quickly replied, putting on my serious face, there will be politics and history, it will be terribly grave and full of significance. Then I thought to myself, what if it *were* all froth and light? What would be so bad about that, if that's what thousands of people love? I took the comment to be a specific dig at popular culture, at 'light' entertainment. It's a weird phenomenon, that the more popular things are, the more they are derided. 'Popular culture' is not something you're supposed to enjoy, *if you know anything*. You're supposed to have 'popular' taste educated out of you. There is definitely a class element at play here, and amateur theatre suffers for that.

Fortunately, 'froth and light' would not be an accurate description of what amateur theatre actually *is*. Yes, some of it is very frivolous, but alongside that there is plenty of work whose intent is higher than 'mere' entertainment – because there are many different types of amateur theatre. It is not one thing. It is not just silly plays in shabby rooms. Sometimes, it can be experimental, and interesting, and challenging. Sometimes, it is absolutely not to my taste, but neither is all professional theatre. There's a whole raft of people making all sorts of amateur theatre in all sorts of places, for the sheer hell of it. Or heaven, rather, because the word 'joy' will absolutely flow through this book, to the point of being annoying. After all, the word 'amateur', with its origins in Latin, Italian and French, means 'from the heart', and there is an abundance of heart in here.

Today, to call someone an amateur is to present them as second-rate, and I want us to look again at that connotation. Some amateurs work very hard *not* to use the word, describing what they do as 'non-professional' or 'community' theatre instead. They feel that 'amateur' describes some other thing, which they are not, something church-hally, or twee. But in refusing the word, they're really not helping. If amateurs won't accept the word 'amateur', why should anyone else? And similarly, some people reject the term 'am-dram' as being demeaning. I make no apologies for using both amateur and am-dram in this book – call it an act of reclamation.

This is a book that puts the amateur back into theatre history. It's about people, and plays, and buildings. It's my story, but it will contain many other people's stories, too. How amateur theatre shaped them, helped them, saved them. Amateur theatre, in all of its forms, has a really strong hold on these islands. This book will tell us why.

NB: Left to my own devices, I would always call both women and men 'actors', because they are equal. In this book, I've used 'actress' where women specifically refer to themselves (or are referred to, in quotes) in that way. Where women call themselves 'actors', I have done the same. Occasionally, using 'actress' has been the path of least confusion in the text, and sometimes I've done it where it would be anachronistic to call them actors.

CHAPTER 1

Setting the Scene

This story starts in 1955, six years before I was born. There was a big freeze, a newspaper strike, Churchill resigned, and for the month of June the UK was in an official State of Emergency because of ongoing rail disputes. It was a summer of heatwave, drought, ITV and the first fish fingers. In July, Ruth Ellis became the last woman in Britain to be hanged, and in September, James Dean died in a car crash, aged twenty-four. He was one year older than my mother but, she told me, she had never really liked him anyway. I think I know why – he'd have been too blatant for her tastes; she was more of a Gregory Peck fan, or Tommy Steele. 'He's still going, you know.'

In 1955, my mum, Hazel Nicholson, was living with her parents in Kingstanding, Birmingham, and had recently graduated in English lit from Manchester University. She was a keen participant in the arts. She went to plays, films and concerts several times a week, hopping buses all over the place, the 33 or the 107 from Beggars Bush. She went to the Pavilion in Boldmere, the Scala in Stockland Green, the Empress in

Sutton and the Gaumont in town. To the Arena Theatre in
Cannon Hill, the (old) Rep and Stratford. She saw everything;
modern, classics, Shakespeare, and things that sound truly
terrible with titles like *The Noble Spaniard* and *Demetrius the
Gladiator* and *The Silver Curlew*. I know these titles, where
she saw them and with whom because she kept a diary and
wrote two-line reviews of everything. My mum did not sit on
the fence.

> Mon 14 Feb 1955: Saw 'Three Coins in a Fountain'. Beau-
> tiful scenery. Story puerile.
> Thurs 5 May 1955: Stratford – 'Twelfth Night' – Lau-
> rence [Olivier] as Malvolio – delightful. Heavy nasal
> tones. Viola – Vivien Leigh – adequate. Poetic moments
> rather false. Wonderful evening.

(Vivien Leigh, adequate! It's no wonder she rejected James
Dean's ostentatious smouldering.)

> Wed 5 Oct 1955: Flicks to see 'Not as a Stranger'. R.
> Mitchum somehow good, in spite of expressionless face.

I was enjoying her reviews. Here was confirmation, if needed,
that the apple does not fall far from the tree. But one entry
really stood out:

> 9 June 1955: Play – went quite well. Bit slow. B'ham Post
> there. Played 'cat's cradle' with Philip!

There's a lot in that sentence that's revealing, not least the final, innocent exclamation mark. You can see from her diary entries that my mother kept her powder very, very dry. She didn't scatter her punctuation, or her feelings, with abandon; they were both rationed. That's not surprising, given that rationing itself had only ended in Britain the year before; people were used to keeping any kind of hunger buttoned down. For my mum to have given something, or someone, the extravagant flourish of an exclamation mark could only mean that it, or he, had significance.

Hindsight also helps.

In a parallel universe to the one in which *Rebel Without a Cause* was heating other young people to a frenzy, my mother was getting her kicks playing cat's cradle with Philip. From our modern perspective you have to work quite hard to understand this, to get a sense of the frisson cat's cradle might have caused between two consenting adults. Is that what counted for fun in the Midlands in the 1950s? Because it doesn't exactly reek of allure, tangling wool round your fingers and hoping it will be seductive. But maybe that's cynical. Maybe it is actually thrilling, to meet someone's eyes over a string pattern, to slide your fingers in under the other person's, make the string taut, then slip it from one to the other, accidentally touching skin as you go. It certainly worked here. Philip was the dentist Mum would marry two years later – my dad.

In 1955, my mum and dad met as members of an amateur theatre company, Highbury Little Theatre, on the outskirts of

Birmingham, between Erdington and its slightly posher neighbour Sutton Coldfield. The cat's cradle was happening in the green room, where the cast hung out when they weren't required onstage. '*The Voysey Inheritance*, I think it was, the first play I started to know him. I played his wife, and I died in childbirth. So that was nice.'

Mum had joined Highbury in 1954 and is still a member in 2020. That makes sixty-six years and counting in the same company, working in every possible capacity, from lead roles to making tea and everything in between. All that drama, all her life, and to this day you will never find her flinging around an unnecessary bit of punctuation.

The game of cat's cradle led to Philip giving her lifts home from the theatre in his car. It would have been a terrible car, he only ever had terrible cars, but it was *his* terrible car. Things moved up a notch, according to Mum's diary, with him 'happening to be in the area' and dropping in on Christmas Day, behaviour which I find a bit appalling, just spontaneously rocking up on this most auspicious day. They wrote to each other all the time, letters passing between them like delicious contraband, each one noted meticulously in her diary.

Early on in their dating life they went to a dinner dance together, and my mum's place card read 'Mrs Philip Landreth' – an innocent mistake but one she saw as a clear message. It felt right. She knew then, she told me, that they'd get married. They did, in 1957, and Highbury remained at the centre of their lives. They had their first child, my sister Sarah, in 1959, then me in '61, then Ruth and Madeleine, also equally spaced.

After that, they mostly took turns to be in plays, to avoid paying for babysitters. Money was always tight, the cars were always terrible. They were memorably cast together in *The Lion in Winter* in 1979, when Madeleine was fourteen and didn't need babysitting. Dad played Henry II and Mum was Eleanor of Aquitaine. A lion cub on a very long lead was borrowed from the zoo to be used in a local newspaper photo, with my parents in the most regal robes the theatre could muster. Lion in winter, you see? This is the kind of stuff publicists dream of.

Highbury was the bedrock of our lives. I am a child of amateur theatre, it raised me, it's in my DNA. But Highbury is not just significant in my life, it's also significant in the history of amateur theatre. It was called a 'Little' theatre and was a founder member of the Little Theatre Guild because it has its own permanent theatre building. A place that was built entirely with the voluntary labour of its members, as recorded in a book by two of Highbury's founders, Mollie Randall and John English. They wrote earnestly, and touchingly:

It is a truism that people and not a building make a theatre. But if a group of competent people, enthusiastic about their art, work together sufficiently hard and for a sufficiently long time, a theatre of real strength will grow from them.

The words 'competent' and 'sufficiently' don't exactly scream 'gaiety of nations', but they reflect the intentions, which were

5

honourable and serious. They were lofty from the off; Highbury's founding group had formed in 1924, with their first play-reading of *X=O*, a one-act, blank-verse drama by John Drinkwater, about the meaninglessness and absurdity of war. If not exactly a barrel of laughs, at least it sounds true to their brand.

In a disused wooden mission hut in Sheffield Road, bought for £200, the 'theatre of real strength' that became Highbury Little Theatre was started. The first bricks were laid in September 1937, the first boards nailed to the stage in 1940, and carpets and seating rescued from Birmingham's bombed-out Prince of Wales Theatre were installed soon after. The first production, *Arms and the Man*, opened on Friday 22 May 1942. War years, you'll note. War might have slowed the players, but it didn't stop them. The site was long and thin, and therefore so was the theatre. Each season they chose four plays from distinct categories: one important new play; an international classic; one that was simply a good piece of theatre; and one English classic, linked to their student group. 'The Highbury Little Theatre,' John and Mollie wrote, 'is primarily devoted to the presentation of plays that cannot normally be seen in the commercial theatre.' Plays like Jean-Paul Sartre's *Huis Clos*, lots of Anton Chekhov and Jean Anouilh, and that classic sixteenth-century English comedy, *Gammer Gurton's Needle*. (No, nor me.) If we need an analogy, Highbury wanted to be BBC4, whereas the big regional theatres and the West End were definitely the shiny-floored ITV. A tiny bit snobbish? Can you almost see the black polo-neck jumpers? I love thinking about them, this gang of sincere intellectuals, giving their all for the arts in the 1940s. Talking the talk, then actually building a theatre with their own hands. By 1947, when Mollie and John first recorded their history in this small hardback volume, the core membership was one hundred strong, and audience numbers stood at a whopping 3,500. Alongside the regular productions and student group, there was a Sunday club, which gave concerts and lectures, and a film group, which had the same purpose as the main theatre – to show films that were not widely available at commercial cinemas. Its aims were to make art, not money; to tell stories of real worth and meaning. On the one hand, it took itself terribly seriously. And on the other – as is clear from the photographic evidence, the stories and the diary entries – everyone seemed to be having a real laugh.

That my parents met at Highbury is not, it turns out, that unusual. Even at this one small theatre in the West Midlands there are other couples who met and married, like Rob and Ros Jones who got together in 1970. Ros told me how they'd both joined one summer, when Rob was put to work painting the ladies' dressing rooms and she was given the job of painting the men's loos front of house. It was her first encounter with a urinal and might have dented her illusion that amateur show business is all glamour. For the theatre's production of *The Crucible*, in which Rob had one line as a guard, Ros was drafted in at the last minute to do props, when the regular person suddenly walked out; she quickly had to learn how to make manacles out of baked-bean tins and parchment out of tea-soaked paper. It was a steep learning curve. In one scene, 'John Proctor was in his cell, and he was supposed to be eating a dish of rabbit stew lovingly brought in by his wife. I used oxtail soup instead of stew but forgot to change the props from fork to spoon, so he was trying to make a moving speech eating stew while watching soup draining through his fork. He came offstage asking where I was, as he wanted to kill me.'

Fortunately, it was just the dress rehearsal, so Ros lived to tell the tale. The day after the play finished, Rob rang to ask her out, and though I'm really reluctant to quote Shakespeare, all's well that ends well. It only makes me cringe a tiny bit, these years later, that Rob played my mum's son in *The Lion in Winter*, and Ros played the role of my dad's mistress.

While the stories of my parents and couples like Rob and Ros are predominantly of romance, there is potentially another narrative. I used the words 'amateur theatre' to a friend and her instant response was 'ah, the knocking shop of doom', which hinted at something I wasn't sure I wanted to hear. I'd been hoping for tales of stage love and skipping through the final curtain together, but her experience, through her parents' local group, was all destroyed marriages and illicit shagging behind the scenery. Amateur theatre has many reputations that are worth challenging, but I talked to a lot of amateurs for this book and came across no other examples that reflect this particular experience. Perhaps that's because 'have you got any good stories about shagging that shouldn't have happened?' is too bold a question for an interview situation.

So, I decided this notion belonged to an era of suburban pampas grass and car keys in bowls, and tiptoed quietly away.

In 1955, when my parents were tantalising each other, Highbury's green room was actually less a room and more a corridor out to the back of the theatre. There were bench seats along each side, and black-framed cast photos and newspaper cuttings hung on nicotine-yellow walls. An old kettle and mismatched cups were stacked in somebody's old kitchen cupboard, and everything was scruffy and chipped. 'The green room then . . .' Mum remembered, 'I mean, you could live in it now.' Could I? I wanted to go back there, to find out.

CHAPTER 2

Never Work With Children

'Did you play an instrument as a child?' my friend Justin asked me recently. Piano, I said, recalling the lessons I had every Friday afternoon from a woman called Mrs Pollock who rapped the top of my head with a wooden ruler in time to the music. I gave up piano lessons when I was barely through Grade 1, because the timing clashed with *The Flintstones* on TV and I couldn't bear to miss it. 'Did your parents make you perform when guests came round?' Justin asked next, perhaps because that was his own experience. Oh no, I chuckled, my parents never did that. We were amateur theatre, darling. The problem was not making us put on a show. The problem was stopping us.

Given that the theatre was so integral to our parents' lives, it was inevitable that it would become part of their four children's too. We were raised in am-dram in the same way other families raise children to support their local football team. I'd say Highbury was our church, except church was our church. And everything about our house seemed well suited to putting on a show. We had the attitude. We knew how plays worked. We had a great dressing-up box, full of faded fancy frocks with puffy skirts made of so much nylon we'd spark off each other like sparrows hitting an active wire. Our sitting room and dining room were separated by sliding double doors, so one room became the auditorium, the other the stage. We'd arrange chairs in the sitting room facing the doors, which we'd open like theatre curtains, using the door frame as our proscenium arch. We'd invite neighbours in, and they'd share a programme, a folded page delicately felt-tipped with the name of the play, a cast list, a brief running order and some decorative flourishes. My sister Ruth would have made that, or Madeleine. That level of attention to detail wasn't in my skillset.

One possible fly in the ointment for our early dramatic endeavours was that we were four girls, and there were no plays that called for only girls. One of us was always required to play the Handsome Prince, or Hansel or Rumpelstiltskin, and that person was inevitably me. I had learned early on that being the princess was passive and boring; being a flashing-eyed evil goblin was much more fun and got you more attention. Don't aim for pretty, I thought, that's a crowded marketplace. Aim for funny. While this needed some finessing, the seeds had been sown. I'd got the bug.

It made sense that it was me who played the boy. You'd have picked me for the boy too. There's not a massive collection of images of the four of us – even owning a camera was quite posh back then. Snaps would be taken cautiously – spontaneity was an expensive risk; the film would be delivered to the chemist, and until you got the envelope back, you'd have no idea which of the pictures would be wonderful and which ones a failure. Someone would invariably say 'yeah, OK, David Bailey', if you tried to frame something in a more experimental way, perhaps by encouraging your subjects not to just stare at the camera blankly. Nevertheless, once a year, my parents got a photographer in to take official family shots, and there's a small collection of these portraits. In most of them we are arrayed in twos, older at the back, younger at the front. One year we were lined up, sitting on a long, low, fifties coffee table, looking back over our shoulders at the camera. My sisters are sweet fluffballs and I, with my bowl haircut and splayed teeth, am more from the dark side.

'Your sisters are pretty,' my great-aunt told me when I was about nine, 'but you're handsome, like a horse.' I probably thanked her. I knew what she said was wrong, but I also knew she was right. Whenever people found out my dad had four daughters, they always expressed pity for him – 'you poor thing, five women!' – but I thought, it's OK, he has me, I'm as much of a son as a girl can be. I was a happy gender-nonconformist, a handsome horse who wore boys' shoes, played with cars not dolls, and slopped about being the fool. I was loud, my limbs shot out everywhere, and I was useless at presenting myself neatly, or even cleanly, as evidenced by the over-greasy fringe I'm sporting in those few precious family photos.

Dining-room theatres were not going to hold handsome horses for long. This stage was too small for me; the neighbours were an insufficient audience. I needed somewhere bigger, so

I graduated to playing the role of 'kid in a crowd' at Highbury. My second home was about to become my first.

Child actors are always annoying, and I was no different. There was a gang of us aged between maybe eight and eleven, the children of actors, playing fill-in ruffians in bustling Restoration market scenes, ready to run on then off again, not at all interested in the rest of the play because it was boring. We'd chase around backstage, giddy with the late-nightness of it all, the freedom of new bedtimes and new friendships and being part of something so adult. We'd sit ready in the theatre's shabby green room, in our tatty old costumes of patched britches or pinnies and thin cotton bonnets, our faces plastered in vibrant stage make-up. (Literally, it was like plaster.) We'd be painted Trumpian orange, with contours striped on in grey, white and brown like the mottled markings of a baby gull. Eyeliner as thick as Cleopatra's. This was no place to be subtle; everything on the stage needed to be big and bold. You had to be seen from the back of the auditorium under fierce, unforgiving lights. Stage make-up came in fat, numbered pan sticks wrapped in thin gold foil which was peeled back sparingly as the stick was used; my father kept his in a blue metal box not intended for this purpose, but perfect nonetheless with its top tier of small compartments, and a space at the bottom for tins of powder and removal cream, as thick and potent as the grease you might put on for a Channel swim.

We'd be called to the wings, where we'd wait, whispering and hopping with excitement. On cue, we'd leapfrog each other

13

across the stage, or stumble through the occasional line – 'Hey, mister! Over here!' or 'Watch it, guvnor!' – and then we'd race off, adrenaline pumping, out of breath and big-eyed. Then, aged about twelve, I got my first big role, as Tom Sawyer's girlfriend Becky in *Huckleberry Finn* – though the idea of being 'a girlfriend' either onstage or in real life was completely distant and unappealing to me. Tom was played by a round, red-haired boy much shorter than me who I didn't like. I remember that I wore long white pop socks, which my leg hair poked through, and cotton bloomers thin from decades of laundering, and that when I sat down onstage I had to make sure there was no gap between the top of the socks and the bottom of the bloomers. One night I got hit on the head by a piece of flying scenery during a scene change but I carried on, semi-concussed. The risk of being seriously injured was a regular part of childhood, exemplified by the dangers of any children's playground. 'The witch's hat' swivelled round so fast and heavy that you'd regularly get thunked on the forehead by it; the rocking log jerked violently back and forward, giving you whiplash. Everything was made of rusted metal or splintered wood. Landing surfaces might as well have been sprinkled with broken glass. It raised us hard, so of *course* I finished the scene.

I remember once I was playing a lout who stole a loaf of bread and got chased across the stage by a fellow actor, an adult, cracking a whip. One night, the whip 'accidentally' caught me. I've never forgotten the actor who did that, and though I could use this opportunity to name and shame him, I won't. He knows who he is.

As a child, I would do anything for my dad's company. I played endless games of backgammon, listened to his Focus albums, and learned to cast a fly in a river. I went to Suffolk with him once to test-drive a Saab we'd never be able to afford and had no intention of buying, both of us delighting in how it raised when Dad started the engine, and lowered when he turned it off. Not having to share my dad with my sisters was the goal and going to the theatre with him was a good way to achieve that. Dad was Head of Sound at Highbury, operating the show from a tiny box at the back of the auditorium accessed via a vertical ladder and a trapdoor. There was barely enough room in it for him and Len, who did the lights, and if I was in there too it was a squash. I watched over Dad's shoulder as he operated all the sound cues on a massive Revox reel-to-reel machine. It was a physical, analogue process. In the dining room at home he'd tape bits of music or effects from his large record collection, then splice the tape with a sharp blade we weren't allowed to touch. Each section of tape contained one sound cue, one piece of music cut to time, one effect. A doorbell, footsteps, a plane flying over. ('Can you specify which kind of plane you want,' he'd say to the director, and quibble pedantically if they suggested one that wasn't historically appropriate.) Then he'd join all the sections together, using clear tape which formed stops; it was pleasingly precise. You could see the neat splices as they spooled from one reel to the other, the machine stopping in the gaps with a very particular clunk I hold as a sound memory. I would sit in the tiny, sweaty sound box, following the action onstage, watching Dad's finger follow the script.

Dad was a heavy smoker, and when the play was finished, we'd lift the trapdoor and smoke would billow out. Home was a permanent cloud too – no one would have dreamed of going outside for a fag. Dad smoked in the car driving us to school every morning, and we'd run into assembly (always late) reeking of tobacco. When I was born, Dad delivered me in their bed at home and I wonder if he was smoking then. I imagine that he was, casually uncoiling the bloody umbilical cord from round my neck, with a fag in the corner of his mouth, anointing my newborn head like it was Ash Wednesday.

By the time I was fourteen I could control the sound desk for a show without him. I'd climb up the ladder into the booth and sit on the left with Len on the right. I'd carefully follow the script, my whole body leaning into it when I knew they were coming up for a phone call, for footsteps on the gravel outside, for something smashing, off. Poised to get it exactly right. It was a matter of pride, of not letting Dad down. I got to know an eclectic range of music, and I knew the plays I worked on inside out, every pause of them. The only ones I wasn't allowed to work on were those with sex scenes in them which were always a risky choice for Sutton Coldfield patrons anyway – except if Alan Ayckbourn wrote them, because that wasn't the sexy kind of sex.

When Highbury started a new youth theatre, my parents might as well have waved me goodbye. I was an outsider at school, but here was a place where I fitted in, where my noise and boy sandals weren't too much. I was attentive to every lesson I could learn here. How to be a fool in public, how to try stuff, how my voice sounded out loud. How there is no such thing as the least important member of a team. How to find your light, and what that even means.

Some people don't need to find their light, they just have an expectation that the light will find them, and so it does. If you've never experienced how cold it is outside, then the warmth of going in will have less meaning for you. But there are plenty of us who aren't given light, or who hide from it, or pass it on immediately to someone else. Amateur theatre can help you find your light, stand in it, and be seen.

In the theatre, I also found my people. Alongside my gang of fellow teens, there were people with a range of experiences and stories. People from factories and universities, people who worked in offices or on assembly lines. A community which shared a goal – the show. This was not the world as represented by my Catholic school, where I was ostracised for being odd, for not being the same as other girls. Here I could find my own role models, outside of the prescribed list. I could stand on a stage and laugh my head off with this disparate collective, and that was a terrific liberation. I could be a great big handsome horse and toss my mane freely. Life became all about Friday-night work parties (a bit of a misnomer, these were weekly sessions when all the other stuff involved in a production happens – set building, costume sorting, prop making, bar stocktakes, maintenance and so on), first lock-ins at the bar, friendships and romance, smoking and getting drunk and hangovers. Oh yeah, and plays.

A photo exists from August 1980, taken for the *Sutton Coldfield News*. I found it recently reproduced in Highbury actor Reg Tolley's self-published memoir, *Memories of a Highbury Ham*. The photo is of six young people who had all started out acting at Highbury and were now pursuing theatre either at university or drama school. The photographer had us all arrayed up a stepladder. (Ladder to fame, get it?) Of the five others I remember three, because they were my great friends – Adrian Middleton, Mike Agnew and Michael Browne (who we always used to tease because he couldn't master the simple art of striding across a stage. I went to a professional musical recently and Jesus had the same issue – once you've seen it, you know it. 'He walks like a hipster in Top Shop,' I whispered to my pal, 'who's spotted a bargain and wants to get there quick without alerting anyone else to it.'). I was also at school with Adrian and Mike, and had starred in the sixth-form play with Adrian, in something called *The Car*. It was mostly about a car. We packed the school hall out, especially after the first night when word got round that Adrian and I kissed onstage, which was shocking, and gave us instant celebrity. In that *Sutton Coldfield News* photo, we are the straightest bunch you ever saw, all flared jeans and V-neck jumpers. Everywhere else, the world had gone absolutely punk, and we had gone absolutely theatre. The shame.

I grew up in those years at Highbury. What would I have done without it? Where else would this outsider child have found any kind of community, as school had not provided one? It became my trajectory, it funnelled me into the rest of my life. Without it, where would I have gone?

Comedian and writer Brenda Gilhooly found her people in amateur theatre, too. 'Literally from the age of five I was telling everyone I wanted to be an actress,' she told me. There was nothing theatrical in her family background, her parents were both nurses. She wasn't taken to the theatre, not even panto. But like me, Brenda grew up in the Catholic Church, which is bursting with theatricality, with its dazzling settings, fancy costumes and rituals, and sometimes-charismatic lead actors. Brenda made the most of every performance opportunity church provided her; she used to read at Mass just as a chance to get up on that altar/stage. Then, aged fourteen, she discovered Epsom Youth Theatre.

'There was a little park just outside the town, steps going down into a sort of space, and they did Shakespeare, in the summer, in this garden. Which I thought was so magical.'

Brenda then joined another group in Dorking that was putting on *The Crucible* and she got the part of Abigail. 'It was just . . . mega. There was no question about it, that was how I was going to make a living. It was everything. I would have done anything for that am-dram group. I really put the hours in. It was my life.'

Also like me, Brenda went to university and studied drama, and she graduated just as the whole stand-up scene was blooming. 'It was 1989, I was twenty-four, and I thought, right, I'm going into stand-up comedy.'

For me and Brenda, the stakes were not that high. It was our lives, but it was not life or death. Other people, like journalist and writer Mic Wright, are certain that amateur theatre was the one thing that got them through very difficult teen years. Mic described himself to me as a 'really sad and upset kid' who was good academically but got picked on, a lot. Then he did some drama at school, liked it, and found out about the Norwich Theatre Royal's arts course. He went as a way to make friends, every Saturday.

'It's how I met my best friend, it's the reunion I go to every year, and before Christmas I go to the pub to meet up with all the people. It was the social part of it that was so important. It's like . . . the Island of Misfit Toys or something.'

The experience sounded really present for him, even now. 'It's still live,' he said. 'We still do that "let's get the band back together" thing.' As well as feeling life-saving, the whole experience has also been central to his work as a journalist. 'I deliver on time, to length, to the brief, and I learned that from the discipline of doing drama. Turn up, and respect everyone in the company by knowing your lines, cos if you don't, you'll get bollocked.'

Mic was realistic about its panacea effect, though. It wasn't some kind of *Billy Elliot* thing, and it didn't fix the damage from being bullied, but it did bring him out of himself. 'The bonds from it are forged in those intensities, those moments, those drama games and warm-ups, that sense we're going into battle now.'

When I left for university at Warwick, just far enough from home, Dad bought me an art-supply box to keep my stage make-up in. It was plastic, not exactly the same as his blue metal one, but near enough. And I was off.

I spent the next four years dressed in boiler suits and chef's chequered trousers and old man's pyjama tops and vests I made out of old sheets, and tie-dyed. I spent my time shagging around and being taught how to cook spaghetti carbonara by a much more sophisticated boyfriend from Goole. I lived in a communal house, and wherever the slugs left trails up the walls, we painted flowers. Apart from sex and spaghetti, my life revolved around being in a lot of plays of all sorts, from Greek tragedies that featured geometrical dancing, to Italian comedies with me as a ruff-necked madam. We toured Denmark with a production of *The Crucible* (I think every single amateur actor in the country has been in *The Crucible* at some point) and performed a compilation we called *Acts of Violence*. We really loved violence. We loved Edward Bond, particularly his play about stoning a baby in a pram, and anything about abused women. I played a sexy murderer in prison in *Chicago*, dancing in heels, a bustier and a strong smoky eye look. We performed on the stage of Warwick Arts Centre with professional technical staff and felt like we were really something. My pal Sally Brookes (she was never just Sally, always Sally Brookes, even though there were no other Sallys) and I wrote ourselves a multi-character play, more of a nascent sketch show really, which got a lot of laughs. Laughs – they were a high to coast home on. We ate, slept and breathed theatre.

When university finished, it was obligatory that we all move to London. We were going to make it. I felt sad for my friends who had been born in London; they were only going home, while the rest of us could experience a sense of having arrived. I believed we'd spend all our time putting on plays and that I'd be an actor.

I moved to London in 1983, aged twenty-two, with my drama gang: Karen, Libby, Dave, Adrian, Paul, Jonty, Mick, Sally Brookes. Karen, Libby and I found a flat in Forest Hill via an ad in the *Guardian* 'Flats to Let' section. We moved into the top floor of a large house right on the busy South Circular. I drive past it occasionally now, wondering if anyone ever sunbathes in the gravelled back garden like we did, the tiny stones leaving dents in our young burnt skin. Forest Hill in 1983 was a long way from the main stage. I hadn't quite arrived, after all. Still, who cared? I knew what kind of acting roles I was good for: the comedy girlfriend, the stooge, the prat-faller. Throwing shade was where I'd found my niche. I didn't mind looking foolish or being physical or ugly, actually I relished it. This was an era packed with fantastic, innovative companies: Complicite, Trestle, Incubus, Paines Plough, Footsbarn – oh, the first time I saw Footsbarn it was absolute magic. Anarchists on stilts, hewn from dirt and fire and sex and masks and filthy imagination, doing Shakespeare. Juggling and fooling with his words to bring them into some new crazy circus theatre life. I wanted to run away and join Footsbarn; I think I still do. These were my heroes, their lives spent on the road in vans, performing in tiny rooms and rackety tents. Radical experimental noisy dirty theatre was thriving. The more energetic, physical, and raw, the better. Who wanted, in those circumstances, to be the romantic lead, the pretty one?

I knew that if there was power in my face it didn't lie in romance. I wanted to be the one who was growling and stamping and getting laughs. That was my currency.

Everyone hit the road running, raring to go, champing at the bit, grasping life by the mettle – all the clichés. Except for me. As I graduated, my beloved dad became seriously ill with a not-entirely-unexpected heart attack. I mentioned, I think, the chain-smoking. I spent the first few weeks of my new London life shuttling between Forest Hill and a hospital in Birmingham. Wherever I was, I was always going home to the other place. Then he died, and nowhere was home any more.

In London the ghost of my dead dad was with me. He sat at the end of my bed chatting to me. In London I kept going, avoiding any kind of emotional conversation about his death because I didn't want to make things difficult for anyone. In Birmingham I was the organiser, the one who got things done, who sorted out Dad's jumper drawer. In neither place was I expressing my feelings, they're still hidden in a tangled mess somewhere along the M40. But then, it's only been thirty-something short years.

Here I was, with a face for comedy and all this sadness. And I fell headlong at the first hurdle. I went up for a couple of fringe acting jobs but didn't get them; I wasn't resilient or talented enough, I know now. I didn't quite have that thrusting ambition – so unattractive in a woman, don't you think? – that one needs to push a career forward. I didn't entirely give up, I learned to drive in the hope of being cast as an ambulance driver on *Casualty*. I wasn't going to auditions for *Casualty*, or anything that might have actually made this happen. I just learned to drive and . . . waited. But I couldn't find my light any more. It had been snuffed out and I lacked the wherewithal to reignite it. I thought I'd just . . . keep waiting, and somebody would rescue me. By the time I was twenty-nine Mum had stopped saying 'you'd be a great *Blue Peter* presenter' and I'd accepted I wasn't going to be discovered, on *Casualty* or anywhere. Over time I have found my light from different sources; not the one big light I'd expected, but more a series of small fairy lights strung together, creating an effect. My years at Highbury gave me a love of making theatre; my love of theatre sent me off to the fringes. I wrote a couple of 'little plays' which had small productions in Edinburgh and London (I've still got the reviews, snipped from newspapers and stashed in a faded yellow cardboard folder). I did press and publicity for a comedy promoter, I wrote reviews for political women's magazines, I worked for a London venue at the start of the stand-up boom. It's what I call a 'patchwork CV' though the smarter term is 'portfolio'. I've lived a creative life in London, which is perhaps what 'making it' really means.

And here I am now, making a decision – I'm going back to Highbury. Will I walk out on that stage and find my original light? I wonder. Everything remains to be seen.

CHAPTER 3

Backstory

One of the most common questions I'm asked about amateur theatre is: 'when did it start?' The answer is easy because, at the start, all theatre was amateur. From the moment humans began telling stories, there would have been one show-off who decided he had to act out exactly how he caught and killed the boar currently roasting over the fire. (I'm not using the word 'show-off' with judgement. Not *much* judgement, at least. Some of my best friends . . . etc.) He'd have leapt off his rock, grunting 'you be the boar, John' to his fellow caveman, 'and I'll be me'. John would have thrown the boar's skin over his shoulders, they'd have done a bit of funny business with the tusks, and between them, improvised a charade of how their skill and cunning had defeated the animal, in a performance full of twists, pathos, jeopardy, drama, comedy and, ultimately, our hero's conquering journey. As the tension mounted someone would have heckled and been told to shut up, and at the end the women would have cheered, and our two performers would have got laid. *Plus ça change*; show business has always had this power.

The first examples of what we now understand as theatre in this country happened in church. In the Middle Ages, Bible stories were brought to life by members of the clergy, not 'actors' as such, just people used to commanding a crowd. There was one slight problem: the villain got all the best lines. The devil, the character most suited to lewd performance (again, no judgement), became a favourite. By necessity, the 'plays' spilled out of the churches into the open spaces around them, where more people could see them and hear the message. A good thing for the church, you'd think, an olden-day version of Alpha courses where vicars try to attract young folk by rapping and handing out bowls of lentil soup. But out in the open, things are harder to control, and once these nascent plays were outside the church boundaries, the clergy no longer had a monopoly on performance. The focus was still religious, though. There were mystery plays, miracle plays and morality plays, all based on telling people how to live via Bible stories and tales about saints. They were performed in cycles all over the country – some of them still are, and get huge crowds. It can be a bit confusing if you're in Trafalgar Square around Easter time and see a man dragging round a huge wooden cross looking pretty pissed off and thirsty – until you realise that it's a passion play, and Mary Magdalene will be along any moment to dab his wounds. Various Middle Ages trade guilds – a cross between a fraternity and a union – chose the Bible stories most relevant to their professions and put those on. The story of Noah's Ark performed by carpenters or mariners was an obvious one; goldsmiths got the Adoration. They performed on double-decker travelling wagons, with the upper floor as the stage, and dressing rooms below. It was the medieval version of *Summer Holiday*.

Free from the restrictions of the Church, things could be a bit more of a laugh. 'The Mystery Plays in the hands of the amateur were a more worldly interpretation of the biblical stories that were rejected by the Church authorities,' wrote George Taylor, and I'm translating 'more worldly', to mean ruder. Possibly a few knob gags, probably some salacious double entendres – our stock-in-trade. These plays were made accessible to the poorly educated audiences, who wouldn't have understood a Latin Mass, by their use of everyday, vernacular language. The Church didn't really like these adaptations, but people's love of jokes won out – as it always has.

In his book *British Drama*, my copy of which has been with me since university and somehow survived quite a few bookshelf culls, Allardyce Nicol wrote that by the late fifteenth century, associations had been formed for the *specific* purpose of putting on plays, rather than a group of guys presenting whatever material their trade guild thought appropriate. (I'm not using the word 'guys' here in any kind of gender-neutral sense. They would have all been men.) So, if the question at the start of the chapter had been 'when did *professional* theatre start?', the answer would be – about now. 'We have not yet reached the world of true professionalism,' Nicol wrote, 'but we are very close to it.' Noble households had groups of minstrels attached to them; inspired entirely by Disney's *Robin Hood*, I imagine being a minstrel involved a lot of gentle strolling and fine lute-strumming. These groups of minstrels 'saw enviously what the amateurs could do, and what the rewards were, and began to follow suit'.

Distinct from mystery plays and players were the more secular, folksy mummers' groups. Mummers, or 'guisers', wore masks, and their plays usually involved two men having a fight, with the loser being revived by a doctor. (Knowing the plot didn't seem to ruin the entertainment. The notion of 'spoilers' didn't exist.) They were all amateurs again, all men, again, and performed in public spaces around festival days like Christmas and Easter. There were countless regional variations telling regional stories, and we're still plagued by remnants of these groups, in the form of morris dancers. To wit: the dreaded jingle-jangle of a jaunty white-trousered man waving his bells-on-a-stick in your face when you're trying to go your way on a peaceful English summer's day. In 2019, Oxford's annual folk weekend proclaimed 'Wherever you are in Oxford you'll never be far from a morris team', which sounds more like a threat than a promise to me.

'As a rule, local [mummers] players did not move far from home,' writes E. K. Chambers. 'The notices of them are sparser in the seventeenth century than the sixteenth, but they never entirely die out.' Indeed, like vampires, they seem impossible to kill. Some of them only stopped performing in blackface a couple of years ago, with some kneejerk 'it's tradition!' uproar. Chambers describes the groups as broadly comedic, but as demonstrated by people's baffling love of Michael McIntyre, comedy is a very subjective thing.

It's well known that Henry VIII had what might be described as a 'tricky relationship' with the Church, and suppressed all religious drama, all the mysteries and the miracles, as part of his Reformation. More people gathered for theatre than for church, so he concluded that it must be the work of that damn devil. He saw theatre as an excuse for laziness and believed that crowds encouraged the spread of the plague. He did like entertainment though, of the wildly extravagant school, and acting companies could be approved as long as they had wealthy patronage (and as long as they weren't religious). In Henry's court, all the best lords owned troupes of actors. Secular drama began to grow and dominate, with the first officially designated playhouses appearing in the 1570s. These were not exclusive places; people of all social classes went. The modern Globe Theatre, recreated on the south bank of the River Thames, with its space for standing, reflects the cheap and uncomfortable 'groundling' experience, though it now discourages the throwing of rotten veg. And alongside official playhouses, the first examples of 'pub theatre', now a thriving part of the fringe scene, were appearing. Chambers tells of an event in February 1653 when three to four hundred people were crammed into the White Hart pub in Witney for a performance; two hours into a three-hour play, the floor collapsed into the shovelboard room below, and several people were killed. I've occasionally wished something similar would happen to me when I've been stuck in an unendingly tedious play and all I want is the interval, a bar, a toilet, something – *anything* – to happen.

It's at this point that I can't avoid mentioning Shakespeare. His plays have been performed by amateurs around the world for hundreds of years, in acts of entertainment, education and colonialism. Actor Simon Callow, giving the keynote speech at the inaugural Amateur Theatre Festival in September 2018, spoke about the first known performance of *Twelfth Night*.

'It was commissioned by amateurs, at the Inns of Court, and performed in the Middle Temple for the very first time by lawyers. As far as we know, none of them went on to become professional actors. They wouldn't have dreamt of it. It was a largely despised profession. The amateurs were the toffs. The amateurs were the really elegant swanky people, the actors were just journeymen, who did a job.'

I am particularly taken with a report of one amateur production of *Hamlet* in 1607, only four years after it was written. It happened onboard an English ship when it docked to get supplies in Sierra Leone, and the images the story throws off are fantastically filmic. In far-off lands, under a beating sun, on a beautiful creaking wooden vessel, I see scruffy deck-hands co-opted into playing ghosts and gravediggers, the fairest among them playing Ophelia (and for that honour, being mocked and yearned for in equal measure), their most handsome and tortured seafarer, their own Ben Whishaw, playing Hamlet.

Performance as a way of displaying wealth created the next big boom in amateur theatre. It happened in the wealthiest Georgian houses up and down the land, in private theatricals that became show-stoppingly flash. The proceedings were private for reasons that went beyond a desire for exclusivity. The Lord Chamberlain, the most senior member of the royal household, presided over the Licensing Act of 1737, which had been brought in to censor theatre. He was responsible for the content of each and every public performance in the country, and had control over all ideas that were presented onstage. He ensured that no seditious messages were spread about the government or royalty and that public morality was kept on a very tight leash. The Act gave him the power to veto new plays, if he saw fit, and any modifications to existing plays. Theatre owners could be prosecuted for staging plays, or parts of plays, without prior approval. The Lord Chamberlain's Office held this responsibility for the next 250 years; and if you hope that its view of society's mores and morals evolved in line with society's changing views of itself, all the evidence suggests otherwise.

The only way around censorship was to create performances that were not open to the public. Private theatres were not subject to the Lord Chamberlain's approval or disapproval. It was not that the eighteenth-century aristocrats wanted to perform dodgy, irreligious or anti-monarchist material, heaven forfend, but having private spaces allowed them to do what they wanted, escape any kind of censure, and retain the element of exclusivity. And their personal delights would not have been seen as appropriate for the lower classes. Ribald debauchery is *so* wasted on the poor.

This love of posh private theatrics started around the mid-1750s, and at its peak, hundreds of houses across Britain had their own performance spaces, frequented by anyone who was anyone in society and, of course, all those who aspired to be. I suspect it bore a strong resemblance to *Hello!* magazine's 'recent party' section; a similar bunch of incomprehensibly named people wearing shiny clothes that cost more than cars, only now with better teeth. There were theatres at all the 'big name' estates, like Alton Towers, Shugborough Hall and Chatsworth House; and there were smaller patrons like Mrs Hobart of Ham Common, Sir Watkins William Wynn of Wynnstay on the Welsh border, and Sir Percy Florence Shelley (son of the poet), who had one theatre at his country residence, Boscombe House, and another at his Chelsea home. According to historian Evelyn Howe, the rural theatres were partly about relieving the boredom after the London season ended, enlivening things among 'dull country neighbours'. As well as giving rich people something to do, private theatricals were a great way of displaying wealth. And, as a bonus, they were a way for families to show off their brilliant offspring – the Fox family, putting on plays at their Kensington residence, cast their own children in various roles. Watching one's own children be amusing is tough enough; being required to applaud other people's is a dreadful chore. But I suppose if my social standing were at stake, I could fake an appreciation of some awful Little Lord Fauntleroy prancing around mangling a classic. I probably already have.

As this part of the story is all about displaying wealth, there are some fantastic characters involved. Some of them are so unlikeable in their ostentation it's hard not to find them compelling. Lord Richard Barry, 7th Earl of Barrymore, for instance. His nickname, 'Hellgate', is a clue. He was, apparently, a 'daring prankster'; one of his favourite tricks was pretending to kidnap young women, and then leaving coffins on their doorsteps to frighten the servants. What a marvellous chap. Barry built a private theatre in his home at Wargrave, Berkshire, modelled on the Covent Garden Opera House. If you're going to do that, you really need to do it properly, and Barry, who wanted to have 'the Compleatest Private Theatre in the Kingdom', used scene painters from Covent Garden itself, plus the best costumiers and some professional actors, for a space that seated seven hundred people and was lit by a mass of glass chandeliers. I'll bet it was utterly fabulous – and it really annoys me that this kidnapping prick had such nice things. Reading about his antics, I imagined him as some kind of paunchy middle-aged UKIP reprobate engaged in a life of sordid lechery, but reports show that he died aged around twenty-four, like James Dean, and, unsurprisingly, insolvent. He lived fast and died young; his equivalent today is probably starring in *Made in Chelsea*.

Hellgate set a low bar, but some of the women involved in this part of history are easier to love – partly because they were the outliers, which is never the easy choice. It's true they were often very posh outliers but, nonetheless, going against their prescribed roles. Take Mrs Anne Damer, who 'with the arrival of the new fashion for amateur plays staged by the

33

aristocracy for the aristocracy . . . found an intellectual niche to which she was particularly fitted', according to her biographer Richard Webb. Richmond House, owned by the Duke of Richmond in (yes) Richmond, just outside London, was the setting for her 'intellectual niche', and as the duke was her brother-in-law, Anne had no problem getting cast in good roles. It's not what you know, it's who, and in this case, 'who' had his own theatre. It was created from two converted rooms, and prided itself on a select audience which included royalty, and on there being no 'intrusion of improper company'. The first play put on in this space was *The Way to Keep Him*, a farce in five acts on the subject of marital infidelity. Every bit of this makes my heart sink. None of it was about dramatic expertise, or talent, or a love of theatre, it was all about society, fashion and being seen in the right place. There were no critics present, though one member of the audience wrote in his diary that 'Mrs Damer in the epilogue had monotony of voice; there was little or no applause', a stinging review worthy of my mum. In 1788, the duke had a new bespoke theatre built and the bad reviews for Mrs Damer's acting continued to roll in. 'Very indifferent,' said one audience member. 'Detestable,' wrote another. You'd think that would be enough to sink a person, but I imagine Mrs Damer sailing on, chin up, impervious to criticism, doing exactly what she wanted. And I feel a sneaking admiration.

The next woman I turn to is the Margravine of Anspach. Born in 1750, her original name was Elizabeth Berkeley, but she didn't hang on to it for long, marrying her first husband, William Craven, at just seventeen. That marriage didn't last, which in itself was fairly controversial, and she quickly established herself in the court of a German count, the Margrave of Anspach. She called him her 'kind and princely adopted brother', though it's not recorded how his wife, the first margravine, felt about this. Elizabeth was described by theatre historian Sybil Rosenfeld as 'a vain and egotistical creature with a strong streak of exhibitionism in her nature, who yet was capable, where her happiness was involved, of showing determination and strength of character'.

On the one hand, she sounds like a total nightmare. On the other, I appreciate the women who didn't play the silent, supplicant role they were ascribed, particularly in an age when strong female role models would have been hard to come by. She was in a world of privilege that gave her the confidence to push herself forward, but she got all her personal agency by allying herself with powerful men. It's an emotional roller coaster, writing about 'difficult' women.

Elizabeth wrote her autobiography, so we have all the details. And I do mean *all* the details, starting with a dramatic retelling of her own premature birth, and onwards in meandering sentences and a maddening narrative that often fixates on her looks and figure, even at the age of ten. Elizabeth saw her first play at twelve years old, 'when I took a most decided passion for acting, which afterwards proved one of the Margrave's greatest pleasures'. Having moved into his court, she wrote that the theatre 'would, if properly arranged, be a source of continual relaxation for the Margrave's mind'. How constantly thoughtful she was.

In 1791, as soon as his first wife was out of the way (dead), Elizabeth married the margrave with what polite society decided was unseemly haste. As his second margravine, she persuaded him to come to London, where they set up Brandenburgh House in Hammersmith, beside the Thames. Elizabeth kept herself busy by being creative. In Volume 2 of her memoirs, she wrote:

> My taste for music and poetry, and my style of imagination in writing, chastened by experience, were great sources of delight to me. I wrote the *Princess of Georgia* [an opera] and the *Twins of Smyrna* [a comedy, apparently] for the Margrave's theatre, beside *Nourjad* and several other pieces, and for these I composed various airs in music.

Little remains of the margravine's scripts and let us give thanks for these small mercies. Sybil Rosenfeld's description of one of their evenings sounds in equal measure glorious and terrible. It was a fete in honour of the Duke of Clarence and after dinner, while guests were in the garden, the dining room was transformed into a theatre. A comedy, burlesque, tragedy and burletta were performed, 'and in them the Margravine displayed "astonishing and diversified accomplishments", singing in French, Italian and English and playing on various instruments. Her son Keppel took part both in male and female attire.' There's no record of how Keppel felt about this.

Like our dining room in Wylde Green, Sutton Coldfield, in the 1960s, where we had unwittingly been a low-brow continuum of Georgian theatrical tradition, the dining room in Brandenburgh House was not enough to hold the margravine's talents for long. She built her own theatre on the bank of the river, a setting that they used to the full, with scenery dramatically rising from the water; there she could entertain her husband and, according to Rosenfeld, 'at the same time indulge in her favourite pastime of taking the centre of the stage'. It opened in April 1793, with performances starring Elizabeth, of course, and Keppel. Their evenings sound suitably and hilariously theatrical; the margravine played an array of roles, including a rustic French boy, Don Juan, Queen Margaret and various romantic heroines; she even played Viola in *Twelfth Night*, with her other son, Sebastian, playing her lover. (Keppel dodged that bullet.) She thought nothing of amending established texts to suit her political and personal tastes, adding epilogues and songs where she fancied, all to perform herself, of course. She was the living embodiment of the words 'prima donna'.

But if it's hard to love her because of all this opulent flamboyance, think for a moment of two things. First, women on the stage were viewed as creatures of immorality, so Elizabeth was on some level flicking a massive V to all that. Second, all the theatrics stopped as soon as the margrave died.

Her taste for it seems to have been, after all, entirely about pleasing him, and being pleasing to him. There is romance in that, if you're willing to allow it.

Part of Elizabeth's life had been spent gallivanting round Europe, as much of the aristocracy did in the eighteenth century. For them, theatre was an international sport, somewhere to be seen, the biggest available stage. But at least the margravine was concerned with the quality of the work. They couldn't just paint it gold and palm her off with any old shit – she knew what she was seeing. For that, at least, let's give her some small credit. But still, it was the poshest version of a gap year it's possible to imagine.

You might deduce from all this that amateur theatre was the pastime of only a few very rich people. But, as ever, it's simply that they're the ones whose lives were deemed worth recording, by themselves as much as anyone else. As theatre historian David Coates says, 'We focus on the rich because that's where the evidence is.' But if we *just* consider the rich, it doesn't give a clear picture of how widespread amateur theatre really was. We know there was some trickle-down from the aristocrats' personal theatres to the aspirational upper-middle classes, people such as Oldfield Bowles, a wealthy amateur painter, Joseph Cradock, the High Sheriff of Leicester, and the Reverend George Austen – Jane's dad. And what we might call the first amateur dramatic society, the elite Pic Nic Club, was founded in London in 1801. It was a combination of amateur theatre and potluck supper club, with an 'exclusive soirée' type of clientele. Here, amateurs recited from writers such as Molière or Racine, and the images that survive suggest the club was full of fat gouty men in powdered wigs watching saucy tits-out burlesque. Because they were constituted as a club, they avoided the censoring strictures of the Lord Chamberlain, but they received a lot of opposition nevertheless. Theatre managers were worried that the club took away their custom and the conservative press attacked them for being louche and debauched – wrapping it all up, as they still do, in some kind of paternal anxiety about public morality.

That trickle-down meant that by the mid nineteenth century, there was what the author Michael Dobson describes as an 'upper middle-class tradition of often all-male drawing room theatricals'. It was very genteel and nice, and stiflingly twee-sounding. All amateur, mostly men. But, while the rich were up to it politely and royally in fabulous surroundings, and the aspiring classes were doing their best to emulate that, ordinary people were putting on plays too. Trickling much further down the social scale, things were bawdier, dirtier and caused more outrage. It was a whole lot more fun here, in other words – for young men. They have all the laughs. These young men could play in what Dobson calls 'the more radical heritage of the early 19th century spouting clubs'. Spouting clubs, popular from the mid eighteenth century, were a kind of theatrical karaoke, where working men gathered to recite (or 'spout') chunks of plays, usually Shakespeare. Because working men were involved, and beer, it's fairly inevitable that the spouting clubs were associated with disorderly behaviour, and the thought of loads of apprentices, mechanics and clerks getting their kicks reading out bits of Shakespeare, everything disintegrating into drunken scandal, is pretty compelling. It's hard to picture that happening now – gangs of twenty-first-century estate agents in Zara suits or data-inputters on Dress-Down Fridays getting together in a local 'Spoons, reciting the bits of *Lear* or *Hamlet* they've downloaded.

This 'radical heritage' was amateur theatre that was private but not exclusive, made by lower- and middle-class young people – clerks, shop boys and law students. For them, spouting clubs had been the influence, rather than the aristocratic drawing-room theatricals. They created unlicensed theatre in shop cellars, playing to audiences made up of their friends. Of the two strands – the polite guys doing polite readings in their staid drawing rooms, versus the louder, more raucous groups, fuelled by cheap beer, giving all they've got to some Shakespeare – I think it's obvious which one sounds better, and was considered corrupting. David Coates tells us that a lot of what we know about these despicable youth can be gleaned from police and newspaper reports, like this one from *The Times* in October 1824:

A smart, dandy-dressed young fellow, apparently about 18, named Charles George Foster ... [had] got connected with a set of amateur performers in some private theatricals, which withdrew his mind altogether from business – kept him out all hours of the night, till at length he absented himself entirely from his master's house.

That notion of being so rapt in a show you can barely focus on work might have been a horror for Charles's 'master', but for Charles and others like him, it meant a life outside work, where theatre was exciting – it belonged to them, it was fun, it was community, it was sociable and it was full of meaning. All in all, it was bloody excellent.

The atmosphere in the unlicensed shop-cellar theatres would have been mostly male, but hiring actresses was costly, so women were finally encouraged to join the ranks, almost as equals. That didn't do much for these places' reputations; anywhere men and women mixed with no chaperones was seen as disreputable and immoral. One step up from this were more educational-sounding places like, among others, the Dramatic Institution, set up by Mr and Mrs Pym in Gough Street in 1832, and Miss Kelly's Theatre and Dramatic School, established by actress Fanny Kelly in 1840 in Soho's Dean Street. It was built in her own back garden, particularly for the training of young women and it is here, in the swirling London fog, that we meet a familiar figure.

Charles Dickens was born in Portsmouth in 1812, moved to London three years later, and started his amateur theatre life in a way that will be familiar to many people – making plays at home in the kitchen with his siblings and friends, and performing in plays at school. Simon Callow writes in his biography of Dickens that 'the making of theatre became a passion for the eight-year-old boy, a passion that would endure till very nearly the day he died'. By the time he was fifteen, Dickens was making appearances at the Minor Theatre in

Catherine Street, where amateurs would pay to be cast in plays. He had a talent for impersonation and for making people laugh, and as he grew up, Callow writes, 'when he wasn't pounding the streets he was at a show. He claimed that for at least three years he went to the theatre every single day of his life.' Dickens had caught the bug. Had he not caught another kind of bug and been too ill to attend an audition at the Covent Garden Theatre, acting could have been his primary profession.

Callow describes how working on a show was a 'balm' to Dickens, who took it incredibly seriously. 'The company and cast were all friends, but there was nothing amateur about his work on the show.' Except, it *was* amateur, and we're certainly not going to go down the road of confusing 'unpaid' for 'poor quality'. Particularly as, by all accounts, Dickens's shows were a resounding hit. As he became better known as a writer, paeans to the importance of theatre would flow from the mouths of his characters, and Dickens and 'his band of literary and painterly amateur actors' would go on meandering tours of the country. Sounds utterly great, the lucky buggers. In the mid 1840s at Miss Kelly's he directed, stage-managed and performed in Ben Jonson's *Every Man in His Humour*, in the role of Captain Bobadil. Fellow cast member John Forster described it as 'a success that out-ran our wildest expectation; and turned our little enterprise into one of the small sensations of the day'. I find Forster's excitement completely relatable. There's nothing like the buzz when everyone is scrapping to get a ticket for a must-see show, and you have one clutched in your hand. And for the makers of those shows, the immediacy, adrenaline and euphoria are not often paralleled in publishing books, even for someone at Dickens's level of renown. No wonder theatre was where he knew his happiest times.

> Let any of us look back upon his past life and say whether he owes no gratitude to the actor's art! . . . In the relief afforded us by [it], we always find some reflection, humorous or pathetic, sombre or grotesque, of all the best things that we feel and know.

To Dickens, it was everything.

This part of the amateur story is not dead heritage. It's not irrelevant nostalgia. It is seeds sown, it is living history, footholds in what was to come. Because at the same time as Dickens was making shows with his literary chums, companies were being established that are still going strong today. All that spouting, reading and acting, whether it was in nice drawing rooms or noisy pub bars, was laying the foundations for today's amateur theatre. Whether theatre was trickling down or along (we know it was not one clear river), these were the early days for groups that are thriving links to our past selves. It's the kind of history that can sometimes be overlooked because it's not royal, or world-changing, but it should be remembered for what it did to enhance the lives of ordinary people. The company that proudly declares itself 'the oldest surviving amateur dramatic company in the world', the Old Stagers of Canterbury, was founded in 1842 by the Hon. Fred Ponsonby to entertain people during Canterbury's annual Cricket Week. They still perform annually. The Manchester Athenaeum Dramatic Society, founded in 1847 for the purpose of 'reading the works of Shakespeare and other authors', is going strong. Both of these examples clearly come from more genteel, middle-class beginnings, but that's not true of all the companies that started then, some of whom we'll see later in the book. The result is the same, though: there is over 170 years of theatre-making in societies that still exist and thrive around the country. It's incredible to think that this simple act of playing, and what it means to people, has remained constant while everything else in the landscape has changed so completely.

CHAPTER 4

Beginners Please

It is a hot Wednesday morning in the summer of 2018, and I am sitting in Highbury's auditorium watching people work onstage while I wait for my mum to come down from the Costume Department. I haven't been here for a long time. In the intervening years, every six weeks without fail, Mum has rung me and said 'This play X is on. I think you'd enjoy it. You should come.' And every single time, also without fail, I'd reply that I was 'too busy'. And sometimes I actually was.

Until recently, I had been certain that my origins in amateur theatre did not matter to me, not a jot. They were embarrassing, actually, particularly because I knew a lot of 'proper' actors, professionals. Then, before I started thinking about this book, when my feelings might best be described as 'dissociated curiosity', I heard John Humphrys on Radio 4's *Today* programme discussing amateur theatre – 'as British as afternoon tea and queuing up' – and ask his guest if it was dying. There were a couple of minutes of standard mock-provocation, where Humphrys talked about how we're all watching more TV and how parking costs have gone up. (You what? What's *parking* got to do with anything?) Then he asked, as his supposedly 'killer' question, does it matter? 'Does it MATTER?' he sneered. Does it MATTER??? I yelled back at Humphrys, from my kitchen table. (I know this to be a common feature of many British breakfasts over many years in many homes.) I started ranting at the radio, about how people shouldn't have allotments because Tesco sells peas, about how because there's ONE way of telling stories we shouldn't find another way of telling stories. About how bringing up parking costs was a ridiculous attempt to derail an art form. In my yelling I furiously mangled a Kurt Vonnegut quote about how creating something is its own reward. Of course it doesn't 'matter', Humphrys. None of it 'matters', I ranted. People fall through cracks in earthquakes and lose everything so no, amateur theatre doesn't 'matter'. But it also matters so deeply, is so much a part of who we ARE, so much about life as a HUMAN . . . And as I ranted at the radio, I realised that I'd shown my hand, rather. It seemed that it mattered to me rather a lot. I'd surprised myself; I hadn't thought about it properly for so long, I'd put it in a box and buried it so deep, and yet here it was, springing out all over the breakfast table. It made me think, maybe it was time I had a proper rummage around, see what I could find in that box. Perhaps, right at the bottom, there would be a light? So, here I am, in the auditorium, waiting for Mum.

Some things about this place have changed totally, other things have not. It is now called Highbury Theatre Centre rather than Highbury Little Theatre, but as it's still part of the Little Theatre organisation, that's just semantics, a bit of a rebrand that makes no odds to anyone. Mum had been wrong and right about the green room – it isn't quite the amazing apartment I'd imagined when she'd said 'you could live it in now', but it is an actual room. The double doors that lead from the foyer into the auditorium still have the same ornamentation. On the left door, there is a silver face in profile, its mouth turned down. On the right door, a silver face in profile, smiling. The dual masks of tragedy and comedy, marking the entrance exactly as they have since 1947. Today, the stage is busy, but not with actors. Wednesday mornings are for work parties – same as I used to go to in my teens, every Friday night. There's a bunch of men building a set, I watch one of them create a pretty convincing L-shaped kitchen, and another one painting sage green on a flimsy wall; I can see someone else creating a fake garden through a fake window. I'm a bit bored just watching, so I wander down and go onto the stage. Nobody pays me any attention. I stand there at the front and look up at the auditorium. The stage feels small. It didn't used to feel small when I was part of it. Now I feel like I could fling my arms out and they'd reach from one side of the proscenium arch to the other.

My mum is a tiny woman, and I sometimes worry that she might fall into a hamper of muffs and ruffles in the Costume Department and never be seen again. But she arrives, safe if a little hot and dusty, and we go to the cafe front of house, to get coffee served in small cups the same sage green as the set. She introduces me to anyone who passes; she is proud. People pretend to remember me, but I could have been any one of my sisters, and that's OK. Brian Hill's dog is working the room, being fed biscuits by everyone. In a perfectly timed theatrical moment, an actor blows in clutching his script for tonight's show, dramatically declaring, 'It's never going to be ready.' I take my coffee and wander through to the foyer, where someone mistakes me for the visiting artist whose work is on the walls. I look like I could be an artist, it is true. I correct her, and she immediately tells me in detail how much she hates the work.

I drift into the bar, where two people are stocking the shelves with ginger wine, and small bottles of tonic. I remember they used to serve Britvic in tiny bottles, each one a couple of mouthfuls of luxury juice. There are production photos hung in rows along the walls, and almost immediately I find one with my father in it. 'Ah, there you are,' I say. Mum comes to find me and bustles me off to see the Costume Department, she wants to show the place off to me. Costume used to be just one room but it's expanded now, with corridors and cupboards absolutely rammed to bursting. Racks of hats and plastic crates of shoes, trunks of oddments, everything sorted into the right era, approximately. Here, a rail of pouffy Victorian dresses; there, a rail of outfits for flappers. A hamper of bright waterproofs, a basket of Ascot hats. Everything you could possibly need in almost any amateur production you could name. Mum spends a lot of her time digging out what producers ask for, then putting things away again. Copious lists are kept in various notebooks, all the entries made in longhand.

Although parts of the building are new to me, they feel very familiar. It's in the smells, the countertops, the carpets, the fixtures and fittings, some of the faces. But deeper than that, something intrinsic. Like when you meet people at a school reunion and they seem to really know you, because they knew the first version of you, the one that time has tried to cover. I still know the core of this place. There is something here that was the making of me, and I am not sure I like the feeling it gives me. I'm conflicted, between this place 'mattering', and the sense that it might be trying to trap me, in my own origin story. Do I want to come 'home'?

That evening, Mum and I go back to Highbury, and it is so hot we all want to die. (Please never doubt my taste for the dramatic.) We are sitting in an extension they call the Upper Foyer. There was a major building programme at the theatre in the 1980s, after I'd gone, and this room is part of it; it sits in the eaves above the front entrance, and has long, low windows right across one wall, which look out at the small terraced houses of Sheffield Road. Tonight, the sun is still blazing at 7 p.m., and it feels like being in front of an oven when you check the Christmas turkey. If someone had set the sprinkler system off, I would have stayed put, for the opportunity to cool down.

I am here for the theatre's 'familiarisation', where they introduce the full programme of plays for the next year. Sandy Haynes, the Arts Director, had already allocated each of the seven plays a director, and these directors are here to 'sell' their play to interested parties. I am here to buy, because I want to follow a production from beginning to end, from first rehearsal to last night, to immerse myself back here, and record the journey. Tonight, I am going to pick the play. There's a little anxiety churn in my stomach: I'm not sure what I'll find, whether it'll be any good, or what performance I'll have to give. I'm here in the role of 'writer' but also 'daughter' and 'past member' and I haven't quite figured out my character's motivation yet. I sip a glass of warm white wine.

There were about eight people here when we arrived. Usually when I'm the youngest in a room, it is a funeral. We all sit and fan ourselves with our own clothes and bus tickets, anything we have to hand, and the wine I'm drinking seems to be thickening in the heat, like gravy. 'Look who's here,' says Mum, gesticulating to a man sitting a few rows back. I turn and recognise the actor who had 'accidentally' whipped me onstage, all those years ago. It's funny what time does; I'd aged so much, from child to middle-aged woman, and this man seems to have barely changed. Then came a series of loud whirrs, clicks and some mechanical whining and an elderly gentleman appears to rise up through the floor into the room. 'That's Dicky Bird,' whispers Mum as he clambers slowly off the stairlift. Brian 'Dicky' Bird is one of the theatre's oldest members, I found his name later as I looked through programmes from 1942. By the time the meeting starts, the room is packed and there are young people here, and an equal mix of men and women. Women's voices are still largely absent from the public, national stage. Amateur theatre, though, is full of them, and this brilliant fact should be acknowledged.

In front of us, between me and the view where blue sky meets the line of Sheffield Road's roofs, is a long table where the directors for the next season, the seventy-seventh in the theatre's history, take their places. Sandy Haynes kicks off proceedings by outlining the play she is going to direct and making the promise of cake for her cast. Just the thought of cake makes me feel hotter. *Absent Friends* is 'a typical Ayckbourn', she says, 'a mix of comedy and poignant drama'. I'll show you poignant drama, I thought, preparing to die of heat. (I warned you I'm fond of exaggeration.) I swigged more 'cooling' wine.

'She doesn't *do* cake,' Sandy says, by way of introduction to Alison Cahill, who would be directing the second play of the season. (I'm averse to this popular use of 'doing', as if cake is a naughty drug. I am happy to hear that Alison doesn't 'do' cake. I didn't want cake, not even future cake, I don't like cake and I feel that it's my duty to rail against the stereotype that any time a woman feels a bit sad or busy or has to leave the house, she 'does' cake.) Alison tells us about her play: Terence Rattigan's *Variation on a Theme*, and how it was inspired by Alexandre Dumas *fils* play *La Dame aux Camélias*, which is not a reference I get. I am aware of Rattigan, of course; Dad had been in one of his most famous plays, *The Browning Version*, at Highbury, so I feel a little jolt of connection and purpose, past meets present. But I don't know this play, or its inspiration. It has a terrible title for a start, as bad as David

51

Mamet's *Bitter Wheat*. There's nothing compelling or enticing to it. Notifications of an Event. Letters from a Friend. Something in a Something Else. It's not a title that tells you anything, except that it is going to be wordy. I know it's not going to be a rough old bit of fury, Rattigan was no Angry Young Man, even though this play was written in 1958 when they were absolutely on-trend. Kitchen-sink dramas, focusing on class, poverty, masculinity, power . . . just from the title I'd have put money on *Variation* not covering that ground. It'd be more gin and it than grime and fury. *Variation* isn't performed often, Alison tells us. That sounds another warning bell: plays often fall out of favour, or remain minor in a play-wright's canon, for one good reason. That they are shit. I wonder to myself why it is going to be performed now.

'This is a play about desire and disillusionment, set on the French Riviera in the 1950s,' Alison goes on. OK, I think, I'm interested in exploring notions of desire. 'It takes place at the home of Rose, a glamorous yet tubercular socialite.' OK, I think again, I'm interested when a woman's desire takes centre stage, even when her role will feature a lot of repressed coughing. The original film starred the beautiful Margaret Leighton, and in another pleasing echo from the past, Dicky Bird tells me later that she came to Highbury in the 1940s, causing a stir. The glamorous Rose falls for Ron, Alison continues, who is ten years younger than her and a ballet dancer from Erdington . . . and hold on, that noise is me screeching to a halt. This has my attention. Terence Rattigan wrote a play about a man called Ron who was a ballet dancer

. . . from Erdington? That needs unpacking. Firstly, the name Ron never denotes 'sexual interest', not in the 1950s, and not now. Ron is your weird uncle who ran off with his mother's hairdresser. At best, Ron is Ron Swanson, from *Parks and Rec*. Ron is not sexy, and Ron is not ballet. Then there's Erdington. If you have an intimate knowledge of the Birmingham suburbs, you'll know Erdington. Otherwise, let me explain. When you come off Spaghetti Junction into Gravelly Hill (and neither of these things are what their names suggest), you hit Erdington, which is *quite* different from the French Riviera. My grandfather was born at 1 Reservoir Road, Erdington, 'when it was a village' my mum says. Highbury is on the edge of Erdington. I can see it over the Sheffield Road roofs. Suddenly *Variation* has local and personal relevance. I perk right up. This is the play I want to follow.

I go and chat to Alison after the familiarisation is finished, and, of course, she knows my youngest sister Madeleine – they were in Highbury Youth Theatre together. More connections, more links. I tell her that I'm writing a book, and that I want to follow her production, beginning to end, and is that OK? It feels like my own small audition, just as 'writer' this time, all the other baggage pushed aside. 'I can be a bit gobby,' she says unapologetically. 'Great,' I say, 'we're going to get on fine. I'll see you at the first rehearsal.'

CHAPTER 5

Exit Stage Left

If the opening scenes of amateur theatre's history are full of the Church, private dramas and ostentatious wealth, this next act is full of acronyms, associations and more politics than you might imagine. The start of the twentieth century is an exciting time where we find plenty of theatres that are still going strong today. Maddermarket Theatre in Norwich, for instance, described by Simon Callow as 'one of the great, great theatres in this country's theatrical heritage, without qualification, professional or amateur'. Based around what was a Roman Catholic chapel, Maddermarket Theatre was founded in 1911 by a man called Nugent Monck, whose original ambition was that his company should perform the entire canon of Shakespeare's plays. He'd achieved that goal by 1933, with strict rules. Actors weren't allowed to be in other amateur companies, there were no names in the programme, and no curtain calls. Personal recognition was not Monck's concern, this was about the team, and *the work*. George Bernard Shaw, whose name pops up all over the place as I research, was as impressed as Callow with the theatre. 'There is nothing in British theatrical history more extraordinary than your creation of the Maddermarket theatre out of nothing,' he wrote to Monck in 1940.

I visited Maddermarket recently to see an adaptation of *The Diary of a Nobody* by George and Weedon Grossmith, a novel which itself teases out ideas about amateur performers. When I walked into their beautiful performance space, I recognised the very smell of it. It hit me: this smells like amateur theatre, I thought. Like home. It's the slight fust of old buildings combined with a stinging singe as stage lamps burn off dust but never quite cover the suspicion of damp, of bodies and greasepaint and historic carpet. On a horrible Monday evening in November, sitting among a full house in this chapel with a changed point of worship, it was clear that Maddermarket is thriving, over a hundred years after Monck founded it.

Then there's the Stockport Garrick Theatre (SGT), which has a plaque at its founding site declaring itself to be the country's 'oldest Little Theatre'. This plaque is SGT's declaration of its point of specialness; staking a claim in the story seems to be important – groups love to make pronouncements about themselves, that they're 'the oldest Georgian theatre' (the Georgian Theatre Royal in Richmond) or 'the oldest am-dram society in the world' (as Canterbury Old Stagers do), and so on. SGT was founded in 1901 by a bunch of actors led by Mr Edwin T. Heys, who'd previously been kicked out of the Stockport Unitarian Church Dramatic Society. His crime? The Unitarian performing space didn't have room for actors to go offstage left and return stage right. You couldn't get from one wing to the other, in the middle of a play. Edwin, being an engineer, sought to solve the problem practically, by tunnelling under the stage. Picture a young actor in flouncy garb marching off stage left, dropping down into a dark hole and crawling quietly under the boards while the play goes on above his head, emerging with mouse droppings and cobwebs in his eyebrows and wig, then appearing back on stage right as if nothing happened, perhaps coughing from dust. It is a commitment to the form, for sure, and one that led to the creation of an important theatre.

Edwin and his gang of tunnelling rebels formed the Stockport Garrick Society at a meeting in a coffee shop that's now a bank. Convening that first meeting, they stated this in a letter:

> There is a great need in Stockport for an energetic society whose aim should be mainly educational, i.e., to perform the best plays by the most capable amateur actors and with the finest scenic effects, and whose efforts should be directed to fostering and furthering the highest forms of dramatic art and literature.

It's so earnest, and I love it. Education was quite the motivator in those days, a desire not for frivolity, but for intellectual aspiration, improving the minds of the working man.

Their first public performance, on Thursday 27 February 1902, was *The Merchant of Venice*, directed by Mr Ryder Boys, with Edwin taking the role of Duke of Venice. The role of Portia was played by Miss Josephine Gaul, who became something of a local role model. It was recommended to her at the time that she either leave her job or leave the theatre, but she dug in her heels, a courage which inspired other women to join. By 1903 the young women of the group were organising fundraising initiatives, where frivolity *could* be indulged. Things like 'Ye Merrie Spinsters Parties', where 'there was much merriment', the press wrote. 'Although partaking largely of the burlesque, [it] was none the less enjoyable . . . A capital vocal and musical programme and a series of waxworks made up an enjoyable evening.' A programme in the archive lists these 'waxworks': 'Mary Had a Little Lamb' was played by Edith Dewhurst, 'Ancient Greece' was Miss Lily Sidebotham, 'Norwegian' was Miss Horrocks. What were these 'waxworks'? Were they tableaux? Were they emulating Madame Tussauds? Were they a precursor to *The Vagina Monologues*, in mime? For balance, SGT also threw Bachelor Parties, had a Cycling section, ran literary and social lectures, and Smoking Parties for Ladies and Gentlemen. 'DON'T BRING YOUR SMOKES,' the announcement yelled. 'Cigars and cigarettes will be provided.' This was living the dream. What all this activity shows us is just what a broad 'offer' amateur theatre presented. Where else could people find artistic endeavour *and* education *and* community *and* fun *and* smoking *and* (this is a big one) women and men hanging out together?

And then, there were the plays. They might have started safe with a Shakespearean comedy, but at Stockport Garrick, they weren't staying that way. They were staging Ibsen's *Pillars of Salt* in 1904, George Bernard Shaw's *Candida* in 1905, *Monna Vanna* by Maeterlinck in 1909 – all considered to be challenging plays. A book, *The Garrick Story*, written in 1951 about the first fifty years of the theatre's history, talked about the role that playwrights like Ibsen and Shaw played.

> The recently departed nineteenth century . . . was essentially an actor's theatre; histrionic achievement in great classical roles was its life blood . . . In the nineties however, Ibsen and Shaw had arrived to introduce the play of ideas, to present arguments on human behaviour, essays in the realistic which demanded acting not of purple patches but of quieter, naturalistic sincerity. And so, in this new mood, the amateur got his chance.

And 'her chance', of course, if we can please remember Miss Josephine Gaul and her sorority. (I yelled 'and her' so much in all my treks through archives and newspaper reports, my throat got sore.) In November 1905 The *Manchester Guardian* wrote:

> Amateur theatricals in provincial towns are not usually a very intellectual hobby, but Stockport is evidently a shining example . . . instead of the depressing revivals of the *Ticket-of-Leave Man*, the *Private Secretary* or *Davy Garrick* that are usual among such societies, they have

decided to take their place at the very front of the independent theatre movement.

This lack of intellectualism bemoaned by the *Guardian* doesn't seem entirely fair. You can't put on radical plays if radical plays haven't been written yet. All you can do is work with what's available. And equally, if putting on radical plays will not attract an audience in these 'provincial' towns, that's another reason to steer clear. Audiences sometimes need leading in slowly. However, the work at SGT, the paper declared, 'gives the society a real function, a place in the world, and in other people's lives, something to live for'. *Something to live for.* The new theatre was a hotbed of improvement and intellectualism, well supported by the people of Stockport. Within their first week, their membership stood at nearly a hundred.

It's not quite the image we have of amateur theatre, is it? And not the image we might guess at, either, from reports of spinsters and waxworks and smokes. Amateur theatre isn't radical, political or progressive, it can't bring about change. It's all farce and laughs and 'depressing revivals' and maintaining the status quo. Isn't that right? Maybe we need to think again. The *Garrick*, SGT's magazine, reported how they stood their ground after a lecture given by Harley Granville Barker, a major theatrical figure, on the foundation of the British Drama League (BDL). 'We all wish the League well,' the *Garrick* reported. 'Our vigorous North will collaborate with but will not be run by London.' That's a powerful 'no ta, Harley'. Theirs was a strong sense of place, theirs was a strong drive for good performance. And their voices would be heard.

By 1920, Stockport Garrick Theatre had moved into their own premises, which they still occupy, converted from an old engineering works, an unwitting but nice homage to their founder, Edwin. It's a long, flattish building budged right up to the pavement on an unconvivial road. As you go round the corner, your eye is drawn not to the theatre, but to the chimney behind it with 'Hat Museum' painted on it vertically in big white letters. SGT continued through two world wars, and is now a busy theatre with a main stage, studio and a youth theatre. Michael Dobson outlines why SGT was so important in its heyday. They were, he writes, the first amateur society to get their own premises, the first to stage Ibsen and Shaw, and they stimulated a revival of 'artistically-inclined' theatre in the North-West more generally. There's not a plaque big enough to put all those achievements on.

Back at the start of the twentieth century, one man, Geoffrey Whitworth, saw amateur theatre as the nation's salvation. Whitworth founded the British Drama League in 1919 (the organisation that Stockport Garrick had no intention of being ruled by), and his aims were 'to assist the development of the Art of the Theatre and its right relationship with the life of the community'. He'd got the idea for the League after watching a play-reading given by munition workers during the First World War, as recorded by E. Martin Browne in *Educational Theatre Journal* in 1953.

There he saw that in a machine-riddled world, millions would find release and delight, not only by watching plays but by trying to express themselves in the doing of them . . . Acting, which had previously been the pastime of a few leisured rich, could become the recreation of the many.

It's such a romantic image, if a little crudely stereotyped: working men and women stepping away from their dirty noisy machinery to indulge in being creative. Going from being physical and wordless to philosophical and expressive; moving from reality to imagination, from labour to dreams. Where machines had robbed people of their personal connections, theatre gave it all back. Drama, Whitworth thought, came to the rescue. And if I am wary of over-romanticising, Whitworth had no such qualms.

As I sat and watched and listened, I felt that I was understanding the fundamental quality of dramatic art in a way that I had never understood it before. Here was the art of the theatre reduced to the simplest terms, yet in this very reduction triumphant.

Whitworth wanted to see if the value of that experience could be fostered across the country, and he was in a good position to try – he was well connected and active in the movement to create a national theatre. The First World War had a profound effect on commercial theatre – rents were high, people sought escapism, the choice of plays narrowed. Whitworth wanted the BDL to counteract all of that. They held their first conference just months after their launch, confirming their objectives to promote and assist theatre in general; to push for the creation of a national theatre policy, and for the establishment of a faculty of theatre in universities and colleges. Any of us who've studied drama either at A level or as undergraduates owe thanks to the BDL's active Education Committee, which fought for it to be seen as a legitimate area of study.

In 1927, the BDL launched the National Festival of Community Drama, and 107 amateur societies took part. By 1959, the festival had over one thousand entrants. Alongside the Education Committee, they ran a library and a training department founded, E. Martin Browne wrote, in response to a new attitude.

> The attitude of the amateur who takes the theatre seriously, as the art through which he will seek to use his leisure for the expression and the enrichment of his whole being, and to make his contribution to the enjoyment of his fellows. Such amateurs in hundreds seek to spend their vacations, their evenings and their weekends in learning how to do better in the theatre.

The first activity run by the Training Department was a nine-day school for amateur producers, attended by eighty students. Nugent Monck, of Maddermarket Theatre, lectured there; his interest in seeing amateurs reach a high standard extended way beyond his own stage. This kind of philanthropy ran through the centre of the amateur world. There was no doubt that Whitworth had achieved his aims.

The BDL was not the only horse in the race. I warned you about acronyms: the National Operatic and Dramatic Association (NODA) had begun in 1899, and the Little Theatre Guild (LTG) formed in 1946. Both of these umbrella companies offered shelter to small communities. The LTG started with nine member groups, including Stockport Garrick and Highbury Little Theatre, and now has a steadfast one hundred; a requirement of membership is that groups must own or lease their own theatre premises. NODA is larger, with a membership of 2,500 amateur theatre groups and 1,000 individuals, but there's no requirement to have your own building, which opens up the field somewhat. Although both of those organisations are flourishing today, received opinion is that things changed for amateur theatre around the 1960s. It went into decline. This was reflected in the slow demise of the British Drama League. It became the British Theatre Association in the 1970s but their public subsidies were cut as a direct result of Thatcher's strategies to reduce inflation by not funding anything nice, which included the Arts Council.

(Thatcher also made an appearance when I spoke to the Stockport Garrick archivist Richard Humphry, a member there since 1973. 'In the 1930s, it got a bit drawing-room comedies. From the 1950s, Shakespeare was our most performed playwright,' he told me. 'And there was a marked change in membership after Thatcher.' We instinctively paused the conversation, like two people of our age invariably do when Thatcher is mentioned for the first time. I gave him a look that asked: 'Are we on the same page?' We were. We had a brief, heated rant, and then Richard carried on. 'There were fewer numbers, the quality went down. People were told when they got a job, that if they worked there, they wouldn't be able to indulge their love of amateur theatre.' That mirrors what Josephine Gaul was told right at the start of the SGT story, only this time it was not specifically aimed at women.)

Some blamed the am-dram decline on the rise of television, which had a broader range of programmes on offer. It is the same argument John Humphrys was making fifty-plus years later so, clearly, concerns about a permanent demise in the sixties were a tad premature. And it's ironic that television can now be seen as contributing to a rise in the celebration of the amateur, with shows like *Britain's Got Talent* and *X Factor*. Alongside television, there was a wider provision of other leisure pursuits – the first sports centres came into existence in the late 1950s, and who wants to make theatre when you can play badminton? (Of course, people did both, but the time they devoted was split between activities.) There was more social mobility, so the old notions of 'community' became fractured, and the whole concept of youth culture was growing. The amateur theatre story here feels like a bit of a microcosm, or a metaphor. It used to be revered, respected and essential. Now everyone is surprised it's still going (except, of course, for the people who are actually going to it, doing it, loving it). The same can be said of working men's clubs – and libraries even. Great institutions that used to form and drive communities and were seen as vital components of cultural life have been replaced or killed off, sometimes by political will. The social offering has been diminished, because society has been fractured and made poor. This lack of social offering then compounds that poverty.

As am-dram declined, the future of professional theatre was looking very bright. In 1960 the Royal Shakespeare Company was founded, then the National Theatre. Fringe theatre companies were beginning to appear, and maybe they were occupying the space that had belonged to the amateur. The actors would certainly have often been paid the same. (Nothing.)

The story is simple: that in the first half of the twentieth century, amateur theatre was booming, it was taken seriously and celebrated, and many groups and associations were formed. Then it all seemed to dwindle. But is this the current situation, and do the statistics bear out that narrative? I wanted to interrogate them, and initially this was not a straightforward task. Even when I asked organisations that exist specifically to promote amateur theatre, they couldn't be more precise than 'there are lots', which wasn't helpful. I wanted hard figures, and I found them by going higher, to the government, to the Department for Culture, Media and Sport's report *Our Creative Talent: the voluntary and amateur arts in England,* published in 2013. If you come to these figures with the word 'dwindling' at the front of your mind, this report will surprise you.

Our Creative Talent opens with this statement:

> Formally organised voluntary and amateur arts groups are a crucially important part of the arts ecology and account for almost one fifth of all arts participation in England, although in some regions it is much higher than that.

The report noted that there are 49,140 groups across the country, with a total of 5.9 million members. Of that figure, 3.5 million are women, and 2.4 million men, a 60/40 split, which wasn't how our history started. Women were largely absent from the drawing rooms and spouting clubs, and even as we moved on into the formation of amateur companies, individual outlier women had taken on the burden of being role models. But this current split was certainly something I'd noticed, at least anecdotally. 'An additional 3.5 million people volunteer as extras or helpers,' the report stated, 'a total of 9.4 million people taking part.' And 'in 2006/7, groups put on 710,000 performances or exhibitions, which attracted 159 million attendances'. Within arts groups 546,000 people have management roles. Hold on, though. Before we get too excited, buoyed by the idea of these hordes of amateur theatre-makers doing hundreds of thousands of plays to unimaginably huge audiences, we need to calm down a bit. Because this figure relates to *all* amateur art forms, including craft, dance, literature and music, the last of which remains the most popular category with 11,220 groups to amateur theatre's 5,380. Broken down, though, the figures are still extraordinary. *Our Creative Talent* states that there are 1,113,000 amateur theatre-makers in the country, with an additional 687,000 helpers giving a total of 1,800,000. The 5,380 groups do an estimated 92,000 performances each year, to an audience of 21,166,000. Amazing! Over 21 million attendances at amateur theatre, in all its various glories, is an extraordinary number. This is clearly no minority sport.

I wanted to compare these figures with earlier ones, to see what that showed me. Perhaps this huge number does actually constitute a massive slump. I started with Edwin Schoell, who wrote in the *Educational Theatre Journal* in May 1963:

It is estimated that there are between twenty and thirty thousand amateur dramatic societies in existence in Great Britain today . . . It is also estimated that more than one-half million people participate in the activities of the amateur stage. George W. Bishop, writing in *The Amateur Dramatics Yearbook* of 1928–29, listed 1700 dramatic societies in Great Britain at that time and estimated that the list comprised about one-half of the active societies of the day. In a period of slightly more than thirty years, therefore, there has been almost a tenfold increase.

A tenfold increase at the start of the sixties contradicts the idea of a downward trend. But then I compared Schoell's delighted figures with those from the *Our Creative Talent* report. They show that we've gone from around 25,000 groups in 1963, to a fifth of that, 5,380, in 2013. Oh. Suddenly our current situation doesn't look so good after all.

In 1979, the Central Council for Amateur Theatre (CCAT) undertook its own statistical survey. They reported that the total overall membership of groups in England was estimated at 479,002. I love the detail of those extra two people. Who were they? My mum and dad? The chair, Arnold Hart, wrote that 'any activity which claims the working participation of half a million adults and has a box-office loyalty of over 14 million, is playing a considerable part in the structure of current British leisure-time pursuits and must be taken very seriously indeed'. In 1996, writers John Pick and Malcolm Anderton estimated that 8,500 amateur dramatic societies in Britain played to 24 million people.

Over the years then, according to these various sources ranging from the 1920s to 2013, the numbers of amateur theatre groups went racing up and then slowly falling down, the number of participants stuck at around the half-million mark for a while, but has now at least doubled, and ticket sales bumped up from 14 million in the late 1970s to 24 million in 1996 and then slumped to 21 million less than twenty years later. There are fewer groups, but more people participating. It is such a mixed message. And it's hard to glean from all this what the direction of travel might currently be. But one thing is clear and indisputable: the figures are now surprisingly large. It might not feel like that if you are standing outside it all, seeing it as a niche hobby, all froth and light. But that is perhaps an issue of perception rather than number-crunching. Because once you start digging and discover all the dedicated magazines, websites, Twitter accounts and Facebook pages of amateur theatre, you can begin to see that actually, currently, there are many thousands of people taking it 'very seriously indeed'. Maybe we need to be much louder about what they do. I'm doing my vocal warm-ups in preparation.

In all these numbers, there is confusion about where the boundary lines are drawn. When writers talk about Great Britain and then give only English figures, that way trouble lies. In his 2000 report, *Luvvies and rude mechanicals? Amateur and Community Theatre in Scotland*, Greg Giesekam gave an overview of the Scottish statistics. The Scottish amateur theatre movement began in the mid nineteenth century with the upper and middle classes, he writes, but spread across the classes, particularly in an inter-war boom, when dozens of amateur companies were set up every year.

By the late 1930s there were about a thousand amateur societies in Scotland . . . often with the aim of developing an indigenous drama. The amateur movement had effectively reached its peak towards the end of the 1930s. After the [Second World] War there was a period during which the movement seemed to be regaining its momentum . . . but a slow decline set in from the late 1950s onward.

Here we are again, with that slow decline; this is familiar territory. But again, Giesekam's contemporary statistics show that the decline was not, actually, terminal. The body might not be in peak condition, but there is certainly still a strong heartbeat.

Whichever way it is measured, the amateur dramatic movement in Scotland is a sector of considerable size and significance for the many thousands who come into contact with it. It annually involves over 26,000 participants performing to a total audience of approximately one million.

The combined audience figures for amateur, youth and community theatre, he points out, easily exceed the audience for professional theatre, and they can't have all been 'shanghaied into going' by the people taking part. We all recognise that shanghaied feeling, I'm sure; the obligation to turn up to something because your child/mum/neighbour will be peering out from onstage, trying to spot you in the crowd, asking eagerly at the end, 'So, what did you think?' And it might be unfair to paint it as obligation, because it can also be one of the main draws, seeing someone you know onstage.

The gender split in Scotland is similarly biased towards women (63/37), and Giesekam also looks at age ranges.

Contrary to popular preconceptions and to a concern which exercised some at one time that the clubs were in danger of becoming dominated by the middle-aged and elderly, there is an almost even balance in the membership between those aged below 40 and those above it.

This deserves a bit of unpacking, this 'danger' that the dominant older people present. On the one hand, it is certainly another reputational issue for amateur theatre – that it's full of old people, which means that it's boring, reactionary, Brexit-voting and will, like all old people, die quite soon. But on the other hand, why should we dismiss something because older people do it? That's called ageism. Do we always have to conclude that anything old people like or do is, by definition, shit? Some old people are absolutely great. Even some middle-aged ones (ahem). Also, and this might be an unexpected plot twist: if we're extremely lucky, we'll all be old people one day, and I'm sure when that's me, I'll hope my contributions will still count for something.

It won't surprise you to learn that the suffragette movement used theatre as a way to spread its message. Founded in 1908, the Actresses Franchise League produced plays and toured them around local communities; the Pioneer Players, a feminist theatre group founded in 1911, explored social, political and moral issues, working in (private) Little Theatres to avoid the cursed censorship of our friend the Lord Chamberlain. Neither of these groups was strictly amateur, but they were lighting the torch for what was coming: the mix of theatre and overt politics. In 1917, the leaders of the Liverpool Independent Labour Party founded a drama society with the stated aims of introducing 'Socialist and Realistic Drama' into their movement, and 'to educate our members . . . to the principles of Socialism through the medium of Drama'. I will admit here that, at first, the thought of this made my heart sink just a small bit. It sounds so deathly earnest, so on-the-nose, and I NEED JOKES. (Or at least the promise of a good story.) The idea of didactic propaganda in the theatre some-times turns me into a resistant child, even when it's good for me, and even from my own side. It's theatrical kale. But then I rallied, because I was so pleased to discover a political strand to the amateur story, and I approve of this drive to provide political drama about and for working men and women. (Some women. But mostly men.) So I decided to relish the purity of the idealism, the sincere endeavour for the good of many, and the optimism. I'd already warmed my hands by the political fire started by Stockport Garrick, when they put on Ibsen and Shaw plays. This is where the flames really start to burn. This is the story of Unity.

Unity is described by its biographer Colin Chambers as a 'unique left-wing theatre that changed the face of British theatre', and that's a pretty phenomenal claim for a bunch of amateurs. But he's right; from Unity you can trace the roots of so much: the rise of political fringe theatre companies; the careers of renowned professional practitioners like Joan Littlewood, who became known as 'the mother of modern theatre'. Unity's players became the leaders in agitprop theatre – where agitation meets propaganda – and from that, you can trace the origins of the political stand-up comedy scene of the 1980s. Like Nugent Monck's actors in Maddermarket, the players remained anonymous within the company to avoid the kind of 'star culture' fetishised by commercial theatre. Some Unity actors, like Bob Hoskins and Warren Mitchell, did go on to have huge professional careers, where they became unlikely members of that star culture. But Unity is where they, and a lot else besides, began.

Rummaging through archives is where history really comes alive. It's in the flowers doodled in the corner of a set of minutes from a committee meeting, in how people sign their names and what they sign with. It's in the way documents have been mimeographed, and what that tells you about effort, and resources and careful collection. It's alive in changing typefaces; the introduction of new fonts. In the way London phone numbers go from being prefaced with their location ('Euston 5391') to 01, then 071, and now 0207. It's alive in the terribly staged and brilliantly revealing old production photos. It's in the heavy dot of a typed full stop which has almost gone through the thin paper. So many full stops. When the world goes up in flames, the paper will burn but these indestructible archived full stops will somehow remain, like the footprints of ants on scorched earth. All the high ideals are detailed in archives, but seeing the material first hand is a reminder that all of this involved real people, who you almost feel you get to know, their names repeatedly written over and again. I fell into the story of Unity Theatre in the V&A Theatre & Performance Archives with the reverence of an archaeologist opening a new tomb in Luxor. I sat reading and staring until the relentlessly pounded full stops danced before my eyes.

One of the first things I looked at was a small maroon notebook with a label stuck on the front on which, in pen, was handwritten in capitals *THE UNITY THEATRE OF GREAT BRITAIN 1936-1946. A DECADE OF PRODUCTION by RON. F. TRAVIS*. With the book lying on a V&A-provided protective grey cushion, I carefully opened the front cover and noted that Travis's thesis, written in 1968, was part of his degree submission at the Southern Illinois University. That made me think. Illinois is very far away from Camden, and it was even further, before the Internet . . . Unity must have really meant something. 'The Unity Theatre,' Travis prefaces, 'laid the groundwork for the modern English drama'; modern for the 1960s means writers like John Osborne, Lionel Bart and Harold Pinter. During its first decade, he writes, 'the small, amateur Communist-dominated workers theatre . . . would foster ideas and goals that would guarantee its existence for the next thirty-two years.'

It's ironic that censorship encouraged political workers' groups like Unity to form. Travis returns us to the Lord Chamberlain. 'The fact that there is still theatre of any kind in England seems remarkable when one examines the archaic rulings governing play production and play writing.' He's right, it *is* remarkable. The Lord Chamberlain's rule ended in the year this thesis was written, but at the time Unity was starting, it was as forceful as ever. For the kind of work they wanted to do, workers needed to organise and become private members' clubs. Even so, Unity fell foul of the rules time and again, by taking work out of a theatre building, and into the open. It almost seems as if the Lord Chamberlain was watching them very closely in the hope they'd slip up. I picture him, fully wigged-up and in swanky red velvet britches, peering round a corner, spying on our miscreants through his opera glasses.

Travis outlines Unity's route into being. In 1922, the Independent Labour Party formed an arts guild for drama societies – the Council for Proletarian Art. And the Workers' Theatre Movement (WTM) of Great Britain, allied to the Communist Party, grew; they took plays out on the streets because that's where they could best serve their audience, and at the same time avoid the dreadful bourgeois trappings of conventional theatres. It wasn't just the practicalities of how people were expected to behave in those theatres (dressed up, clutching expensive tickets and revelling in a sense of exclusivity), the WTM were against the type of work that was on offer, and how it was staged. They wanted to be radical in every sense. Various groups splintered (this is a story about the left – of *course* there was splintering) and amalgamated, but by 1926, the WTM had associations in London, Glasgow and Manchester and were in touch with similar workers' theatres in Germany and New York. They premiered *The Ragged Trousered Philanthropist* in 1927, an incredible play which became synonymous with the movement, and which I vividly remember seeing at the Half Moon in Mile End sixty years later. In 1933, a group called the Rebel Players formed from the merger of several units of the WTM; in their work, they wanted to stress the artistic as much as the political. And Unity came next, in 1936. All these words – rebel, workers, proletarian, communist; we need only a 'comrade' and a 'brother' to have the full Old Lefty bingo – are not only deeply unfashionable now, but also seem so unthinkable in relation to amateur theatre. My preconceptions have been blown out of the water.

The first two years of Unity's life were spent in planning and organising, the next two years focused on production. Looking at archived committee minutes, surviving from 1936 and packed with those indestructibly hefty full stops, I got both a sense of reverence and a reminder of the tiny details that go into an endeavour like this. And let's be realistic – the tedium of meetings that may be enthusiastic, but sometimes feel interminable. That dread moment when you think the end is in sight, when the chair says, 'Any other business?' and someone puts up their hand, 'Well, yes, actually . . .' Here, the big things have as much prominence as the small. Every now and again, a seemingly simple item drew a vivid picture. One piece of business noted that 'Mrs Buckland is typing copies of *Bread In The Waters*', and in that, I could see her laboriously typing the same page over and over, to save on copying or purchasing costs. The minutes talked about the perpetual problem of budgets, in which there were always serious deficits. 'This leaves about £10 to be found,' they recorded, 'which must, I presume, come from God.' It seems unlikely to me that a communist organisation might look to God for cash, so I assume a level of sarcasm was at play. 'Our main aim during this period has been to build up a reputation . . . We have achieved this.' And then some, without the help of any higher powers.

In its first year, Unity had 60 members and 300 associates (who would have been able to buy tickets to shows). One year later, membership was already at 184 full members and 1,409 associates, and there had been a total of 48 shows given at the club, and 65 outside it, when productions were taken to labour meetings and town halls. The play *Waiting for Lefty* by American author Clifford Odets, a series of vignettes around cab drivers planning to strike, was becoming their 'signature dish'; writer Amber Massie-Blomfield, in her fantastic book *Twenty Theatres to See Before You Die*, recounts that when H. G. Wells, an avid supporter of Unity, saw *Waiting for Lefty*, 'he leapt up on his chair, waving his umbrella around and joining in with the chanting "Strike! Strike! Strike!"'

As I looked at page after page of archive material, plays and players became familiar. Alongside *Waiting for Lefty*, both *Till the Day I Die* (also by Odets) and *Private Hicks* were regulars in the repertoire, as were titles that clearly knew their market, like *Playing to the Factory Audience* and *Winkles and Champagne*, the latter written by Terry Newman and William Rowbotham – who you might know as the actor Bill Owen. By 1937, Unity had their own theatre premises that seated 330 people, converted from a former chapel in St Pancras and built by voluntary labour donated by trade unions in London; it was their home for the next forty years. 'Soon Unity began to sell its product, namely political theatre,' Travis proclaims in his thesis. They did a version of *Babes in the Wood*, Massie-Blomfield writes, 'which satirised appeasement, and in particular Neville Chamberlain. A question was raised in the House of Commons; there was discussion of shutting the Unity Theatre down; but nothing came of it, and the play was a smash hit.'

They took an active role in Spanish politics during the Civil War, campaigned against Oswald Mosley back home, and supported the transport strike in 1937 with productions they called 'Living Newspapers' – which remind me of the topical satire shows which boomed in the 1980s and 90s. Remember, Unity in the 1930s were playing in a culture otherwise domi-nated by light entertainment. In 1938, American star Paul Robeson turned down West End work to appear in their production of *Plant in the Sun*, announcing that 'as an artist, I must have a working-class audience'. That play became one of Unity's greatest achievements. The group kept growing, forming into two acting units, with a summer school, a PR department, a play department, a writing group, a revue committee, the Living Newspaper group and, by 1943, one of their lead actors, Una Brandon Jones, was asked to direct a Women's Company. In her memoirs, she wrote:

By the time the war was started in earnest, late in 1940, the shortage of males at Unity was becoming more and

more noticeable ... although there was a certain fluctua-
tion among the women ... more and more the main brunt
of keeping the theatre open was falling upon the women.

Another wartime memoir in the archives talked of how
'there was only one voice on the boards pleading for action to
help the Jews, to save Europe from war. We needed a stronger
lead than the Cliveden set of appeasement. Unity Theatre gave
that lead here in Camden.' This was the theatre of the left, the
theatre of the working class, and their voice was loud. Sybil
Thorndike, who had also been a member of the Actresses
Franchise League, declared that 'the greatest hope for the stage
in this country is the rise of the Unity Theatre, realising that
the real art of the theatre always was, and always must be,
bound up with the life of the people of the time.'

Influential political writers played an important role in
their programming. They were the first theatre in the country
to perform Bertolt Brecht, and Jean-Paul Sartre chose them
for the British premiere of *Nekrassov*; they brought a wider
audience to Maxim Gorky and Sean O'Casey. By the end of
their first decade, London Unity had spawned a national movement, with theatres in Glasgow, Liverpool, Manchester and
other cities. The amateurs, the communists – they did that.
Absolutely bloody marvellous.

In 1975, Unity's theatre in Camden burned down. There's
no suggestion it was anything other than accidental. Bill
Owen, who'd begun at Unity, later recalled how 'we looked at
the four walls, and up at the sky. It was a frightening

experience. All my memories raced through my mind, full of ghosts. It was my life.' Although Unity continued, as Unity Theatre Trust and Unity Theatre Society, things would never be the same again. One memo I found, written in the 1980s, stated with certainty that 'the old standards are no longer acceptable. The well-meaning, politically-motivated amateur performance has no place at the present time.' In those few words, all of that rich and wonderful past had become bundled up into 'well-meaning' and 'politically-motivated'. Irrelevant, damned, chucked out. To the modern Unity, amateurs were outdated and wrong; but without them, things fell away.

Sometimes when you're looking for connections they appear in the most unlikely places. What or who, I wondered, can pull all this history together? Is there something, or someone, who can bring us all the way from Charles Dickens to the present day? Then I found the connection, in Essex. It is the one, and only, Chesney Hawkes.

In 2018, Brentwood Leisure Trust, under the production leadership of Mark Reed, put on a community production of *Joseph and the Amazing Technicolor Dreamcoat*. The original intention had been to only use 'community' performers – or amateurs, a word we are not backing away from. 'But Chesney was in panto and someone suggested he'd make a very good Joseph,' Mark told me. Chesney was cast in the lead role, as the only paid performer. The rest of the cast were amateurs, and they had to pay to be in the production, £35 per adult. This was exactly what Dickens had done, let's not forget – paid to be on stage in the Minor Theatre in Catherine Street, in the nineteenth century.

From the way Mark defended his decision, it was clear there had been a backlash. Amateur theatre is a hobby, he said, and with all hobbies, there is cost involved. 'We have to look after local people's money and what we spend it on. Some goes into sports, and some goes into theatre. If your hobby happened to be judo or badminton, you're paying out every week. That's what you're doing in amateur theatre.'

Mark reckoned they got the fee for Chesney, which he described as 'really not a lot', back within a week of announcing that he was in the show, selling out two nights in a hall that could seat around two thousand. 'They came from all over the country to see him.'

It was an experiment that went right, so they are repeating it; when I spoke to Mark, he was about to announce Chesney's return to Brentwood in 2019, in *Godspell*. 'For *Godspell* we'll have five months rehearsal, two hours a week, and people will be taught all sorts of skills – balloon modelling, juggling, fire breathing. We're going to be pushing ourselves and learning stuff. The money people pay to be in it works out at around a pound an hour.'

Mark talked with passion about the ethos of inclusion at Brentwood. 'The people in *Joseph* had a range of needs and wants. And there was so much community in it. It was wholeheartedly beautiful and supportive and positive. We can show that we're bringing people together and helping individuals. We are going to do that again.'

There are people who want to work with Chesney, who want to make a show, need help boosting their self-confidence or want to find a way to help their loneliness or access. It sounds like a win–win. And it's fitting that they are unknowingly providing a bridge in amateur history. From Dickens to Chesney via some radical proletarians. Who would have thought it?

CHAPTER 6

Cast List

At the inaugural Amateur Theatre Festival, held at Questors Theatre in London in September 2018, Matt Applewhite, managing director of publisher Nick Hern Books, kicked off proceedings by saying: 'Everyone who makes a living from working in the theatre almost certainly started off involved in some capacity for free, for the love of it.'

It's not hard to find names that fit that statement from every rung of the professional acting ladder. At the very top, we have Ian McKellen, who was patron of the Little Theatre Guild from 2008 to 2016, a role now taken by Kenneth Branagh. Judi Dench started off in a 1951 amateur revival of the York Mystery Plays, working up to star billing as the Virgin Mary. On *Desert Island Discs* in 2015, Judi talked with evident enjoyment about her first performance in a school play where, aged about five, she played a snail.

'My father made me a huge shell, which I had to creep under, and at one point creep out of, and when it came to the day that the parents came, I stood up, looking out at everybody, and I heard the principal of the school saying "Get down, Judith!" I remember it absolutely vividly.'

After Glenda Jackson finished school at sixteen, she got involved with amateur theatre in her home town of Hoylake, in Cheshire – 'usually playing maids and things like that'. Ben Kingsley was a lab technician when he started with the Salford Players, and describes being 'transported' by the thrill of the audience response when he performed. Patrick Stewart's mother, Gladys, was a weaver in the West Yorkshire mills and active in amateur theatre; she and Patrick's English and drama teacher, Cecil Dormand, encouraged him to take part. Tom Bateman, a patron of Oxford's Tomahawk Theatre, told me, 'I loved my am-dram days!' Brenda Blethyn was working as a secretary for British Rail when she got her first role with the Euston Players. And Simon Callow, in his keynote speech at that Amateur Theatre Festival, mentioned that Charles Laughton, his hero, was an amateur in Scarborough 'and he said they were the happiest and most creative days of his life'.

Professional actors get plenty of space to talk about their journeys and their roots, how it all started and who they'd like to thank. It seems right, then, that amateurs take centre stage here.

It's as if there's a secret code – if you say the words 'amateur theatre', all kinds of people appear. It's our version of a Masonic handshake, only without the patriarchal bullshit and the little knife down your sock. When I began thinking about this book and used the secret code a few times, it unlocked a load of surprises even in my immediate circle of friends. I didn't have to tie anyone to a chair and shine a lamp in their face; all I did was start talking about amateur theatre and people readily confessed to being involved, without any need for interrogation. Among my friends, the code revealed Lucy B, Sue, Brenda, two Barbaras, one Dave, a Dick and Wendy. The secret code unlocked another tier, too, the friends-of-friends. Everybody knew somebody. It began to look suspiciously like amateur theatre reached much further than I'd ever thought. If you use the code, be prepared for a massive amount of 'my uncle/neighbour/mother/colleague does that'. And if you talk to the uncle/neighbour/mother/colleague, you can learn all sorts of stuff – about theatre, of course, but also about people, life, relationships, purpose and joy. So often, there was joy. If joy was a fuel, I'd shove everyone onto the amateur stage and we'd be as rich as Norway.

One of the women I found was Barbara Hughes. Like me, Barbara performed to her neighbours as a child, only she used a sheet across a washing line as the curtain to her theatre, which was in her small back garden on a new council estate in Rutherglen, near Glasgow. There she'd perform with her friends what she called 'little plays' that she wrote, charging a penny each to the audience. 'The first time I did that,' she said, 'my mum made me take all the pennies back.'

Barbara and I were talking over a pre-show gin and tonic at a pub in Richmond, North Yorkshire. That night she was in charge of props for *A Bunch of Amateurs*, a play by Ian Hislop and Nick Newman about a bunch of amateur actors.

(Plays about amateur actors are always a hit with amateur actors. It's a bit of a double bluff, a wink and a nod. 'We know.') I was going to be in the audience at the Georgian Theatre Royal. I asked Barbara if the performing gene was in her family, and the picture she paints is evocative.

'I come from a family that all sing. My mum sang, my aunt Bet played the piano, my great-aunt sang in one of the Glasgow choirs, my grandfather wanted to join the music hall, but his parents were Plymouth Brethren and the music hall was a great big NO. My great-grandfather made my grandfather, my pappy, go on the coal wagons, and for a while he was the Singing Coalman in Bridgetown. One of my deep memories of my pappy was him singing to me. And my nanna was in the Townswomen's Guild in Rutherglen. They had a dramatic society and I went to watch her.'

From a really young age, then, Barbara knew what theatre was, and how it looked. When she was performing in the garden, with the sheet as a curtain, she knew how to construct a play, because she'd seen them onstage.

'And those days you went to the cinema a lot; I used to go and see musicals. That's what I wanted to do. I wanted to sing and be in musicals . . . The sixties were starting, it was quite feasible I could have ended up singing in a little band in Glasgow. That's not off-the-wall stuff, that's feasible.' What happened? I wondered aloud. 'My dad happened. And by the time I was sixteen I had no confidence, nothing. I couldn't do it.'

Barbara was talking about the physical abuse that her father inflicted on the family, and particularly his sexual abuse of her. The family had moved to Portsmouth when she was nine, because of his naval posting; when she was sixteen, they escaped from him, and Portsmouth, and returned to Scotland.

'That last year we were with him, there were many, many times I thought he was going to kill us all. By the time we'd left him and gone back to Rutherglen, none of us were in a fit state for anything. I was so wrecked. I was a mess. And I started drinking.' But still, those women, that fierce creative matriarchy, were around her. 'They saved me. They kept a light lit within me.'

When Barbara moved to Richmond in 1974 aged twenty-nine, she joined a group called the Housewives Register. I wondered how I could match the Barbara sitting here, a radical feminist with dyed red hair, with the jangling image the word 'housewife' conjures up. But by her description, it sounded more like a social gathering than the ghastly 'how to please your husband' frippery I'd imagined. A woman in the Register, Judy, encouraged Barbara to join the Richmond Amateur Dramatic Society. 'That theatre changed my life'. It gave her confidence, long-lasting friendships and some fabulous parts.

'We put on *Daisy Pulls It Off*, and I was Daisy! Then I was Sister George when we did *The Killing of Sister George*, and Mrs Wicksteed in *Habeas Corpus*. I was the Wife of Bath, when we did *Canterbury Tales*. I was Mrs Lovett, when we did *Sweeney Todd*. I was Lettice, when we did *Lettice and Lovage*. I've had absolutely . . . it's just been wonderful.' Barbara's face, as she reeled off these roles, shone as if she couldn't quite believe her luck. 'Oh yes, and *Calendar Girls*! It had been released for amateur rights, and I got a part in it. On the first night, they told me after the performance, the original Calendar Girl that I was playing, she was in the bar and she wanted to meet me! In there!' Barbara gestured to the theatre across from the pub. Working in a theatre of such distinction was a big part of her sense of extraordinary good fortune.

Amateur theatre satisfied something in Barbara; it answered her performing dream. When she realised that being either in a band or in musical theatre might not happen, she revised her expectations but still wanted to get up in front of an audience, in whatever way she could. 'The other thing I wanted to do was go to domestic science college and then get a job with the Gas Board and be a demonstrator.' That rattled a few bars of my memory. I'd seen those demonstrator women on TV, displaying new ingredients to the housewives standing in front of them, their shopping baskets ready, all wondering what to try out that night. It took me back to the days of liver and haslet and fish on Fridays and stretching things out to last. Of only having satsumas at Christmas. Of always doing a rice pudding if you're putting the oven on for baked potatoes. Of fruit in salads and savoury jelly moulds. Barbara had jolted her own memory, too.

'Now I'm looking back, it's as if everywhere I've gone, I've tried to find somewhere I can go and perform. I love theatre. Sometimes you do something in a play and you can feel the audience, and you think, oh, I'm giving them the sort of pleasure that plays have given me, and that is a wonderful feeling. And it's a really, really good hobby to have, I don't lose sight of that.'

The word 'hobby' is one I've consciously avoided; for me, it conjures up making Christmas cards out of pasta shapes. And I wouldn't want to trivialise an experience that is so important to so many people. Amateur theatre has been a big part of Barbara's life for decades, there's so much emotion and salvation tied up in it, and still she chooses to see it as a hobby. She describes her life as 'very ordinary' though, and I wonder if she'd swap it all for a life in lights.

'If I was suddenly discovered now? Like Liz Smith? Yes. Absolutely. If *EastEnders* were looking for a Scottish grandmother I'd be there like a shot.'

Hilary Jennings was another woman who appeared when I used the code, down at the lido in south London where we both swim. (That's another community. Life is about finding these communities, however and wherever they appear.) When I told her I'd grown up in amateur theatre, she planted a seed. 'Is this an instinct you've been squashing down for years?' she asked. 'Has it lain dormant? Are you going to end up coming back to amateur theatre?' I couldn't get that image out of my mind, of a person physically squashing something down as it tried to rise in them. I just wasn't sure if the person I was imagining was me.

I discovered that Hilary is part of the Southside Players, so I went to watch them perform *The Herd* by Rory Kinnear, in Chestnut Grove Academy's modern hall in Balham. Hilary was there selling cans of drink and home-made cupcakes. 'It's so dull, doing front of house,' she told me, 'except for the five minutes before everyone goes in. It's because you're the only ones with no adrenaline.' I'd never thought about it that way. 'Amateur theatre is so bonding because it's one of the few times in life where everybody involved has adrenaline. If it's your birthday, you have some but nobody else really does. But at a cast party, for instance, everyone has it, which is why it's so crazy at times. Remind me to tell you about the nudity and jelly party.'

Already we'd gone off in a direction I hadn't expected.

I asked Hilary how she'd come to Southside Players. In her mid-twenties, she'd moved to London, wanted to meet people, and gone along to a drama group with a friend. But it was hard to see where she fitted in, because she didn't want to be onstage. (That's often the assumption, that you're doing this because you're some kind of show-off. Not everybody in amateur theatre is a show-off.) Then she joined another group, and they were short of actors so she read in, ending up onstage in a tiny part. I wondered if they'd played a trick on her, finding a devious way to get her up on that stage. 'I think it was more that I was about the right age, and I could speak,' she replied. This is amateur theatre we're talking about, after all.

'My direction was "walk in and sit down over there" and I remember thinking, my character would not have done that. Then someone asked if I was interested in directing. It was a Sue Townsend play, *Womberang*, set in a doctor's waiting room.

Then I did *Two* by Jim Cartwright, then *An Ideal Husband*. But I was out of my depth. I wasn't confident enough to cut it, and Wilde does go on a bit.'

She started to understand that directing was the right path for her. It made sense of the fact she loved performance but didn't want to perform, which means she's happy to support the actors without any desire to replace them onstage. She's not one of those directors who knows how they want each individual line to be said, down to the tiniest intonation. That's when performing becomes an exercise in 'repeat after me'. She sees herself as the person who holds the space and the time, and puts enough structure into it for the actors to find the best way to tell the story. She frees them up to create the characters.

'At first, I was quite nervous and concerned if I didn't know what I wanted. Now, I love the process. I like not knowing quite how it's going to be. I get to shape it and watch it happen. Make sure it all fits together.'

I bet she's a great director. I bet she never yells. 'No, I've never yelled. Apparently, it's all in the click of my pen.'

Not every person who moves to London would want to join an amateur drama group for a ready-made social life. But theatre had been part of Hilary's childhood, she'd gone to pretty much everything at the Liverpool Everyman.

'Theatre in Liverpool was really important, and it was radical and interesting. I went back recently to the Everyman, and going back into that space, it made me realise . . . That first play I did, *Womberang*, we started with the curtains open, which was radical, to not have the creaky curtains. And the second play I did, I did on the floor of the hall, with the audience sitting round it. And that was all coming from watching plays at an early age, in the 1970s. I was unaware of it, but it had sunk in.'

Hilary knows that amateur theatre has enriched her life hugely, giving her everything from plenty of really good friends to all that adrenaline. 'My partner always says that the heat of the production forges your friendship, they become quite deep quite quickly,' and she clasps her hands together in illustration. 'And I've got friends of all ages, and it doesn't matter where you come from or what your job is, or if you have one. As long as you do your bit, everything else is equal.'

Given that Hilary and I also share a love of swimming, the concept of 'flow' seems appropriate here. It's the idea that being so engrossed in something – whether it's making theatre or playing an instrument, or cooking, or swimming – that you forget anything else is going on. It's really good for your mental health, and sense of well-being. 'If I start directing, three hours later I have not given a single thought to anything else in the world. It's great just to be able to do that,' Hilary said, palpably happy. 'I could talk about amateur dramatics for hours,' she said. 'It's such a joy.' There's that word again. Hilary puts it like this: 'Theatre is about us understanding humanity. You're picking down to the tiniest minutiae, of why people are the way they are, and what they say.' I want to repeat that loudly, for the people in the cheap seats, the people who think that amateur theatre is second-rate. It's not. It's about under-standing humanity.

Southside Players call themselves non-professional, or a 'community' group, but not amateur. What's wrong with the word amateur?

'Nothing, per se. But we've noticed at Southside that people come with the perception, still, that amateur theatre is not given the same attention, it's not taken seriously, it's slapdash, the scenery will be falling over, it'll be wooden, and there's the idea that "they don't care about the audience because they're just having fun on the stage". People come expecting it to be not very good. And then afterwards, the same people say "I've enjoyed that, I might come again".' Southside Players, Hilary feels, have proved themselves beyond the perception of what the word amateur might represent. 'And there isn't this kind of divide between professional and amateur anywhere else. In music, for instance, there's hierarchy, but there isn't that divide. People are more tolerant of the range.'

What should we call it, I asked, if not amateur? 'Theatre,' she said. 'We might just call it all theatre.' You've slightly blown my mind, I said.

I was so taken with this that I left Hilary without reminding her she was going to tell me about the nudity and jelly party. Maybe that was best for all of us.

How about we just call it theatre? I asked writer and performer Hannah Maxwell, whose solo show *I, AmDram* is about identity, belonging and her experiences in amateur theatre. She gave the question about two seconds thought, then: 'No,' she declared. 'It is its own world, and it can be mapped. So, reclaim amateur.' She thought for another two seconds. 'In fact, give it a capital A. I think the word amateur should be held with pride. Professional stuff is all well and good, but take away the monetary reason for doing it, and amateur seems more pure to me. It seems to go back to the classic Greek version, being about the joy. I think it's a critically overlooked area of society. A massively overlooked world.'

Hannah and I both came from that world and rejected it, on my part for a long time, so are we part of a cultural snobbery? 'Maybe, we *were*.' Maybe we've seen the light, I said. It's only later that I realise I sound a bit born-again and am slightly embarrassed.

Like me, Hannah Maxwell grew up in am-dram, she was a child of the stage. Her 'home' was the Welwyn Thalians Musical and Dramatic Society, in Welwyn Garden City and it was a fate she couldn't avoid.

'The two founding members were Millie Thompson and Harold Dunham. Their kids, my grandparents, married and had my mum. So the whole of my mum's side have been in the society for four generations. Growing up, Mondays and Thursdays were always rehearsal nights; if they couldn't get a babysitter, me and my little brother would go and hang out at rehearsal.'

This felt totally normal to her; it does to me too.

'I can't think of things in years, I only think "oh, that's when we were doing *The Mikado*". At one point we stopped getting babysitters so they just made up small parts for my brother so he could come along. My mum played Annie Oakley and me and my brother were her siblings.'

Only in the amateur world would this be entirely normal, and given that we've already encountered the Margravine of Anspach playing opposite her own son as her lover, this feels relatively tame.

If Hannah's family was the beating heart of the Welwyn Thalians, the society is also the beating heart of her family.

'Their whole lives are about doing these shows. There were periods when my mum and nan stopped talking to each other, around arguments about who was going to direct *My Fair Lady*. On the one hand I can go '"it's so silly and cute", and on the other, there's serious raw emotion flowing through the seam of it.'

It was this suggestion, that there was an important and serious element to it, that I was interested in uncovering.

'The Thalians are really white, because of the area and the kind of shows they do, but at the same time anyone who walks through that door, if they can vaguely hold a tune, they're in. No elitist "you're not good enough, you don't look right". All ages. It's close-knit, there's all the dramas. People get vulnerable and closer to each other than in other suburban contexts. Most people, they have their job, their work friends, the PTA, etc. But this is their world, and it has all the colour and texture in it. It's where they get that life source.'

It's a wonderful idea, that this derided, undervalued and mocked world is actually where people are creating a vibrant tapestry for themselves. I'm seeing an amateurs' Bayeux.

Hannah was articulate and clear-eyed about her experience and its context partly because she has a degree in English and drama, and therefore the vocabulary to view it all as an academic artist, and partly because she made a personal show about it. Is that about your journey? I asked, taking a risk with that cliché.

'It's more generally about your relationship to where you're from, before you settle on an idea of your own identity, but for me that is entirely wrapped up in am-dram and musical theatre, so that's how the story is told. My journey was: I was very much in it all, until I was eighteen. I thought it was all marvellous and hilarious. Then I went to uni and started to push back a bit. Now, a lot of stuff has been reconciled. I can have a warmth and a nostalgia and a fondness for the Thalians while seeing the foibles and also being happy where I am, doing different things.'

That sounded familiar. Hannah views her childhood, being incubated in that kind of space, as 'wonderful', mostly.

'I've got odd things, like I don't have any particular music tastes because I didn't spend my teenage years listening to albums and working out what I was into. I just knew show tunes. If anyone says "who has a song request?" I have no idea. I often find myself drawn to songs with narrative. And a key change. But I can harmonise with almost anything.'

I grew up harmonising in a Catholic school choir, but I suspect my own skills pale in comparison. I was a bit jealous.

In talking to these three women, I inadvertently bump up against one of amateur theatre's reputational issues, the over-representation of women. As we've seen, the recent statistics, the 60/40 split, bear this out. It might have started out as a male activity, but over the years, am-dram has become 'notoriously' female. (It's funny how the statistics only need to tip a tiny bit for this perception to take hold.) And it's a conundrum for me, this. Areas where women form the majority stakeholders are often undervalued. If there were a plethora of men in amateur theatre, it would, I have no doubt, be taken more seriously. And there's a double bind – if women like an activity, it becomes 'women's interest' which means minority or domestic. Serve cake and prosecco and they'll all turn up, bless them. But as Hannah Maxwell said, it's not just silly or cute. A serious vein runs through it, *even though* it is mostly women involved. As I'm a lazy feminist, my amateur theatre manifesto would encourage more men to join in rather than take on the onerous task of changing perceptions of 'women's interests'. My advertising slogan would be 'you'll never have to wait around for a good part'. As Hilary explained, 'It's always a bit harder to get men, because they're always cast in things. Partly because historically plays are written by men about men. Men's lives are seen as more interesting.' And historic plays, those with reams of men, are the lifeblood of a lot of amateur theatre. For one thing, once they're out of copyright, they're free to perform. For another, audiences to *all* theatre, professional and amateur, love the classics. Even when women are in charge, they can't magically produce classic or historic plays featuring lots of women, when those plays are non-existent. And young men are the golden geese. If you

97

are a young man, you'll get cast again and again whatever your level of talent, because that's how it skews. In that sense, amateur theatre is no different from the rest of the world, in terms of what is considered precious.

But Hilary also said, 'I think absolutely anybody could find a place in a dramatic production.' If a village is putting on a play, there's going to be something for everyone. There's room for quieter people like Hilary, who want to be involved but not in what she called the 'flashy or flamboyant way'. It's there if you want to add some colour and texture to your life, if you want to make friends and find some understanding of the process of being human. Go with the flow. Heal the pain. Get some joy. The repeated, unprompted use of the word 'joy' cannot be denied. Maybe my favourite point was Hannah's. 'It also sticks all the weirdos together so they can't cause trouble elsewhere.' I remember my noisiness, and my boy sandals, and am very happy to declare myself to be Team Weirdo, every step of the way.

CHAPTER 7

The Fourth Wall

At the start of their book about Highbury Little Theatre, John English and Mollie Randall wrote, 'It is a truism that people and not a building make a theatre.' And of course, they were right. People are at the heart of all of this. But however much we say 'it's the people, the people', it is also, without a doubt, 'the places, the places'. Theatres are buildings that hold a sort of magic.

There are two experiences to be had at the theatre. The first is as a member of the audience. Now, I love a gilded Frank Matcham ceiling as much as the next person, and I love the plush bounce of a fat seat, that satisfying thwunk as it swings shut when you stand up. Those fancy ones that recline slightly when you sit down. The cool leather in the main auditorium at the Barbican. The refurbished Victoria Palace Theatre, where there are enough women's loos. All the trappings. And I've had performances ruined by being squashed into rows as cramped as a budget airline, or my arse numbed by the plank I was sitting on. So, yes, I see how buildings matter. But, as in life, it's often not the fanciest ones that draw my eye. I love glitz, but I also love a shed. I have felt powerful emotions in a damp box with sweat pouring down the walls; I've been absorbed in a story in derelict knackered rooms; I've sat cross-legged on the floor, goddammit. Magic where you least expect it has so much more value. If you ask people what their favourite theatres are, they will often have one, two, possibly a list. Because these are spaces where we create memories, and if we visit again and again, those memories get embedded in the fabric of our lives.

The second experience of the theatre is as a player. And when we talk about 'place', the accepted hierarchy for amateurs and professionals is reversed. It is very rare that professional actors get as rooted to one place as amateurs often are. Professionals move theatres from play to play, season to season; they might return, but it's more likely that they won't. They don't form a relationship with those bricks, that mortar. They might be in a show for months on end, but that's nothing compared to the amateurs who have access to a permanent theatre, who can work perhaps all of their adult lives under the same roof. And it feels fundamental, the knowledge created by time and repetition. It's security. Understanding the tread of a building, how it breathes at night, where the cool air is and where it's hot – that's an intimacy that can feed your art. Contemporary theatre architecture is all about creating spaces that will be as open as possible, as comfortable as possible, as accessible for the audience; those are the priorities, as they should be. The building itself becomes a player, which the actors get cast with, over and over again. In terms of buildings, amateur players are top of the hierarchy.

When I wrote 'memories get embedded in the fabric', I hadn't meant it literally. But one theatre has taken it that way, as author Amber Massie-Blomfield told me. We were talking about current theatre design and she mentioned the work that architects Haworth Tompkins had done for the Liverpool Everyman in their recent refurbishment. It was the first theatre to win RIBA's Stirling Prize.

'Part of that was because of this radical accessibility in the architecture of the building. One of the things I really love is that when they put the velvet on the theatre seats, they laid the velvet upside down, so that when people sat on the seats, they'd imprint them. The seats would wear quicker, the patina of people's touch would wear into the seats more quickly.'

Memories and arses, both embedded. Of course, if you're a visitor to a theatre you may neither see nor care about such things. But it'll happen anyway, which seems to be a great metaphor for all the unseen stuff that happens in performance.

One of the most extraordinary amateur theatre spaces is the Minack in Cornwall. When Amber told me that there's a webcam at the Minack, it was a useful thing to know. Watching it was a great distraction on a rainy day when next door's kids started crying at around 8 a.m. and didn't stop. It was tantalising on a day when the whole of London seemed to be operating at a high-pitched screech, I could feel the pollution in my mouth and all I wanted was to be near the sea, wearing a baggy fleece. I turned to the webcam on a closed-in day when the weather at home had gone prematurely grey and I needed to put myself somewhere with a big sky, just to hang on to summer before everything fell. I peered in; there was a whole world going on three hundred miles away, a life where people in fold-up macs and zip-off trousers sat on cliffside terracing, watching a play happening down a vertiginous slope in a stone bowl, below them. Even squinting at my computer screen I could almost fall into the maw of this stage. Some of the audience had blankets on their laps – the wind was clearly up. My own horizon was a Post-it-covered wall about two feet from my nose, theirs was where the sea meets the sky. At least I hadn't had to park in a field, I consoled myself. (Whenever I go to Cornwall on holiday, I seem to spend quite a lot of time bumping my unsuitable car around fields co-opted into seasonal car parks.)

Almost a quarter of a million people visit Minack each year. That figure is made up of around 150,000 who just go to look round, and about 80,000 who go to a performance – a phenomenal number that makes an amateur theatre one of Cornwall's top tourist attractions. In the simplest terms, Minack is an outdoor theatre on the top of a cliff just up from Porthcurno beach. Of course, it is much more than that. It's actually an extraordinary space – and that's what you have most of, in this theatre, space, up and away as far as you want. Looking at the jumbling, falling ancient rocks around the grounds, you could almost imagine you are looking at an original amphitheatre, built maybe by men wearing Roman

Boden on their annual two weeks in Cornwall. Then common sense will kick in. If this was an actual Roman amphitheatre, do you think the heritage industry would allow you to scramble all over it, then sit there on a flowery holiday-cottage cushion, with the dog's rug from the car over your knees, having a terrible picnic of claggy pasties and a plum? No, they would not allow that. This theatre was actually built in the 1930s, which means that it is now old enough to have become a historic site in its own right. The main buildings – the box office, cafe, loos and an exhibition space – sit at the top of the cliff, and then tumbling down the side is a spill of paths and terraced seating and crumbling archways and, at the bottom, a stage. Behind the stage, a low wall, an arch, and then – the stunning view. Dotted around are massive rocks and Cornish planting; for all the structural stuff, it still feels like it's rising out of nature. It is a unique space, in a unique place, and the cherry on this cake is that it was built by a woman. Literally built with her own hands, and I love that. And hers is a story that bounces about all over our history of amateur theatre.

Rowena Cade, born in 1893, got her first taste of amateur theatre at her home in Derby, in her mother's production of *Alice Through the Looking Glass*. (That's our first 'bounce' – the idea that Rowena was doing what lots of upper-middle-class gals were doing; am-dram with mummy in the drawing room.) She and her mother moved to Cornwall after their family was torn apart by the First World War, and while renting rooms, Rowena 'found' the Minack headland. She bought it, for £100. (Inflation calculators tell me that the current equivalent price would be just over £5,500, at which I had a quiet sob at how cheaply Cornwall sold itself at the time.) She had a house built on the site – Minack House – and set up home.

Amateur theatre was a big part of the local community around them (the second bounce). In Porthcurno, the Cable and Wireless Company ran a theatre for their staff (the third bounce – in Chapter 10 I look at theatre at work). Rowena got involved with making costumes for a production of *A Midsummer Night's Dream*, which was put on in a nearby field. When *The Tempest* was suggested as their next production, Rowena volunteered her garden for the performance – it made perfect sense for that play to be performed in a place clinging to the edge of the land, a heady dramatic landscape with backdrops of stormy seas and massive skies. From those humble beginnings, this incredible venue was born. In her book *Twenty Theatres*, Amber Massie-Blomfield writes about how Rowena set to work with the help of her gardener Billy Rawlings (and by this point, I'm busy thinking up my fantasy cast for the film script).

> Together they blasted the site and used the granite they extracted to craft the first green-cuticled terraces of seating. Rowena would harvest sand from Porthcurno beach below the site and climb the headland, goat-like, with the sack of sand slung over her narrow back.

That image of Rowena, lone woman, working the land, persists throughout the story of Minack. It was she who added seating and dressing rooms, she who hauled all the timber up from the beach. This was Rowena's theatre, even the smallest part of it built by her hands.

Rowena created what became, pretty quickly, a prestigious venue. Over the years, she added to it as and when she chose. If she wanted an extra arch or a pillar, she'd blast away what was there, and put the new feature in. She mixed and poured and etched every bit of concrete. She created Minack with passion and commitment, falling into amateur theatre the way other people fall into the Church.

On my first visit to Minack some years ago, I didn't really appreciate all her creative brilliance. It was a rain-spotted, breezy evening and I was not as well prepared as I could have been. (I never am – it's a combination of laziness and bad management.) I had two kids with a disastrous five-year age gap. The small one was too young to go to the theatre, but I didn't want to go alone, so the big one, probably aged seven or eight, was roped into being my trusted companion, even though he found 'sitting down' quite a challenge. A good start. The play began; minutes dragged by. He was really trying to be good. We were in cheap raincoats that made our backs sweat and we didn't have any cushions to soften our seats, so the ground got quite hard, quite quickly. If I were a proper mother, I'd have crafted a fun and fabulous picnic. Instead, ours was measly and unsatisfying, prepared on the hoof, and we ate it way too early. I can't remember what the play was, it might as well have been Shakespeare. We huddled together, I put my arms round my son in a way that looked like warm cuddling but was actually an attempt to pin him down. Everyone around us was rapt, and we were damp and cold to the bone, struggling and shuffling in some kind of mortal combat. I wanted a drink. When I momentarily stopped paying attention to what was happening onstage, the whole play slipped out of my tenuous grip, and time slowed almost to a stop. The interval finally came, and I asked, in that forcedly cheerful tone, 'Are you enjoying it?' praying he'd say 'no', even though I knew it would be better parenting if I *forced* us to stay to the end, to teach us both something British about keeping going and persistence and tolerance. 'Can we go home now?' he said. 'OK, if you want,' I replied, deeply grateful. We went. I pretended we were going because he was fidgety. 'It's past his bedtime,' I said as we crept out. 'He's only small.' But it was me too. I was really thirsty.

I know that my Minack experience would have been significantly better in the right clothes, with older companions, and a drink. It was my own inadequacies that had made it less than successful. Even with those inadequacies, though, seeing theatre outside has a particular and resounding charm. We all know it can be rendered disastrous within seconds by a downpour, but that can add a sense of delicious jeopardy. 'It didn't rain! Woo-hoo!' Or even, 'We got absolutely soaked! Woo-hoo!' There is something special in the way voices carry, projected in the open air; in how actors are affected by a cold breeze or the sun in their eyes; in how our view of it all can be changed by a cloud, or darkness falling; in how the sound of a rustling tree or a bird flying across a stage can add a frisson. It creates a closeness, a conspiracy; a feeling that you're all, audience and cast, in it together.

There is also the question of children at the theatre. There is no doubt that other people's children can spoil things. The way they kick the back of your seat or rustle sweets or ruin a poignant moment by asking loud questions. (I say 'other people's' children. I probably mean 'your own'. I'm remembering, here, a time I took my young daughter to see a play at the Edinburgh fringe. One of the cast sat on the stage a few metres from our front-row seats, cradling her own leg, as she might a baby. All was silent, until my daughter's clear voice piped up. 'Is that woman eating her leg?' Shhh, darling, I'll explain later.) We spent most of our summers when the children were young at the Edinburgh fringe with both of them in tow, at a time when there was very little on that was suitable for them. Fortunately that's changed now, and it's become a fantastic opportunity to introduce small people to a whole raft of performances, including kid-friendly stand-up, puppet shows, and some great physical theatre and mime. (Another 'fond' memory: taking my daughter to some mime at Edinburgh when she was about twelve and well versed by then in theatre-going. She was sitting between me and her dad. The first five minutes of this mime show involved a fully naked man dancing onstage, his dick pranging about like a crazy daisy. We all sat staring straight ahead, mortified, not one of us daring to turn to the other. I knew she was wishing herself anywhere but here and, to be fair, so was I. She's never forgotten it. Theatre can *scar*, people.) In general, I think taking kids to the theatre is a good idea. I always thought *other* people taking my kids to the theatre was a *really* good idea.

The glory of the Minack story is that it began with amateurs, and it is still mostly amateurs who form a large part of its schedule. Phil Jackson, the theatre manager, told me that 'the programme is still solidly based around amateur companies but we use professional companies on the fringe of the season when it's more difficult for the fully amateur companies to come'. I love how it's that way round – amateurs get the best slots and they graciously allow the professionals in at the less popular times. And Phil pointed out that for a place like Minack, 'the line between amateur and professional is quite blurred nowadays. There were only four fully professional companies in the 2018 season, but a few other companies had a mix of professional and community actors.' In their twenty-week season, with a different production each week, they map it out to make sure there is a mix of musicals, Shakespeare, comedy and drama. 'We introduce new companies when existing groups can no longer meet the required standard, but that's not very often.' I imagine the queue to perform there is pretty long. It would be an amazing experience.

The next theatre we turn to is the opposite of Minack, geographically, socially and architecturally. It has a roof, for starters. It is set on a coast road, but this one is the A1058, a busy dual carriageway into Newcastle. It's a nowhere –

everywhere place, right on the cusp of urban, suburban, industrial heritage and the parkland of Jesmond Dene. The People's Theatre comes upon you so suddenly it's almost leering into your face from the pavement. As my friend Sheetal dropped me off outside, she said, 'I remember this place. I did a student revue here in 1998. It was called *Stool Trek: The Next Defecation*.' Ah, the famed black humour of medics, I thought, a pained grin on my face. She waved, as she cheerily drove away.

The not-quite-any-one-thing location seems to tally with the building itself. It's a massive block, with a half-hexagon jutting out front with bright green roof tiles and huge squares of contemporary glazing. There's a bit over on the left that used to be something else, and then a bit to the back, a sixties section, that wasn't part of the original building. Often these theatre buildings will have a small original hub that was added on to in the sixties, the eighties, whenever there was a bit of money floating around. Maddermarket in Norwich is the same, and the Georgian Theatre Royal in Richmond. When I walked in, past the new box office and into the enormous foyer/bar/exhibition space created in their recent £1.5 million refit, I think I might have gasped out loud. It's unexpected, stylish, part industrial design (all the ducting visible in great steel tubes across the ceiling) and part shabby charm, fitted out with mismatched chairs and tables from their props department. There's a massive sign behind the bar made by a local blacksmith that says 'The People's Theatre presents THE BAR' in a curlicue frame with large light bulbs around it in the style of an old fairground. The front of the bar is horizontally stacked scaffold boards, made by volunteers with the same attention to detail that Rowena Cade put into her home-made cement pillars. No wonder people feel they belong to a place, when they build it. It's as understandable as feeling pride in the home you've created.

'This is so classy,' I said to Tony Childs, a theatre committee member who'd agreed to show me round. 'It's also a great performance area,' he told me, which was the first hint that this is a confident place, not afraid to try new things. 'Are you sure it's an *amateur* theatre?' I asked, a question I was to repeat several times during my tour. If you ever think that amateur must mean second-tier, you haven't been to the People's.

For the first forty years of its existence, the People's Theatre in Newcastle would have definitely fitted the 'it's about people, not places' argument, and not just because of the name. Founded in 1911, it started out as the Clarion Dramatic Club, 'an offshoot of the Fabian Society', Tony explained. 'Just a group of people interested in putting on plays.' The first venue they used was in a building in town that's now a tea shop and still has a tiny stage in the corner; the company moved in 1915 to the old Royal Arcades, then again in 1929 into a disused church in Rye Hill, in the West End, and finally, here, to Heaton. This venue started life as a cinema in 1933, and in 1961, the People's raised £180,000 to buy it and turn it into an arts centre. Their emblem is a phoenix; their archive says: 'This move made the legendary symbol of rebirth and resurrection an appropriate one.' Looking around at this latest 'rebirth', it's clear that raising money and transforming buildings is something they're very good at.

'Are you absolutely sure this is an amateur theatre?' I asked Tony again, as he showed me into the new studio. It wasn't finished at the time, and on its unplastered walls I could see the remnants of previous lives. Old strips of curled and flaking wallpaper, a section of fake panelling, half a square-tiled wall, with bright new wiring across the top of it all, ready to be bedded in. Then we moved to the main theatre auditorium, and there's no doubt that when we walked in, I did gasp. Tony gave me a moment to take it in then said, 'Good, isn't it?' in an understatedly proud way. Good? It's bloody brilliant.

'Up there is the old studio.' He pointed to the back of the auditorium. 'That's now a prop store. There used to be the old projectors up there. It used to be nine hundred seats, it's now 480. We don't always fill them. We sell out for panto. When we did *39 Steps*, twelve hundred people were in, over a week. We used to put on shows because we hoped a lot of people would come, because we needed the money. But hopefully now we're going back to doing shows because we want to do them, as a theatre.'

We clambered up onstage, and I stood and looked at the auditorium. Tony stood next to me. 'If you're here talking to the audience,' he said, speaking as an actor not a committee man, 'they're here, with you.' Next minute, he was at the back of the stage, calling me to join him. 'You can see the depth of it, look. You can do anything, it's so deep. I did *They Shoot Horses* and had forty people onstage. And how many theatres can do *Nicholas Nickleby*? It's two plays, twenty-three actors playing a hundred parts, they shifted stuff all the time, it never stopped. I started rehearsing it in May, we went on in October, it was so big. Professional theatres have to pay all the actors, we don't.'

There was a hint of tension or competition between amateur and professional theatre in what he said, but it's not one that really exists, beyond this shorthand way of expressing pride in achievements. Setting out the differences between the two, sometimes a defence mechanism comes into play, the idea that in order to big one up, you have to denigrate the other. Defence is understandable, given the perceptions amateur theatre is always having to counter. But the two are actually very different beasts. Still, I joined in. I'm starting to believe it's better to be in amateur theatre, than professional, I half joked.

'If you were a professional actor, you wouldn't play Lear, Prospero, Joe Keller, Willie Mossop . . . I got to do all those, with good actors, in this theatre. I've been in some rubbish as well, but still. And I can be in a play with people who are ten, twenty, thirty years younger than me.'

That kind of social mixing can keep a person engaged with life, I thought, with my mum in my mind.

I marvelled once more at the stage and auditorium. If I say it was better than many professional spaces I've seen, am I, too, guilty of stoking that competitive fire? Then we went off to tour the rest of the estate, talking about the young people who come through this theatre, as we went.

'Some of them will stay forever. You recognise those ones, when they first join, they want to do everything. Some of them move, or whatever. And some of them decide to be professional. Kevin Whateley, he came through here, Jack Shepherd. Andrea Riseborough. Ed Wiseman, he's another one. He played a fairy for me in *Midsummer Night's Dream* when he was eleven.'

I wondered if their very active youth theatre was the key. 'Some of them come through that way. But not all. They just come. You never quite know why.' Are you sure you're an amateur . . . ? I started to ask again. 'We are an amateur theatre,' Tony replied firmly.

People's Theatre encourage writers too, putting on new plays and running a play competition, which attracted ninety entries in 2018, for a cash prize and a week's performance.

'Alison in box office, she's a playwright, she wrote *My Mam Was An Ice-Cream Blonde*, it won the People's Play.'

We went up to the rehearsal spaces, which feel as good as any drama school. You can understand why people would come, and why they'd stay. It is a phenomenal resource. We ended up in the green-room bar which is also enormous. Everything here is scaled up, even their membership list. We chatted about the challenges of this recent refit, still being completed around us, which Tony helped oversee.

'We decided to do all this because ten years ago, we were doing OK but in an ageing building. And in ten years, if we did nothing, the bills would overtake the money. We had to do it.'

You didn't have to, Tony, I said, I've seen some beautiful golf courses out there. Why did you stay? 'Because I love it,' he replied. Simple as that.

Building work has meant sleepless nights, firing emails off at 3.30 a.m. and getting replies ten minutes later, and a lot of stress. 'At the opening,' he said 'it was the panto, and the first show goes up on the Friday night, at 7 p.m. We got permission to open at half five.' I love this sense of drama, it seems so appropriate, as if normal life events have a three-act structure. The increased audience figures show all the work was worthwhile. 'I think the building has a lot to do with it. Everyone who comes past can see this thriving hub. We've risen from the ashes again.' I look at my notebook later, and see that I'd written, in thick capitals, DYNAMIC and PROGRESSIVE. And it's true, it feels like a particularly expansive theatre that has the foresight and energy to keep moving forward.

'You become a church, in a way, in the sense that it's a community,' Tony said. And here we are again with church, back at the start of the story. I agree with him, that local theatre, like church, can provide structure, a shared belief and a sense of not being alone. There is a theatricality in the 'performance' of religion – as Brenda Gilhooly mentioned, the altar was her first stage. And both places are chock-full of ritual. I realised I should celebrate the similarities, and that this place could be taken as seriously as a church. That a theatrical calling can provide an interior light. That the sense of belonging that some people feel about their church community is so present in the theatre too.

When I spoke to Amber Massie-Blomfield, she told me how 'theatre buildings have a lot of controversial political issues about them. They carry a set of associations that might present a barrier to some people crossing the threshold.' People's Theatre has worked hard to breach those barriers. And I'd take the passion and commitment of this amateur place, on its busy main road into Newcastle, a hundred times over London's new Bridge Theatre, where the paint colours might be exactly on point but an egg sandwich costs £6.50. Amber reminded me that 'you can't get too sentimental about this stuff, we need well-equipped theatres and we shouldn't get too nostalgic about the crap ones'. She told me about an extreme example, a new theatre in Shanghai, where there's a forest of great big cones you have to weave through, making it more difficult to get in. It's theatre of the elite. 'Here, [in Britain currently] the impulse is to strip so much of that away. But maybe people like going to a place that's distinct from their everyday world, where they have to dress up.'

In her book, Amber quotes Lynne Kendrick, one of the founder members of Camden People's Theatre, talking about their building. 'It's absolutely and utterly unfit for purpose in terms of the real business of making theatre, but that's what made it make great theatre.' Amber feels there's a kind of permission to those spaces, especially for artists starting out, that doesn't exist in spaces that are very slick and technical.

So what would she choose? Shanghai or Camden? Or some-where in between?

'I love the idea of a building coming to belong to a place and a community, more than any one individual. It comes to belong to the people who build their lives there, their narra-tives there. That's why I'm a passionate advocate for theatre buildings, they come to speak in the local dialect.'

Newcastle's People's Theatre is exactly that. The perfect amateur theatre, in terms of people *and* building. It's like finding a church you want to belong to.

CHAPTER 8

First Rehearsal

I am sitting on a low wall in front of a locked Highbury Theatre Centre on a Sunday evening in the dregs of summer, and I am early. There are two types of people in this world: people who are early, and people who don't care about anyone else. I am in the first category. It would be impossible to count the hours I've spent waiting for people in the second category, and impossible to quantify how much I've moaned about it. I've tried to be late to things, to artificially stimulate the insouciant quality of those late people. Because I know that being early is not cool. But I can never override my natural 'early' instinct, and always end up bursting in, sweaty and apologetic, the very latest I can bear, which is: exactly on time. It means I've spent a lot of time on train platforms, in cinema foyers reading the small print on the posters, and in cafes 'just waiting for my friend before I order.' Being late to a play is too awful to contemplate, I'd almost rather go home than suffer the shame of squeezing along a full row of seats, muttering, 'Sorry. Sorry. Sorry. Not my fault. Sorry.' At least now I can pretend to be busy with my phone – imagine all of this in a world before mobiles, when people couldn't text you to say 'just leaving now' when you'd already arrived. Those times were an absolute horror.

If I could get back all the hours I've spent being early, I'd probably use them being early for something else instead. I'm happier that way.

Tonight, church bells are ringing, the sky is still light, and sitting here on this wall, I am remembering being a teenager at this theatre, hanging out with adults who had disposable income. After a rehearsal, or in the middle of a work party, these adults – who were probably only in their mid-twenties, but still, an unbreachable gap – would often go to eat at the Cork & Bottle wine bar, at the end of Sheffield Road. It was done out in stripped pine and looked more like an old-fashioned corner shop than a pub, in that you could actually see through the windows. At the Cork & Bottle, they served lunches, like a ploughman's, or quiche and salad – and these fat wobbling slices of quiche were aspirational. Quite unlike the thin utilitarian ones I had at home, they had fat chunks of salty bacon and, radically, courgette. For my family, with four children, no income was disposable, and eating out was a rare event for which suitable gratitude was expected. The thought of us all sitting in there, entirely relaxed, casually ordering six plates of quiche and salad – unthinkable. Wine bars themselves were a new thing. Wine was for fancy dickheads or people who went to France; red was for men, white for women. My normal pubs – the Boldmere, the Station, the

Cup – were proper old, sticky-carpet boozers, kept dark inside, and with loud music, bikers and heavy chairs. Instead of quiche, they had bags of pork scratchings hanging on cardboard strips that gradually revealed a naked woman – the more you bought, the more you saw. We drank rum and black, snakebites, pints of cider, Bacardi and Coke. Not wine. The Cork & Bottle was out of my league.

I am at Highbury, early, for the first read-through of *Variation on a Theme*. Auditions took place in the middle of August, height of the holiday season, a risky time for an unknown play. Mum had gone as my proxy as I too was on holiday; I'd imagined a queue of people and fierce competition, but only two people had turned up, she reported, including her. Casting this play was going to be less of a big reveal and more of a slow burn. So I wasn't surprised when the director Alison warned me that it wasn't going to be a full cast tonight. There were two men still to find, and Ron, our young ballet dancer from Erdington, was a particular challenge. 'The two boys are proving troublesome,' said Alison drily. Our golden goose was being elusive.

Alison arrives and we head down the long narrow driveway along the side of the theatre which leads to a car park and a Victorian detached house. I glance surreptitiously up at its large, first-floor bay window; this is where my first proper boyfriend, who I met at the theatre, had a bedsit, which is another story for another kind of book. There are some garages and what looks like a young offenders institute, all breeze blocks and council-green paint. This is a new addition to the theatre, and it's where we are going to be rehearsing. They've called it the Harlequin Room in an attempt to give it a theatrical feel, but you could cover it in glitter and call it Pearl, it would still look like a young offenders institute.

Alison flicks on the overhead strip lights, which further emphasise the correctional facility vibe, and we get out the chairs, student chairs with those small fold-down tables on one side. We arrange them in a semicircle in front of Alison's table, and I take one off to the side, to be discreet. Maura arrives first – 'like Laura', she tells me, 'only with an M'. Then Sean, who has the look of a man modelling a cardigan for a knitting pattern. He says he's only taken on the role of Kurt because 'we share the same birthday', which seems like as good a reason as any. We are lucky to have Sean, he'd cancelled being in another play with another group because the dates clashed. Good men are in demand; if you find one, hang on to him. (In theatre, so in life.) Louise pitches up, our Rose; she's also in another local drama group. Then just as we are about to start, a young woman in a Hard Rock Café T-shirt bounces in. She is Kim, and she is younger than all of us by at least twenty-five years, I guess. All I have about these people, at this point, are a few guesses.

Before we start, Alison explains how she works. 'First thing we'll do is block the whole thing, beginning to end, so everyone knows it, more or less. It's useful to know where the play is headed. Then we'll go back, split it up, run it in small sections. That's when we'll start to drill down into character and interactions.'

Alison has already decided some of the detail of how this play will look, and she shows us an early drawing of the set. We're two months away from technical rehearsals: out in the professional world that would be a very tight deadline, but here, things seem to happen both much slower and much faster, and I'm not sure which pace I prefer. When the 'troublesome boys' were cast, which would be very soon, I thought, they'd be flung straight into eight weeks of rehearsals, three nights a week, then a two-week run, Tuesday to Saturday. They would hardly know what had hit them before it was all over.

We crack straight into the first reading; everyone already has their own lines highlighted in their scripts, and I am trying to get my bearings. I know that Sean's character Kurt is German, and that Sean is worried, he tells us, about 'going too 'Allo 'Allo'. (That's a generation-specific reference if ever I heard one, but it's shorthand for 'terrible stereotypes of accents'.) Kurt is Rose's current boyfriend, but it takes me a while to suss that Hettie, Maura's character, is a kind of housemaid to Rose, played by Louise. Kim is playing Fiona, Rose's daughter. I am starting with the same information that the audience will be, but it's tangling me up a bit; figuring out the relationships stops me focusing on the dialogue. Everybody has questions, and Alison talks through a lot of the period detail. The first scene of Act One takes quite a while to get through.

By the time we start reading the second scene of Act One, I can see through the barred windows that it is getting dark. Nights are already drawing in. Alison is reading in the extra parts – both the troublesome boys, and another female character whose purpose escapes me. I had this tiny germ of an idea, right at the back of my mind, that she'd ask me to read in for that one, and that my talent would be so overwhelming she would beg me, they *all* would, to join the cast. 'We can't go on without you, Jenny,' they'd plead. Maybe get up a small petition. But that doesn't happen. It's just my overdramatic side, rearing its head again. Instead, I sit quietly, discreetly, in my seat at the side. This isn't going to be my moment. If only I'd been a young man, even one with a horsey face, I could have been their hero.

Once I'm more familiar with who the characters are, I can pay closer attention to what they are saying. I am drawn to Fiona and Rose's relationship, amused at how familiar their mother–daughter arguments are, sixty years on. Tiny bells chime when Rose attempts to cajole Fiona into spending time with her. I try and connect in the same way with my own daughter, getting her to do my eyes if I'm going out. 'You're so much better at this than I am.' 'I could wear slacks and do my hair in a fringe,' Rose says. Slacks and a fringe were the very model of modernity for young women in the late fifties, set against the more traditional chic of the older woman. This, by the way, was Rattigan setting out his stall in opposition to the way theatre was changing. The same year that *Variation* was first performed, 1958, Joan Littlewood's Theatre Workshop premiered Shelagh Delaney's *A Taste of Honey*, a kitchen-sink drama about class, sex and race in Britain. Delaney was a million miles away from Rattigan and also, culturally, where my heart more honestly lies.

As I listen to Rose and Fiona, I take a mental step back and observe. Even sitting in these uncomfortable student chairs in this baldly lit box, these four actors, focused on their scripts, are intent on creating something with meaning. I am at the start of something. Against the odds, with this material, there is a feeling brewing. It is in the concentration, in the little looks between the cast and the pencil marks they make on their scripts. 'Leave a pause,' Alison directs. 'You'll find that out about me. I like a pause.' 'I like being able to pause without the prompt leaping in,' replies Louise, and in those small exchanges, it begins to build.

These people sat here – who are they? Who is Maura, or Louise, or Sean, or Kim? I don't know anything about them, except that they are amateur actors. I am starting to know about Kurt and Hettie and Rose and Fiona; I am at the early stages of being able to make guesses about how the characters work, their motivations and emotional arcs. But not these people in front of me. And why would I? What does it matter? When I watch something on the professional stage, I'm not thinking about the actors, 'real lives' offstage. So why is my interest piqued here, about what *this* cast do when they're not in the theatre? I want to know what makes them tick, what brought them here. Because it's not work, they are here for pleasure. And I wonder – will I think differently about Sean if I find out that in real life he's a chiropodist, or an estate agent? What will I feel about Louise's depiction of Rose, if I discover that Monday to Friday, nine to five, she's a teacher, or a management consultant, or a radiologist?

Our willingness as audience members to suspend disbelief is the absolute crux of what going to the theatre is actually all about. Am I less willing to do that here, in an amateur context, than I am at the professional theatre? Or, conversely, more willing? Do these amateurs have to work harder for me to suspend my disbelief? Or will I give it more readily? Do I come in with a different mindset because I know that acting is not their actual job but their 'hobby'? This relationship between actor and audience – do they need to be paid in order for me – and perhaps you – to take it seriously? Do we all come to an amateur play feeling, in our heart of hearts, that amateur really does mean second best? Does that mean that whatever they do, however brilliantly, they don't actually stand a chance?

In amateur theatre the connection between actor and audience certainly works in a way that it simply does not in a professional production. But that is an advantage, theatre academic Helen Nicholson explained to me. 'There is something about that sense of "ownership" of the theatrical product, that the audience is *part* of the product, that you don't see unless its actively constructed in the professional theatre.' Being 'part of the product' can mean all sorts of things in amateur theatre. It can mean knowing someone in the cast or crew, or it can mean that the theatre is your 'local', that you've been coming here twenty or so years, that the building feels like yours, in some way. That you were in a play there once, maybe. That you donated your old curtains or came to a fundraiser. That this hub in your neighbourhood has served you culture, whether you've chosen to take it or not. Belonging to the same community as a member of the cast is not an irrelevant position, or one to be minimised. It makes a difference to the quality of your engagement. You feel part of this event, your role is not as a passive spectator, but an active one. You occupy a different space to the one you might take up at a repertory theatre, or the National, or anywhere that the ushers are paid and the bar is corporate. You're less a visitor, and more a participant. You are inside, not out. Me, coming to Highbury, was part of this process of going inside.

For Helen, the idea that knowing what people do outside the theatre does make you commit to them differently, changes the actual nature of your engagement. 'When you see an amateur production, there's a double ontology. You're imagining what they do in the rest of their lives. When you discover that Sir Andrew Aguecheek works in the sandwich shop, it creates a different relationship with place that I think is really interesting.'

Helen was expressing something academically that I am experiencing 'live' at Highbury, that feeling that I wanted to know things about this cast, about their lives outside the theatre. Ontology is the study of being, so a double ontology, in the amateur theatre context, means you're enmeshed with the figures onstage both as the characters they are playing, and as people you know, at the same time. Drama professor Michael Mangan writes how 'for this audience, part of the pleasure is the double consciousness provided by the experience of watching people whom they know in everyday life play fictional parts'.

Two days later I am back at Highbury for the first *Variation* production meeting. A phrase comes into my head: 'dramaturgical design'. It's not the snappiest but I wish I'd invented it. Let me explain where I got it from.

In 2017, I went to a show called *Wild Bore* at Soho Theatre, created by three performers – Zoe Coombs Marr, Ursula Martinez and Adrienne Truscott. The idea was simple: they talk out of their naked arses onstage. (The idea was simple, the explanation less so: the performers are bent over with their trousers down, their bare bums towards the audience. Between them and us is a table, and the performers prop their bums on it, facing us. They reach their arms behind and tweak their buttocks, to simulate talking. Get it?) Nudity neither endeared nor deterred me. I've seen heaps of experimental stuff – Chris Lynam in his prime 'firework up the arse' days, performance artist Trevor Stuart tugging a boom box on a skateboard across a stage by a rope tied round his penis (made more trepidatious when the stage has a steep rake, which makes the skateboard veer off towards the audience), and shows where women pulled all the props out of their vaginas. So I was thinking 'this better be more than just three sets of bum cheeks with stuck-on googly eyes. I'll tire of *that* pretty quickly'.

The show was based around the arses reading out bad reviews the performers had received – throwing hostile criticisms back out and turning them into performance. It could have been massively self-indulgent; maybe this will all be one huge revenge fart, I thought. But these three experienced artists know how to create a hilarious, physical show. Lyn Gardner's *Guardian* review called it 'a sharply satirical hour that arrives at a crucial juncture in the debate about how we talk and write about culture'. All from three arses. Incredible.

Two points were particularly memorable. The first was when Ursula Martinez's bum cheeks read out a review of a show where she'd built a brick wall at the front of the stage. The sensible among us would assume that if a thoughtful, seasoned artist is building a brick wall at the front of the stage, there will be a point to it. They're not exactly subtle metaphors, brick walls. But one critic's review said that Martinez 'assembled a breeze block wall . . . for no apparent reason'. Her reading of that, and our reaction to it, was golden. 'For no apparent reason'! What a fucking idiot. The second was the recounting of another critic, wondering if a particular scene was there by accident or by 'dramaturgical design'. The idea was farcical – as if something, anything, that happens on a stage might not be a choice, not totally deliberate, however tiny a detail. As if things just *happen* onstage, entirely spontaneously, rather than by carefully crafted design . . . (you can see where I'm going) . . . by the dramaturg. For an audience member not to be aware of the level of planning a show entails, that's one thing. For a professional critic, absolutely absurd. This wilful stupidity gave me the phrase 'dramaturgical design' and I fling it about in any context I can get away with.

Tonight's production meeting is held in the 'club room', a name that's a bit misleading. If large armchairs, dark panelling and big lamps with tasselled shades come to mind, think again. This is amateur theatre, not Pall Mall. There is nothing remotely clubby about this room; it is a tiny box with a small table, a noticeboard and a row of kitchen units clearly rescued from a member who was throwing them out – amateur backstage spaces are often full of people's refurbishing rejects. It feels like a staffroom for the warders from the young offenders institute we are rehearsing in. I am a bit early to the meeting (natch) as is Malcolm, the set designer, so we chat. He thinks I'm writing a novel about amateur theatre, so obviously word is getting around, Chinese whispers style. He doesn't know me, he says, but he does know my mum, 'obviously', and my sister Sarah because he was in a play with her twenty years ago.

Others arrive, and we budge up our chairs. Richard, the workshop manager, and Steve, I think his name is. They all look a bit alike, to be honest, a bunch of middle-aged men in fleeces or casual knitwear. Since I'm a middle-aged woman in casual knitwear, I feel I'm with my people. Another man, Andrew, arrives and the average age of the room drops ten years. Steve, Richard and Malcolm start discussing the set design for *Absent Friends*, which is currently in rehearsal, and while they talk, I look at Andrew, smile, and think I should fill the silence by asking questions. That is never a good idea. The only advice I ever give people if they're going for an interview is: don't fill the gaps, because that's when you'll start revealing more than

you intend to. 'I am experienced with Excel spreadsheets
. . . [long pause while an interview panel waits for you to
say more but you *have* no more so you panic] . . . and I
want this job so I can steal the stationery.' Also, I'm a soli-
tary writer, so all meeting etiquette is a dim and distant
memory. AND I'm a woman, socialised to make things easy
for everyone, damn it. So, I press on and ask Andrew what
he does in his real life. It's been on my mind, that question,
since the first read-through a couple of days before, and as
I've already got my notebook and pen out I feel obliged to
perform as advertised. He's an ex-teacher, he tells me,
currently spending time wondering what to do next. Then
he stops talking. He feels no responsibility for the silence,
exactly as I would have recommended. Admirable restraint.
I can't ask any more questions without sounding like a
careers adviser, so I too shut up, and pretend I'm busy
making important observations in my notebook. Sometimes
having props is extremely handy.

Margaret, Head of Costume, and Ann, Head of Props,
arrive, and finally Alison rocks up, a bit late because she's had
a hellish day at work. No one asks why; I'd have asked a few
questions because that's polite (see note above about socialisa-
tion) but we are ready to start. Steve is running the meeting,
and Steve has a list.

First up is a discussion about lights, about sunrise and
sunset and whether the lights would come on at the back of
the auditorium and move to the front, or go from side to side.
It feels like the work you have to do, shuffling your feet about

on the soil, before you can lay a lawn, and let's be honest, prep work is the boring bit. Some of us do not handle boredom well. Some of us are excellent at walking in when all the prep is done, being our best magnificent and creative selves, then walking out again, leaving someone else to do the cleaning up. I admit it – 'some of us' is me. I am bored.

Malcolm, an architect, pulls out an A3 drawing he's made; it's a plan of the stage, where the rostra will be, solid walls, railings. All the sight lines are dotted. I don't really get it, I can't 'read' it, I want to turn the page round to get my bearings. I am getting left behind and already they are talking decorative finishes, Mediterranean colours and shutters at the windows. I stare at the plan some more, frowning. 'You having woodchip?' asks Steve. 'I might get something posh,' replies Alison, 'but I promise I won't blow my budget on wallpaper.' (Every show has a small production budget.) She turns to me and says, conspiratorially, 'I blew my budget on wallpaper for *The Winslow Boy* but it was lovely.' I am still staring at the plan trying to work out where the audience sit and what's a wall and what's not. Malcolm pulls out another drawing, this one with a swathe of deepest blue. 'That took a lot of blue!' says someone who knows the price of printer ink, impressed with the profligacy. I am even more confused. I know it's a drawing, but of what? Malcolm explains. 'The villa the play is set in sits on a promontory in the South of France. That means there's sea all around. When the actors stand on the terrace, they're looking out to sea.' 'So, the audience is in the sea?' Alison clarifies. 'Yes,' he says. What he's drawn is our stage from a distance; a pulled-out shot from above. He wanted to give everything context, to breathe life into something flat. It all begins to make sense and, again, I get that feeling, the one I got watching the actors together on their first encounter with the script, that this is the start of something. Where the light comes from and what the quality of that light will be – it matters. This is dramaturgical design! And it is the shared responsibility of everyone on this team.

The discussion turns to costume, and Margaret. As Alison describes the setting of the play, Margaret takes notes in tiny precise handwriting, exactly the kind I'd have given her if she were a character I'd written. 'Ron will need sportswear,' she says, not meaning a tracksuit. 'Slacks.' I can picture Ron on the front of an illustrated fifties magazine in some slacks, a cricket sweater casually tied round his neck, his hair Brylcreemed, his gaze out across the audience sea. Now all he needs to do is turn up. Next, they discuss the type of swimsuit Fiona would wear, something I know a bit about. But I don't want to sound like a know-it-all so I keep quiet. Margaret thinks that for Rose they could use 'the wig we had for Ruth Ellis in *The Thrill of Love*'. Then we move on to set dressing. Steve asks, 'Is there anything to be made?' and 'Well, no. Yes. No. Maybe. You know me,' Alison replies. 'Let's see if Tony can make us something,' Steve says. 'Tony is our star carpenter,' Richard explains, for my benefit. 'He worked at Birmingham Rep, at Central, he even worked at *Spitting Images*,' says Steve. Oh, me too! I reply, delighted to make a connection. The whole table turns to look at me. I stare back. 'Tony Huggins,' says

Steve pointedly like, you know, Tony Huggins? I shrug. 'I was more in the office.' They all turn away and I get the feeling I've disappointed them somehow.

Steve goes through the rest of his list, asking Alison who was doing what in her stage crew. 'What about Mark?' he asks. 'He's at Sutton Arts,' she explains. 'They dragged all our men over.' Sutton Arts is the other amateur theatre company in the area. There's a rivalry between the two groups that's publicly described as 'healthy', but when I was looking at Mum's diaries as I began my research, I'd asked her if she ever went to Sutton Arts and she'd replied with a vehement 'Good lord, no!' Steve wraps up the meeting by discussing a group of visiting Americans. 'They'll love us,' he says confidently. 'Why will they?' asks Richard, and it is a good question. 'Because we're quirky, and British. And a bit weird,' Steve replies. It's not a compelling slogan, but it reminds me of being part of Team Weirdo, so I can hear some truth in it.

I go back to Mum's after the meeting, driving past what used to be the Cork & Bottle, and is now called the Boldmere, and then past what used to be called the Boldmere and is now the Bishop Vesey, which is also the name of a local school. I'd recently succeeded in persuading Mum to get the Internet installed at home, and she'd rung me a few days earlier, to tell me the hub had arrived. 'I've put the Internet under the coffee table,' she said. Mum is worried about having the Internet; worried that whenever she uses her phone, her information will be hacked and her identity stolen. I point out that as she's texted me twice in her life and one of those times was a mistake, there is no information on her phone *to* be hacked. Still, I understand how confusing new things can be. That night, going up to bed, she points at the blue glowing hub and asks me, 'Should I turn it off?' 'No, leave it,' I say. 'Won't it get hot?' she asks. 'No, Mum, it won't get hot,' I reply. We go up to our rooms, and I use the new Wi-Fi to tweet about my mum.

CHAPTER 9

He's Behind You

All roads lead to Ealing.

Specifically, all roads of enquiry into amateur theatre seem to lead to Questors Theatre, Mattock Lane, London W5. The name pops up again and again, peppering so many conversations, covering so many aspects of this story. The theatre was a key player in the start of the Little Theatre movement, alongside Highbury; it took part in British Drama League drama competitions. They regularly took work to the Minack Theatre, in Cornwall. Michael Green's *The Art of Coarse Acting*, a book which featured heavily in my young amateur life, was conceived there, as was its contemporary grandchild, the smash-hit franchise *The Play That Went Wrong*. On top of that, the Questors origin story includes 'renegade Catholic priests, missionaries, spinsters, shady drinking clubs and the Scouts', the current artistic director Alex Marker told me, so that's some potent intrigue added to the mix. A renegade priest? My favourite sort.

On 5 September 1929 a new theatre company formed in Ealing, with seventeen enthusiastic young members and a bank balance with the princely sum of 7s 11½ d (around £15 today). Founder member Alfred Emmet, quoted in a biography of Questors, recalled:

We had very big ideas . . . we solemnly christened ourselves The Ealing Junior Arts Club (Dramatic Section). This was a great impertinence because it was done without any reference to the well-established and active Ealing Arts Club . . . So the name had to be changed, and at an historic meeting over lunch in a Soho Restaurant one Sunday in November, it was decided, for no particular reason except that by the coffee stage no-one had thought of anything better, to change the name to The Questors.

Emmet went on to be their most noted personality, and has a room in the current theatre building named after him. But Alex noted firmly that Emmet was just one of the players. Amateur theatre is about building teams, not empires.

Their first few productions were staged at the Park Theatre in Hanwell, and they decided to do only plays that were 'worthwhile'. That's a loaded word. It tells us what was likely to be excluded from their repertoire: anything 'frothy and light'. This team of questors were clearly serious in their mission to present interesting, challenging work, in interesting, challenging ways. It reminded me of Highbury's first production, $X=O$, that blank-verse drama about the meaninglessness of war.

In their fourth year, with a bank balance described as 'precarious', the Questors began to look for their own premises. This is where our priest comes in. In 1895, a man called Father Richard O'Halloran had been suspended from the Catholic church, so he bought a substantial Victorian house in Mattock Lane and built a church of his own in its grounds, at a cost of £2,000. As 'fuck yous' go, this is a pretty good one. Where he got the money to do it, nobody knows. And while Alex Marker assured me that he was suspended because of his fervent support for the Irish Home Rule bill of the 1880s, which put him at odds with his lords and masters, there are also words like 'troublesome priest', 'immorality' and 'go to Australia' in archive reports, which muddy the waters somewhat. (I'm not taken to praying but may have resorted to a quick 'please don't let him be dodgy' here.) His church was constructed out of those wavy sheets of tin you see on old allotments or air-raid shelters, and was called, rather grandly, 'The Iron Church'. It must have been boiling in summer and freezing in winter but a bit of physical discomfort would have been entirely on-brand. He built up a congregation there, even when the decree that he was to be excommunicated had gone all the way to Rome.

On his death in 1925, Father O'Halloran left 12 Mattock Lane to his carer, Miss Ann Webb; by 1930 she was living there with her sister, so here are the 'spinsters' in our tale. These two were canny. The Iron Church had been let out to the Ealing Scouts, and in June 1933, Questors moved in to share their premises and costs; the Iron Church became affectionately and more accurately known as the Tin Hut. Highbury also started life in a mission hut, remember. Six months later, on 6 December 1933, the first Questors production at this site opened. It was the English premiere of an experimental play by Shirland Quin, *Dragons' Teeth*, which *Amateur Theatre* magazine called 'undoubtedly the most experimental work done by a London society in recent months, if not years'. According to the theatre's biography (called *A Few Drops of Water* because in 1950 Emmet had described the theatre's achievements as 'the adding of a few drops of water to the mainstream of theatre'), the play had 'an elaborate and expressionistic dream sequence in the last act'. Dream sequences, in whatever creative medium they appear, are always dreadful. Elaborate and expressionistic ones are actual hell. Worse – or better, depending on your viewpoint – the production involved around seventy characters, which meant members of the cast had to double, treble, quadruple and even quintuple their roles. It sounds less 'expressionistic dream' and more 'who the hell am I *now*?' nightmare. 'It was not staged,' the book drily said, 'without some considerable difficulties.' Those difficulties included two members of the cast, who played nine characters between them, dropping out on the afternoon of the first performance. Of course, the show still went on, their experimentation continued, and the theatre grew.

Which brings us on to the 'shady drinking club'. The canny spinsters were letting out a separate building at 12 Mattock

Lane to 'a drinking club of notorious repute', known as Ye Olde Mattock Barn Club. But the Questors wanted to expand. Emmet described their negotiations:

> We would plead with Miss Webb how desperately we needed to take over the Barn Club and she would promise us that next quarterday we could. Then the proprietress of the Barn Club would get wind of this and in her turn would visit Miss Webb. She would leave behind her a £5 note on the mantelpiece. Come quarterday Miss Webb would explain, almost with tears in her eyes, that she 'hadn't the heart' to turn Mrs Whatever-her-name-was out, and we had to start all over again ...

By 1947, with the company now in its teens, they finally managed to obtain the lease and Questors expanded. Over time, it acquired the site fully, and a new theatre was built, with the labour provided by members, just as it had been in the creation of Highbury Little Theatre. This new building was so exciting it was celebrated with national and international publicity, even featuring on the BBC – I can't imagine any theatre (with the exception of the National, perhaps) getting that much attention these days, let alone a place for amateurs.

Questors Theatre still stands on the site where it started. Now, you'd be hard pushed to see the difference between this and a professional theatre, and hard pushed to believe it all began in a religious tin hut. They have full-time staff, and alongside their annual productions they rent out rehearsal rooms and studios and run a thriving youth theatre with around five hundred attendees. When I walked in to meet Alex Marker, I could hear a group of young drama students in one of the studios, the familiar noise of their warm-up game, tossing plosive sounds to each other. As I waited for him, a woman came into the reception area with two children – I suspect she was their gran, in charge of them for half-term – to enquire whether there was room in the youth theatre for, she pointed to the smaller of the two children, a girl aged about six. As Gran chatted to the woman behind the counter about classes and timetables, the small girl put her arms on the counter and laid her head on them. She began to sob. The adults carried on enthusing. Her big brother touched her back, briefly, consolingly. She continued sobbing. The woman behind the counter went to find a leaflet, and the small girl lifted her head. 'Is that it? Am I in?' she asked tragically, hardly needing acting training at all. 'We're just enquiring,' said Gran. 'So I don't have to go?' the girl asked. 'You don't have to. But I think it sounds fun, don't you?' 'No,' the girl sobbed heavily, 'I don't.' 'It's really good for their confidence,' the woman behind the desk said, to their departing backs. Questors is undoubtedly a success; but still, it's not for everyone.

It's a success that goes way beyond its own postcode. Lucy Neal, theatre-maker, writer and co-founder, with Rose Fenton, of the London International Festival of Theatre (LIFT), told me how Alfred Emmet had influenced LIFT. Their first festival was in 1981 and in the process of setting it up, Lucy and Rose went to Questors looking for suitable venues and met Alfred.

'We were following our noses and Alfred was in the throes of inviting a show from India, a production he would host at Questors,' she told me. He had, by this stage, been active in the theatre for an astonishing fifty-plus years; he travelled a lot for his work in the tea industry, so was able to follow his passion, and see a variety of different performance abroad. Lucy described Alfred as open-hearted, generous and professional, particularly in how he managed, produced and hosted artists. Lucy and Rose went to Questors several times to see international shows he was presenting, which would have been amateur productions, obviously. So beyond *how* producers look after people, Alfred also helped LIFT think differently about who those people might be. About how relevant and important amateurs are, in work from outside the UK.

'Alfred helped us see beyond the label and that was absolutely foundational for LIFT. He was on the hunt for people, companies, communities, who between them had created a mesmerising, dynamic piece of theatre and that's what we were looking for. So we never went "eurgh, that's amateur", we just went WOW. I believe that theatre is the place where the darkest, darkest things can be acted out, the truth of people's different political cultural situations wherever they are in the world – Palestine, Chile, apartheid South Africa . . .'

In terms of telling political and personal truths, if you decry the amateur, you miss some vital contributions. Lucy told me about the Polish theatre they saw in 1980 when they were setting up LIFT, when companies actively *preferred* the student theatre or amateur label as it meant they avoided the censorship that professionals were subjected to. Rose Fenton's 2006 report on theatre in Iran quotes a young artist who says:

To make theatre in Iran is a form of resistance. We are part of a generation who did not participate in the revolution of 1979 because we were too young or not even born. The Fadjr Festival offers us a greater freedom to express our thoughts.

Rose writes how that festival, launched in 1982 and still going, presents a 'surprisingly eclectic mix of local shows from Iran's thriving, largely amateur theatre constituency'. 'I come above all to seek what I cannot read in the press,' said one student attendee. 'The theatre offers me a barometer of the situation in my country.' If you forget the amateur, you forget that story. The story is what matters, and its telling. In influencing LIFT at its start, Emmet helped to shape what would be presented on future London stages: amateurs from round the world who continue to give us some of the most radical, engaged and necessary work. 'Got to keep it political, Jenny,' Lucy tells me, signing off an email.

About as far from 'keeping it political' as it's possible to get, it was time for one of my toughest assignments for this book: the Questors panto.

I am not a fan of panto. I'm not even going to do the 'oh yes you are' joke. I view adults who go to panto with the same suspicion that I view adults who go to Disneyland without children. Enforced fun brings out my most snobbish and judgemental self; enforced fun aimed at children that adults also appear to enjoy – well, I just don't get it. It was in this open, accepting mood that I turned up, mid-festive season, to see a show where the majority of the audience didn't reach my knees. And if you're thinking I was grumpy, I was a ray of sunshine compared to my companion for the night – my teenage daughter. If there is anything to strike fear into the hearts of even the most seasoned performer, it is the 'go on, entertain me' face of a young goth raised on sarcasm, sat right in the front row.

I went to the panto because it's good to confront your fears, and because a big Christmas show is very important to lots of amateur theatres. There are several reasons, one of them being the obvious financial benefit of selling a lot of seats; Tony at People's Theatre had already told me they pack their space out with the panto. And it brings an audience that might have been tempted through the doors for the first time. Creating habit and familiarity, getting people in with something accessible, is a good way to build audiences who might not otherwise contemplate amateur theatre. If you come here as a child, to see shows aimed at you, you just might keep coming. Pantos are also a great way to get young people onstage, and for a theatre with a huge youth group, that is an obvious attraction. If the quality of the show is comparable with anything you could see in the professional theatre but tickets are a fraction of the price, so much the better.

The panto at Questors certainly hit those marks. The last one I'd been to, on a duty visit to a professional theatre because a friend was in it, they'd run TV-style adverts on a large screen before the main show, and I felt sullied. Tonight, I made a conscious decision to relax and join in, to leave my judgemental self propping up the bar. It wasn't actually that hard. Here was a large top-notch cast, including lots of kids, taking our night of silliness very seriously. The stage effects weren't lavish but they were effective, and it occurred to me – this *should* be right up my street. I've been to plenty of big shows where you can see the money onstage, and while that's impressive in the short term, it can feel like posh food. Ultimately unfilling. It's refreshing to be more home-made, a kick against the idea that big money is the answer to everything. When the scenery creaked and juddered a bit, nobody pretended that wasn't happening, we were complicit with it. The comedy was broad, and in our groaning at the dame's puns, we were complicit with that, too. I even joined in with some booing and hissing as the villain appeared. In all, it was a hit with the whole audience. Apart from one. The interval came and I asked her, 'Are you enjoying it?' She looked at me. 'Can we go home now?' she said, deadpan. I remembered Minack. We went home.

Even though they'd done a great job, I hadn't come out of the Questors panto as a true convert. It had all been so silly and noisy, and that was just the audience. But it's a lonely place, being the anti-panto grinch. I wanted to understand its attraction to people I might otherwise think of as right-minded. So I talked to David Simpkin, by day a mild-mannered independent bookseller in Winchester; by night an amateur panto wizard since 1994. I confessed my feelings about panto-mime to him upfront. 'I am gutted and bereft,' he replied, clearly resisting the urge to boo me. And then he went on to tell me why I'm wrong.

'It's a form that lends itself to both the best and the worst. It's very, very easy to do lazy, lowest-common denominator panto. And it's quite difficult to not do that, but still be extremely funny. One of the ways to do that is to look back. Part of my mission as a panto performer is to teach young kids old jokes.'

In that sense, David is Winchester's answer to Barry Cryer, a comparison nobody who knows their comedy could possibly object to.

'One of my heroes! I use a combination of storytelling and knowingness and deliberately referencing things; every year, I will stick in a joke that only I will get, and it'll be a fifties radio catchphrase. It's a way of reaching back and reaching forward. And it was important to me that it wouldn't be cheap. I said I wouldn't do *Aladdin* until I learned how to eradicate the casual racism.'

He had touched on an issue which troubles me. Some companies don't bother to adapt their shows and call any attempts to change things 'political correctness gone mad', which is a personal red flag. Why would anyone be proud of being wrong? Why would casual racism and other prejudices be worth clinging on to? Is panto where our veneer of tolerance slips, and we show our true colours? *Sardines*, a magazine for the amateur theatre world, produced a panto issue where one contributor wrote about 'being PC' referencing *Aladdin*. 'Who exactly are we offending? Not, I think, the Chinese people who I suspect don't see much pantomime.' (Take a deep breath, Jenny, reply calmly.) Well, Mr Contributor, here's the thing. This comment, 'we're not offending them, they don't even come to panto', reveals more than you think it does. If Chinese people tell you they are offended, please listen. Listen to, for instance, Daniel York Loh, a British East Asian theatre artist, who asked, 'Are we actually arguing that racist jokes and reducing other races to exotic fancy-dress costume is wholesome entertainment for Caucasian families in the British provinces?' Panto is an equal-opportunities offender; no group is left unmocked. But this isn't much of a defence. And it doesn't have to be this way. York Loh highlighted Theatre Royal Stratford East's production of *Rapunzel*, 'which managed to be fast, fun, bold and rude in a truly exhilarating and riotously joyous fashion, without ever once crossing the line into cultural insensitivity'. You see, Mr Contributor? Please move gracefully into this century, you are welcome here.

The dame is one of the staples of British panto. 'I'm very much in Les Dawson's camp on this one,' David Simpkin explained. 'The dame is not drag. The dame is clown, and clowning has been a massive part of panto's history. It's not a man pretending to be a woman. It's a clown pretending to be a woman. It's a subtle distinction. For instance, I don't wear breasts, and I don't do much with my voice – I posh it up a bit but I don't go squeaky. Because it's me. One of my big fat theories on panto is that the audience's reaction to the show is moderated through their knowledge of the performers, whether it's in a big professional show, recognising him off the TV and having their television persona be the character, or actually knowing it's the vicar or the postman.'

Or the local bookseller, of course. David's theory echoed what Helen Nicholson had said about double ontology. Where people have a relationship with the actors onstage, their involvement in the group dynamic is heightened. David brought in social anthropologist Victor Turner.

'His theory in the study of ritual is this idea of communities – the idea that everyone present is a participant. And whether that's a religious ritual, or a football match, or a piece of theatre – it's true. That everyone who is present is in some way part of the group dynamic. And what's different about panto is that there is no suspension of disbelief really. It's possibly the most Brechtian form of theatre outside Brecht, in that the audience know the story.'

My interest was definitely piqued now. I'm so easily reeled in. Just one mention of Brecht and I'm right back to my days of prancing around in a boiler suit and Doc Martens proclaiming how very, very important theatre is. To David, the lead comic figure has the role of providing that Brechtian distance, even though the political intent might be completely gone. Understanding how theatre works has allowed David a better understanding of how panto works.

'There's a lovely description I heard in a documentary. It was of Herod in the mystery plays, and it said, "They cast the best actor, and encourage the audience to boo and hiss," and I'm like – really? That sounds familiar. This is old, deep stuff, and if you can take an audience with you, they love it. The great thing with panto done well is that it involves the audience in the laughter-making process. You're letting the audience in on a secret.'

I am constantly finding connections; today, David took me right to the start of amateur theatre's history, to the devil being the most popular character. It's where we started, and it gave me a little panto moment. 'He's behind you!'

After talking with Alex Marker at Questors in mid-February, I had noticed a poster on the wall. It was advertising the next Christmas panto already. Having listened to David speak so passionately and convincingly about panto, I decided I needed to give it another try. Next year. If I'm free. I'm pretty busy. Maybe the year after. Soon, anyway.

CHAPTER 10

The Day Job

If Highbury's 'club room' did not fit the traditional image, the Army & Navy Club, where I was having lunch one particular July Tuesday, absolutely did. It is situated just off Pall Mall, a fancy London street with shops that don't sell anything I will ever need. (Somehow, I have never found fine art, fishing waders, or cigars more expensive than houses on my 'essentials' list.) The Army & Navy Club is not my normal kind of lunch venue. I'm less a white linen tablecloth and heavy cutlery type, more a wipe-down surface and things-with-chips kind of person. 'I will be in the Ribbon Bar,' Noel Rands had emailed in advance, 'which is informal.' Some people are better turned out to go to work than I was for my wedding, so I know that one person's 'informal' can be another person's 'how can I manage this without borrowing stuff?'. I googled it to be sure. The Army & Navy Club website stated that the dress code for the Ribbon Bar was smart casual: 'polo shirts, smart/designer jeans and loafers (equivalent for ladies)', which confused me. Aren't all jeans designed? And what is the 'lady' equivalent of loafers? Wasn't that just . . . loafers? Or are loafers only for men? Clearly, I was out of my comfort zone. When that happens, I find it helps to go in character, so today I was appearing as 'confident woman totally at home in the Army & Navy Club'. I affected a kind of entitled don't-give-a-shit-ness. I'd have casually flung a scarf over my shoulder, if I had a scarf that wasn't woolly.

When I arrived, Noel was already there having a Bloody Mary. I decided not to drink – one vodka and I'd have dropped character and been all noisy. Our other lunch guests arrived and we ordered food. I chose a club sandwich. This was a stupid thing to do; 'confident woman' wasn't thinking straight. This club sandwich was so long it had to lie down. I wasn't sure about the etiquette, so I faffed around deconstructing it, picking through the innards, dripping tomato pips all down my white shirt and eating bits of bacon with my fingers, all the while holding back the urge to take the long skewer holding the whole bloody thing together and go on a small rampage round the Ribbon Bar.

I'd recently been introduced to Noel by my old Highbury compadres, Rob and Ros Jones, and something he'd dropped into the conversation had caught my attention. Noel had spent a year at Highbury in the 1970s, it's how he knew the Joneses, but most of his involvement with amateur dramatics, he said, had been 'when I worked for Midland Bank'. What do you mean, 'when you worked for Midland Bank'? I'd asked. 'They had an amateur dramatic society, for employees. I was in one in London, in Liverpool, in Cairo,

Bombay . . .' I wanted to know more, so he'd offered to have lunch with me to talk about it, along with two of his former colleagues and fellow thespians, Brian Hocken and Josephine Hinde.

Noel's casual comment about having been in the Midland Bank Dramatic Society, had reminded me of something from a few years back: the time I'd snuck into the old Shell building on London's South Bank for a swim. I say 'snuck into' – I'd been signed in by an employee but it was all very hush-hush. I'd had to leave my politics (which could be loosely defined as 'anti-Shell') at home and I constantly felt like my true left-leaning identity was going to be revealed by a throwaway comment about profits and planets, and I'd be chucked out by the London Eye wearing only a costume and goggles. Despite that, I'd had a splendid visit to a beautiful space. Dating, like me, from 1961, it was an architectural and design gem; at the time I described it as 'Mad Men in swimming pool form.' The pool, several floors beneath a busy Thames-side street, was thirty-three metres long and had a full-size diving board, which might give you some idea of the grandeur of the space. This was no cramped, dark underground cavern. The pool had been part of Shell's staff 'offering', alongside gyms, squash courts, a rifle range (of course, that's entirely natural and not at all worrying), and a variety of on-site beauty salons. It was demolished when Shell were revamping their iconic building, which to me was a kind of corporate vandalism.

I am not a fool. I'm well aware that when employees get given stuff, this is rarely pure benevolence. There's always a pay-off for employers. They're buying your loyalty, or perhaps acknowledging that your well-being might need boosting because you work for them. Anyone's attitude might be improved if they felt that their boss cared about them holistically, encouraged them to get fit, or let them do some target practice. Let's not romanticise the on-site hairdresser. Stuff like that can appear to be generous, but it keeps staff on-site and on-side, when recognition of a union, or paying a living wage might be more useful in the long term. Shell might have been upmarket in giving their staff an incredible pool and a rifle range but providing facilities for the workforce used to be quite normal at the time their offices were built. The surprise for me that Noel introduced was that, at one time, 'facilities' could have included a company theatre. I'm not talking about a couple of milk crates turned upside down and a few rows of company chairs. I'm talking about proper stages, proscenium arches, auditoria. Amateur theatre definitely used to be part of 'what I did today at work'.

I started looking and found stories of workplace amateur dramatic societies across all sorts of businesses, at all levels. Harrods, Barclays Bank, British Leyland, British Rail, Unilever. The Cable and Wireless Company in Porthcurno, which had been right at the start of Rowena Cade's Minack story. The Dunlop Players in Birmingham, based at their massive factory, a mini-city which had ten thousand workers at its peak, had their own theatre. Reg Tolley worked there in the early fifties, and wrote about it in *Memories of a Highbury Ham*.

Dunlop's, I used to joke, made tyres as a sideline, it was the Dramatic Society that counted. After two or three days working for Dunlop, I discovered they had a dramatic society and was immediately a French waiter in *The Magistrate*. Most critics agreed it was one of the best groups attached to industry.

Reg's remark tells us that there were many similar groups attached to industry, and that critics took them seriously. In a few words, he had conjured up that idealised vision that had pushed Geoffrey Whitworth to start the British Drama League. Men in boiler suits, grimy from their work on a factory line producing tyres, wiping off the dirt when the whistle signalled the end of the day, and acting together in a Shakespeare, or a Coward, or *The Magistrate*.

In the 1920s, the dramatic society at the Shredded Wheat factory in Welwyn Garden City was run by a young woman in the personnel department who had trained as an actor and who later went back to the professional stage – Dame Flora Robson. Another company formed in 1905 by a group of senior members of the Stock Exchange, to 'take advantage of the great variety of stage talent they saw scattered around the house', is still going strong. I was told there used to be a British Embassy drama club in Paris.

When I used the secret code on my friend Wendy Lee, she told me that she used to be in a drama group, at the ad agency where she worked. 'We were called TITS,' she said. Er, what? 'TITS. Theatre in the Square. We were based in St

James's Square and it was clearly too seaside humoury to resist. It was run mostly by a copywriter and an art director, Reg Farrier and Pete Oliver. It was all comedic sketches – we never did a play or anything like that; it was about having fun, we just wanted to get to the laugh. I was the only one who ended up doing it professionally.' Wendy left advertising to go into the world of stand-up in the late 1980s, one of the few women to brave it at the time. And of course there was the Midland Bank Dramatic Society – which is where we came in.

I continued to fiddle with my club sandwich as Noel, Brian and Josephine reminisced. Noel and Brian looked and sounded alike; they'd been a bit of a double act in their day, they said, and the old routines were clearly still at their fingertips. Noel had already told me that he and Brian were once the cabaret at Quaglino's at an annual dinner for the Midland Bank Dramatic Society, and seeing them together, I could see how. They were blustery and avuncular, full of good humour. Josephine was their physical opposite. An orchid between two trees. She needed to raise her voice a little to get her stories heard, but she didn't shy away from that, she held her line; the two men were respectful of her, and clearly full of affection. It reminded me of how men of a certain generation go a bit soppy around the Queen, and actually Josephine would be a great double for her, if that role wasn't already taken by my mum.

As the three of them talked, the picture they conjured sounded pretty halcyon. I've never wanted to work for a bank in the 1960s and 70s so much. Josephine told me that her bank career had begun when she was a young woman. 'When I first joined the bank, the operatic society was just starting to audition and I said, "Lead me to it!" A few years later the dramatic society was starting up again, and I joined that.' It had closed down during the war, and restarted in 1946; you could join from any rank if you auditioned. The chief general manager, Mr Charles Trott, was a keen member but you could be a star at whatever level you were. 'That sounds great,' I said. 'Wonderful,' said Josephine.

The three friends had met at the Midland Bank head-quarters, at 27 Poultry (this is an actual address, if you needed a reminder that the City of London is weird). Initially, the bank used to hire various venues for their productions – the Fortune Theatre, the Scala, the Vanburgh Theatre, Toynbee Hall. 'We had the bank's resources behind us. The costumes, scenery. We'd send the bill to the bank,' said Brian. 'Even in those days, the operatic society would spend over £1,000 to put on a show,' said Josephine; this was clearly not done in a half-arsed fashion, the good name of the Midland Bank was at stake. 'You'd design a set, and the bank would build that set,' Noel said. 'You had the pick of directors too. Whatever you wanted, it was there,' Brian added. 'You knew you were going to run at a loss but as far as the bank was concerned it was a philanthropic thing we all did. If you didn't play rugby, you went into the amateur dramatics. You were encour-aged to do it.' Then the Midland Bank built their own theatre, in-house. Facilities like this were completely normal, every bank had sports and social clubs. If Shell could have their own huge pool, deep underground, why the hell should the Midland not have a theatre, slap bang in the heart of the City? 'We had our own theatre, our own bar. It was lovely,' said Josephine. 'We used the smoking room too,' chipped in Brian. 'We used to rehearse in there,' said Noel. 'No, no, we used to rehearse down in the safe deposit,' Josephine corrected him, and I liked that image. 'I always felt terribly, terribly happy. It was a lovely feeling,' said Josephine. 'It was a big family,' said Brian. Can you imagine feeling that way about working in a bank? I can't.

One aspect of this life was summarily ended. The building that was Midland's headquarters is now a smart hotel, though the theatre had been ripped out earlier, when Midland became HSBC in the early 1990s. 'HSBC was huge,' Noel said, 'but they never had a dramatic society because they weren't interested. Any kind of family, that disappeared.' Theatre makes family, family makes theatre. 'If you go there now, that safe deposit is a bar,' Brian said. 'Have they kept the fishpond?' asked Josephine. (There was a fishpond?) 'They have a piano on top of it,' replied Noel. The way they talk, it *is* like family – or maybe 'community' is the word. Josephine radiated a respectful fondness for this place, this time and these people. She gave the impression it was the happiest time of her life. For the last thirteen years of her career, she was the secretary of the operatic and dramatic society, and the art society. Not as an addendum to her regular duties in the bank, these *were* her regular duties. Such was the importance of these societies within the bank, they employed someone to run them properly. One could almost say, then, that she was doing it professionally – this kind of slippage shows that the distinctions can be blurry.

'I had my own office, I did everything. I was answerable to my committees and the hierarchy of the bank. Barclays Bank was the same, except their secretary had an assistant. Mr Mather, who was the chief and a very nice gentleman, he really was, he came to everything. He would ring me up the day after he'd been to a show. "Is that Miss Hinde? We enjoyed the show last night." It felt very genuine.'

Josephine's parents had been involved in amateur theatre, so it was part of her upbringing, though acting wasn't something she considered doing professionally, because in the amateur world she got such good roles. This was becoming a theme for me; Barbara Hughes had felt the same, and Tony at People's Theatre. Josephine was clearly a bit of a shining star, because other companies tried to poach her, she told me, and she sounded proud of that, but not boastful. Brian was in the National Youth Theatre in 1960, but had realised that acting was a precarious profession, and that it was all about who you knew. He didn't have the right connections. 'I was a Home Counties boy, from a comprehensive school, but I was on the stage from aged four, tap dancing.' He's still on the stage now, mostly in the form of a barbershop quartet. It's all about performing though. 'In the fifties and early sixties, this is what it was about. We all did things like gang shows [revue/variety shows]. It was part of life.' Noel chimed in, singing

'I'm riding along on the crest of a wave . . ." Still quite the double act.

Noel's route to the theatre was via school. 'Various people change your life,' he said, and for him, one of them was a teacher who cast him in the title role in *Toad of Toad Hall*. From that, his acting career was started.

'The first society I joined was in Liverpool, I acted there. There was one in Manchester, and Birmingham. We did *The Drums of Deliverance*. When I went to London, I joined the Midland Bank Dramatic Society. I met Josephine, got the part in *Deep Blue Sea*.'

'And *Present Laughter*,' added Josephine, twinkling, 'that was wonderful, wasn't it?'

'As I wandered round the world with the bank – Liverpool, Manchester, Birmingham, Tehran, Cairo, Bombay, Hong Kong – I joined the local am-drams as a means of getting to know people rather than join the football club or the rugby club. They were there wherever you went. When I was in Tehran, after the revolution, they said to me "Noel, we're doing play readings at the embassy", and so it continued.' It became a central part of Noel's life but his devotion to drama caused ructions. 'Someone had been asked, "What does Midland Bank get out of Noel's acting?" And they'd replied, "what we get out of it is, he's the best-known correspondent banker in India and he can get an appointment any time he likes." They all knew who I was.'

This was never about hustling for promotion or being seen as a good loyal employee. 'I think the fundamental thing about all of this,' Brian said, 'is that we did it for pleasure. We wanted to do it.' Their evocation of the patrician company and its happy, loyal, theatrical workforce, fair made me nostalgic for the olden days. It's simply not as binary as 'boss and workers', when you hear these people's experiences. The sense of belonging to a family, a community, was important. The Midland Bank didn't kindly 'give' their employees a dramatic society. People formed a dramatic society with their work colleagues, and they were supported in it by their employers. They were allowed and encouraged. It was an entirely normal thing to do, with no downside for either party.

After I'd murdered the last bit of my club sandwich and we'd moved on to coffee, I asked what else they'd got out of amateur theatre. Noel spoke first. He had already questioned why he was an actor, and come to a conclusion.

'I could be someone else. I could learn a part and go onstage and for a while, the insecurities I have . . . If I'm invited somewhere as myself, I'm absolutely tied up with nerves. But going there in a part . . .'

Josephine helped us through the sympathetic silence that came when he stopped talking.

'I'm not saying Noel or Brian or I were always shy people but shyness was behind some of it. You become somebody, and you'd do things onstage you wouldn't dare do offstage. It gave me confidence offstage.' She told me about a theatrical trick she'd learned. 'Early on, before I felt I could speak up, if I came into a room, I would always, in those days we were always wearing gloves, I would start taking my gloves off. By the time I'd taken them off I was going round talking to people. And I'd learned how to take gloves off by watching Peggy Ashcroft onstage. Oh, to see her take off a pair of gloves was fantastic.'

As she talked, she mimed removing a pair of lady's gloves, rather delicately, with finesse, like I've seen women do in films. This was a whole 1950s London life she was conjuring up, and I was taken with it, the thought of this gentle woman mesmerised in her theatre seat watching Peggy Ashcroft, the whole audience rapt. It's a romantic vision, still powerful as Josephine invokes it more than half a century later.

Can you see Josephine, well turned out and always polite and kind, trotting up the marble steps to her office, at 27 Poultry? Can you see her, answering the phone on her desk to Mr Mather when he calls to compliment the show, and her feeling a little giddy with it all? I can. This play-acting, it gave her a voice. I was charmed by it all. Weeks later, Noel emailed to ask if he could give Josephine my number; she'd told him that our lunch was the happiest day she'd had for a long time. That was something to think about. All it had taken was for someone to listen, to help her go back to this wonderful time again. If amateur theatre gave her so much all those years back, I was pleased to have been able to help her relive it. To hear someone's stories, told with love, is such an honour.

I came across the Unilever amateur dramatic company via the *Guardian* obituary of actor Carmel McSharry. 'Carmel was evacuated to Surrey during the second world war and, on leaving school, worked as a secretary for Unilever in London,' it blithely said. 'The acting talent she displayed in the company's drama group led her to gain a scholarship to Rada, and she won its silver medal on leaving in 1947.' I started digging into the Unilever archives to find out more, and absolute wonders spilled out.

Port Sunlight sounds like a made-up place, but it's not. It is a 'model village', where 'model' means perfect rather than miniature, on the Wirral Peninsula opposite Liverpool. This is where Unilever started, and the village was conceived and built by industrialist William Hesketh Lever in the late nineteenth century, as a place where employees of all levels from his factories could live. It butted up right next to Lever's soap factory (hence 'Sunlight', the name of the soap) and had its own dock facilities (hence 'Port'), an explanation which takes the shine off. The location might not sound as promising as the name, but the records of its earliest incarnations are extraordinary. I stared at the drawn plan from 1914, marvelling at the idealism brought to life. The village had plenty of allotment gardens, recreation grounds, wide roads and space between houses; it had bowling greens, wooded parkland, a (temperance) pub, a gym and an open-air swimming pool. Naturally, they also had a theatre, Gladstone Hall. I thought it might be heaven, until I read that it was only men who got to use everything on offer, including the pool. I wonder if I'd have been as furious then as this makes me now. There was a club in the village, which, Edward William

Beeson wrote in his 1911 collection of photographs, 'shows that men in different positions can mix successfully and be drawn together for their mutual benefit'. And that was the point of it all, a kind of cooperation, a partnership. I'm not usually susceptible to 'the glorious gentleman generously taking care of his workers out of the sheer goodness of his heart' message. It's the kind of thing that belongs in a propaganda film. But still, I fell for it. Because by all accounts, this project was Lever's genuine philanthropy, his desire for a new way of working, it was respectful of how people could lead good lives, whatever their work status. It was a happy place.

Port Sunlight News, the monthly magazine for employees, makes this abundantly clear. It reported in great detail both the working life of the factory and people's lives there. Things like this from 1922:

> There was a delightful gathering in the Men's Dining Hall, when the girls of Number 2 Stamping Room assembled to do honour to Mr "Teddy" Williams, who, after being foreman of the room for 21 years, has been given a post in the new Stocks Control Department.

He wasn't leaving, you'll note, he was just moving department, but his colleagues thought it was worth a party, and *Port Sunlight News* thought it worth reporting on. Every time a woman 'left to get married' or went to live abroad (which was not uncommon), it was noted and often accompanied by posed photos of people who clearly didn't face the camera often. Here is Miss Millie Crompton, for instance, 'who for the past eleven years was engaged in the Fancy Cardbox Department' (the what?) and was off to Cairo to get married. Millie stares out from the shiny page, with a slight smile and an almost-raised eyebrow, in a simple embroidered shirt and with messy hair. Here is Miss Martha Griffiths on her retirement; she warranted a page-long article, which in itself was a history lesson about working lives and women and the early days of soap manufacture. 'Martha has taken leave of her beloved Printing Department with which she has been associated since 1889.' She'd joined the company 'over thirty-four years ago, before the first boiling of soap in No. 1'. There was the Number 1 Soapery, the Number 3 Soapery, the Number 1 Stamping Room, the Number 2 Stamping Room. Each a small glimpse.

The *News* also reported all the things that went on outside work, which makes for a glorious record of the sheer quantity of opportunities employees had. Education, the arts, sport, social activities, charity, horticulture – you name it. There were reports on the bowling seasons and whist drives, the billiards trophies and the dances that are run by every department – the Traffic Department Dance, the Time and Wages Department Dance, the Service Department Dance – and about all the holiday camps, Old Boys' Associations and Girls' Social Clubs. There were ambulance classes and the Women's Helpful League, gala days and presentations. These people were busy. So was the *News* writing style, which ranges from florid to fever pitch. In December 1922, a royal visit gave one journalist a meltdown. 'One of the greatest days in the history of Port Sunlight was Saturday December 16th,' he hyperventilated, 'and it was also the greatest of the many great days in the life of Viscount Leverhulme.' There are even pages listing every new book put on the shelves of the Lever Library.

There are articles, too, on how to live your life as the perfect Port Sunlight resident. They could read about the importance of temperance, or life insurance, or gardening. One article, 'Teeth as Arbiters of Health', reminded me that my father's last place of employment in the late seventies was the dental surgery of Hardy Spicers, a Birmingham car factory which felt very far from the charms of Port Sunlight. There are articles on how to pronounce 'margarine' (with a hard 'g', surprisingly. I've been doing it wrong all my life) and lectures on whaling, including graphic detail on how to kill a whale. Impossible to believe that would be useful to many people, but there it was. They reported on the development of radio – 'I HEAR AMERICA ON WIRELESS' proclaimed one headline, as momentously as it could. Through it all, there was a sense of encouragement, to learn, to enjoy art, and to improve oneself. It's obvious what all this was doing. Creating a workforce that took pride in its position, one that worked hard, and actively *wanted* to work hard for the bosses and, seemingly, for themselves.

As an extra bonus, *Port Sunlight News* is also a fount of absolutely brilliant names. Gertrude Penkyman. Cherry Tinning. Bunty Cliffe and Mr Spool. Mary Seed (married to

Dick) and Anita Loon. I long for a name with the punch of a Jeanie Quail or a Minnie Lever.

It will be no surprise, given the activities with which Port Sunlight employees were engaged, that they also had an amateur operatic and dramatic society. But that's not all. The Old Boy's Association also put on plays, as did the Staff Training College, and theatre was found in more unexpected places. 'An enjoyable evening was recently spent by members of the Adult Bible Class, when they and their friends, to the number of 150, held a social in the Collegium. After tea a concert was given, a sketch entitled "Mixed Pickles" presented by four of the committee, providing great amusement.' (As I've said, comedy is subjective.) Performance was everywhere, amateur theatre was really popular, and the *Port Sunlight News* reported every production in microscopic detail.

For example, *A Snug Little Kingdom* by Mr Mark Ambient, put on in the Gladstone Hall from 14 to 16 February 1924. It billed itself as 'A Comedy of Bohemia in Three Acts', and while 'comedy' and 'bohemia' are fairly promising, anything billed as 'in three acts' makes even the keenest theatregoer slump. It's the perennial conundrum: I love going to the theatre, but why do I have to be there so damn long? The production 'gave exceptional enjoyment to a large number of the Society's supporters', the review stated. This is important, they go on, because 'there are critics so consecrated to the classical conception of dramatic principles that they overlook the function of the theatre as a place of entertainment'. Translated: it's all very well doing the serious stuff, but people want laughs. Again, a conundrum that's as old as theatre itself. I bet in early Greek times, when someone put on a production of *The Iliad*, there was a heckler yelling for Aristophanes, and vice versa. The reviewer loved the performances. Mr W. R. Pringle was described as 'an amateur virtuoso of acting', Miss Cowper's portrayal of a Soho landlady was 'highly satisfying in its humour and fidelity of voice and deportment', and Miss A. D. Minshall 'combines with histrionic instinct and pre-possessing presence the talent for employing them gracefully and effectively; and adds to her versatility a singing voice utilised with agreeable effect'.

Pan From the Past was always going to be well reviewed. The writer was the Hon. W. Hesketh Lever himself. His play is 'a "fantasy of the future" and a study of advanced feminism'. As I read that, I thought, blimey, could I love the honourable gentleman more? It deals with the reversed roles of men and women – hardly an exciting premise now, but then a really daring undertaking – and depicted the Martyn family, with Mrs Martyn going out to work and Mr Martyn left to worry about things of 'domestic import'. The play was a hit – of course it was. Anything Mr Lever turned his hand to, he was a master of. I can barely think about him without blushing.

Over time, Unilever became so big they had enough drama societies to host their own drama festival. As well as Port Sunlight's Amateur Operatic and Dramatic Society, there was the Blackfriars Society – the drama group for their London office where Carmel McSharry had started out. T. Wall & Sons (the ice-cream company bought by Lever in 1922) had an amdram society, as did British Oil and Cake Mills Ltd (I had no idea that oil and cakes were milled, but whatever this company did, they were acquired by Lever in 1925). *Port Sunlight News*, in its original overblown, overwritten, overextensive and thoroughly delightful format, shrunk though. It became a more 'fashionable' magazine, like a thin Sunday supplement, and only marriage notices remained steady. In this 1950s slimmed-down version, I spotted a review of the farce *Sailor Beware!* which gave me pause. Amateur theatre seems to have spun this invisible web over me; I was constantly finding sticky connections, constantly being thrown back to memories and childhood. My mum was in *Sailor Beware!* at Highbury, playing the role of Edie, a spinster aunt who read teacups. In one scene Mum sat on a very low stool, at a dining table where everyone else was on normal chairs. Night after night, her chin resting on the table sent the audience into hoots of laughter. She has a great sense of comedic timing, my mum. The phrase 'doing an Aunt Edie' joined our family lexicon, and is used whenever there's too many people round and someone is required to take the small, uncomfortable chair.

There's a memorial to William Hesketh, 1st Viscount Leverhulme outside the art gallery he built at Port Sunlight in honour of his late wife. On the front, it reads:

Founder of Lever Brothers Limited and of Port Sunlight.
A man remarkable for his business ability, his public

benefactions and his love of beauty and art. The monument is erected by his fellow workers.

Don't spoil this moment of reverie for me; I'm just taking a minute for an imagined romance with a remarkable man, one who'd build an art gallery for me when I die. Surely that's not too much to ask.

CHAPTER 11

Don't Say Macbeth

I was on the Eurostar on my way to Antwerp, sitting across from a man who would, later, snore so loudly that the whole carriage turned to look. The man's outfit had already put me on high alert. He was dressed in cotton trousers ('slacks', as Margaret from Highbury would have called them) and a matching V-neck, both the colour of tinned salmon, and he was engaged in the act of eating a Pret sandwich neatly, which was impossible because it had tomato in it. People should cut tomatoes up before they put them in sandwiches (as demonstrated by my performance at the Army & Navy Club). The man was hunched over, using his teeth and tongue to corral the dangling tomato into his mouth, dripping pips onto his copy of *The Times*, which he'd spread right across our supposedly shared table. Also, he was sitting in the outside seat, his bag on the window seat next to him, and we all know that is a twat's move. Despite all of this, I was in a pretty good mood.

For my journey, I was rereading Michael Green's 1964 book *The Art of Coarse Acting*, which I'd been reminded of by my trip to Questors Theatre. It was the amateur theatre bible when I was just the right age to be amused by the same things as my parents. It's a sweet spot, that one, the few years when you share a sense of humour, before you race ahead and discover *Not the Nine O'Clock News* (in my case) or BBC Three (in my children's), leaving parents bemused and 'too old to get it'. For a while, though, you stand on the same platform. I remember finding the book absolutely hilarious, we all did. Copies were passed round among a cast, everyone read their favourite bits aloud in the bar after rehearsals, the company jokers made their own attempts at coarse acting - or upstaging, you could call it. The main thrust of the book is 'how can I make myself conspicuous?' - and we all know people who've made that their life motto, whether they're in the theatre or not. The paperback copy I was reading on the train was a 1984 reprint the same size and colour as a Findus Crispy Pancake, and from roughly the same era. I wanted to find out if I still found it funny. Did it have the staying power of an *Adrian Mole*, or would I feel the same way my children did when I'd shown them Victor Borge's punctuation routine on YouTube? (That had been my dad's favourite comedy routine, which absolutely speaks to his character.) Was I going to reread this and end up questioning my own taste, and the taste of all people in the seventies?

The answer, of course, was 'no more than I already have done'. The taste of people in the seventies was notoriously terrible. Trousers so high-waisted they doubled up as bras, the colours cream and brown frequently put together, in bathroom suites or in stripes on the side of platform shoes, and Gary Glitter. In that context this book is relatively benign. And although I came to *The Art of Coarse Acting* with a real yearning to love it again, I didn't enjoy much of it this time round, not even for nostalgia's sake. It's not that the humour has dated – some of it still wrung an affectionate chuckle from me. What Green wrote about the way some amateurs believe professional actors have nothing to teach them, well, there are some arrogant amateurs who *do* still feel that. 'My friend Askew,' Green wrote, 'always maintains that Laurence Olivier is not a great actor "because he has cold eyes". "He doesn't *feel* it," says Askew, who has never in his life remembered a line correctly.' That sounded like something my mother could have written. Green wrote about the 'wonderful friendships one makes in the amateur theatre', and of course that resonated with me, it's been a theme in almost every conversation I've had with amateurs and will have on the weekend ahead of me. But the attitude to women felt old-fashioned and demeaning, and it reminded me of what I'd grown up with, attitudes which still proliferate where they're not wanted, like buddleia on a building site.

On this reread, what I hadn't banked on was getting two very visceral memories. The first came right at the start of the book, when Green stated that 'coarse acting is not, of course, restricted to the amateur world'. Flashback to 1979, my friend Adrian and me sitting in a theatre, watching a production of *Othello* starring Donald Sinden. Yes, *Othello*, and yes, *that* Donald Sinden, the one who played a quintessentially pompous English butler in a sitcom, then moved seamlessly on to play the role of a black prince on the Shakespearean stage. I say 'seamlessly', I mean 'stumblingly and hilariously badly'. It was the last time the RSC cast a white actor in that role, so we were waving a terrible slice of history off on its final death cruise. Had we known that, Adrian and I might have let our laughter out rather than spending a large portion of the play with our jumpers shoved in our mouths, trying to muffle it. It remains one of the worst things I've ever seen.

Memory Two. Halfway through the book, smiling at a picture caption ('How to steal a scene, though unconscious'), I suddenly had an enveloping feeling of my father's laugh. His proper, can't-hold-this laugh, where his whole body got involved. A laugh that we'd observe with the kind of confused horror children feel when their parents reveal themselves in some physical way. Kissing, dancing, laughing – observed in delight with an undertow of revulsion. I remembered Dad's face going puce, his shoulders heaving, his belly jiggling, the sweat on his brow, his breath wheezing like Muttley and tears rolling down his face. It was a laugh that produced a lot of movement but not a lot of noise, apart from that eternal wheeze and a jangling sound from the coins and keys in his jacket as it bounced up and down. Dad's laugh was all about suppression, about keeping the dam from bursting, and the effort of that paradoxically heightened everything until it became a maelstrom. Laughter overwhelmed him only occasionally, but it was the physicality of it that slammed into me on that train to Antwerp. I listened attentively as the memory played; I was sure I had heard it, actually heard it. The spell was broken by a louder sound, as the man in salmon-pink slacks started snoring.

I was in a good mood because I was headed to Antwerp. Planning this book, I'd expected to visit amateur theatres in the far-flung regions of Basildon and Newcastle, so the opportunity of a proper mini-break abroad was not to be missed. I was off to do something I've never knowingly done before – celebrate a spot of Britishness. A *spot* of Britishness? It's a bloody huge spot, this one; it stretches right across mainland Europe.

If you're involved in the world of amateur theatre, you won't need reminding that it has many tentacles. It is political, personal, persistent and, above all, present. It exists in all sorts of public and private places, everywhere from Glasgow to Cornwall, from prisons to cruise ships, from Dunlop Tyres to the Athenaeum Club. But even someone of great am-dram knowledge might be surprised to learn about FEATS – the Festival of European Anglophone Theatrical Societies. Because it *is* quite surprising, the fact that there is an annual competition between English-speaking European-based amateur theatre groups. It's surprising, delightful, and potentially a bit baffling. I am travelling with a lot of questions. Why are there so many English-speaking amateur groups in Europe? Why do they exist? Who are these people? Why do they get together? Why why why? I was on my way to find out.

In my mind, this was going to be the amateur theatre version of Eurovision. I was excited for a Graham Norton-style compère, a load of glitter, pointless dance acts, little films introducing every country, flag-waving and null points. I wanted something tacky and glorious, something with terrible outfits and hilarious-and-yet-unexpectedly moving performances, massive jingoistic crowds and people pronouncing English words in new and interesting ways. It didn't turn out like that, at all.

I should have guessed from their name. The Festival of European Anglophone Theatrical Societies sounds a little clunky and old-fashioned because the organisation has been going since 1976 and they chose their name a year later. It's a bit grandiose, one imagines it properly pronounced, accompanied by the wave of a hand and a deep bow. At first, as I'm an idiot, the word 'Anglophone' was slightly troubling me. It sounded suspiciously close to 'Anglophile', and when I wasn't excited about it being like Eurovision, I was worried I might step into a world that was all UKIP and copies of the *Daily Mail* a day late, full English breakfasts in Union Jack cafes, and Marks and Sparks. I was worried it might be like being in Gibraltar. Nothing like Eurovision at all.

Now, I am English, my parents are English, I am from bang in the middle of England. But I don't feel stirred at the sight of the flag of St George. I don't feel proud, or the sense of belonging that others loudly report. I am wary of all evocations that we should feel national pride based on the accident of where we are born. I don't support much about being English, and even though my mother gets booked for local events where she turns up as the Queen, I am not a fan of the royals. I understand that there is a certain level of privilege, even for a person from Birmingham, that comes with never having to examine or explain one's roots, at never having had a mean finger pointed and the question asked, 'Yes, but where are you *really* from?' So I struggle to connect with the idea that were I living abroad, I'd want to hang out with people purely based on their ability to speak my language. But what else would I do – remain silent? That wouldn't go well. And also, what experience do I have to bring to this table? None. I've never lived more than a hundred miles from where I was born. And aside from my recall of French being pretty good when I'm in Greece, and vice versa, I don't speak any other languages. It's almost as if I'm quintessentially English. How annoying is that, for me?

And then, it wasn't like being in Gibraltar or at Eurovision at all. It was exactly like being in Antwerp.

For a start, 'Anglophone' is not 'Anglophile'. It simply means 'English-speaking' and having an agreed common language when you're gathering people from across a continent makes sense. Not everyone taking part in the festival is English, but all the plays are performed in English, as are all the discussions, forums and adjudications. (Imagine having to perform in a second language, by the way. That's an actual recurring nightmare I often have.) But it's more than that, of course. It's not just that the language is agreed. There wasn't a vote and English won. It's an absolute reflection of what we have. Which other country has such a tradition of theatre, such a tradition of amateur theatre, and such a vast library of work? Our writers are one of our most successful exports; Shakespeare is known in practically every country in the world – name me any other playwright that we could say the same of. For English people living and working abroad, what else could remind them so effectively of home? I only realised when I was on my way back to England that everything about FEATS underlined what I was coming to feel about amateur theatre being such an important part of this country's cultural landscape. I had to come away, to see it clearly.

So, what is FEATS? At an organisational level, it is a collection of amateur theatre companies from all over mainland Europe. Every year they run a competition between twelve member groups. (Theatre companies from the UK used to take part but not any more – there's just too many of them. I can just about remember waving off a group from Highbury Little Theatre in the late 1970s, being dazzled by the unbelievable glamour of foreign travel and the unimaginable riches of having a passport.) FEATS is a growing organisation, or at least 'growing in some ways, shrinking in others', according to David Crowe, the organisation's permanent secretary. Tight budgets mean they're performing in smaller spaces, but there are new groups from new countries wanting to take part. The actors' age range is very mixed, while the audience demographic is getting older. There's a rolling schedule of host companies for the competition, and this year, it had fallen to BATS (British American Theatrical Society) who present 'English-speaking theatre in Antwerp' and have a clubhouse with rehearsal rooms, a small theatre and bar that gets used for meetings, forums and the festival 'fringe'. You could have been to Antwerp twenty times and never known their splendid building was there. Sometimes, amateur theatre feels like the Gothic ornamentation under the eaves of grand buildings. You don't see the gargoyles until you're looking, and then once you've started noticing them, they are everywhere.

Each of the twelve participating groups performs a one-act play of under fifty-five minutes, three plays a night over four nights. At the end of each evening, an adjudicator gives their opinion, delivered in the best tradition of 'critical friend': compliment, compliment, HARSH TRUTH, compliment. The adjudicator, from the Guild of Drama Adjudicators, is one of the only non-amateurs taking part; they sit in the middle of the auditorium at a kind of desk/lamp arrangement taking up several seats, a low-rent version of an *X Factor* judge. This may be amateur, but it would be a mistake to think that adjudicators don't take it seriously. Boxes are ticked, marking is vigorous, the rules are set in stone, internationally. Each group has the same short amount of time to set their scenery and lights and do any final checks. It's run on a tight schedule, and points are at stake.

One might think that a competitive element is antithetical to the whole nature of theatre, performance, self-expression and creating. And surely if any art form were created to fit the statement 'it's not the winning, it's the taking part', it's amateur theatre. But we judge all the time in every art form, and certainly in professional theatre, so why should amateurs be any different? You can judge the quality and the effort, you can reward talent, and competition gives FEATS a kind of *raison d'être*. The whole thing would feel very different if it were just a showcase or a gathering. As it is, over the four days, tension mounts, speculation builds, and the atmosphere grows as people root for their own shows and anxiously watch their competitors. Performances are dissected in a way that they wouldn't be if nothing were at stake. Gossip and whispers abound. If there were bets being taken, odds would be shifting and swivelling all over the place, but it's all done in a spirit of camaraderie and support. Can you imagine if someone suggested you play cricket just for the hell of it, and not keep score? This feels the same. And, actually, competitions are absolutely booming in the amateur theatre world. There are so many in the UK it's become multi-tiered, culminating in an ultimate 'All Winners' festival, and creating a kind of am-dram Premier League. In Ireland the competition circuit is essential to the livelihood of amateur theatre. In that context, one European competition doesn't seem unreasonable. Keep it competitive, I say. What are we, hippies?

This year's festival performances were on at Fakkeltheater, another building I'd have barely noticed if I were visiting Antwerp as a tourist. It has an unassuming air, the kind of place you'd visit on a rainy holiday when you've been to all the museums and shops and art galleries, in the same way that we once ended up seeing *Norbit* at a beaten-up old cinema in St Ives because we'd shuffled through all the shops and galleries and could not face another watercolour of the sea, rack of stripy fisherman jumpers or tuna sweetcorn sandwich at an indoor adventure park. At Fakkeltheater there are 'forthcoming attraction' posters on the wall, advertising plays like Noël Coward's *Heel Geestig*, which we know as *Blithe Spirit*. Their website translated the title as 'Very Spiritual' and I loved their brilliant caps-locked description – 'SECOND WOMAN, YEARS ON THE SPIRIT OF THE FIRST WOMAN? MANY TOO COMPLEX FOR A MAN!' The image on the poster was a woman wearing a turban and long strings of beads, beside a man looking aghast and perplexed, and it thrilled me in the same way that finding a terrible shirt in a vintage shop would. 'This is the worst shirt I have ever seen, I must buy it immediately.' There are more women in turbans on amateur theatre posters than I've ever seen in any sphere of actual life. They're used as shorthand, for a specific kind of woman. Somebody *geestig*, maybe, or *heel*.

The FEATS programme made it clear that if I'd been expecting something as dated and clunky as their acronym, this festival was not delivering it. There were a few original pieces of work, some extracts, and some complete short plays. Two of the entries immediately stood out. The first was a play called *The Hunchback Variations* by Mickle Maher, in which 'Beethoven and Quasimodo . . . invite you to a panel discussion on the search for the impossible sound'. If there was a performance I was most dreading, it was this one. It sounded like it might be intellectual high jinks and, apart from Shakespeare, there is nothing worse.

The second was an extract from *4.48 Psychosis*, by Sarah Kane. Kane was a compelling, challenging and complex writer; she took her life in 1999 before this play could be performed. It's about clinical depression, suicidal thoughts and ideation, and it's a mix of the abstract, naturalistic and poetic. To give a sense of what it's confronting, the cast list of the main characters, aside from three doctors simply numbered 1, 2 and 3, are Disgust, Fear and Loneliness. In what would turn out to be her final interview, with theatre academic Dan Rebellato, Kane talked about this play, then a work-in-progress. Rebellato wrote that Kane

describes the collapse of boundaries between self and other, between self and world that is characteristic of psychosis and says she is trying to find a form for a play that will express that experience but refused to say what that form would be.

It's a brutally challenging work, and the extract from it was being presented at FEATS by the English Youth Theatre from Brussels, a group of actors aged from seventeen to twenty-two years old. I felt humbled by its inclusion; Lucy Neal had reminded me to 'keep it political', and here these young actors were telling me forcefully that amateur theatre is not outdated or middle class or safe.

Before the evening's performances started, I grabbed a beer and a chat with David Crowe. I asked him who these FEATS people are, trying to get a handle on a bunch who perhaps started out as giddy adventurers working abroad and ended up doing am-dram.

'On the whole, they're people who work for international European companies. Or they're students, or ex-students. But often, they're people who are away from home for three years or so, and don't get a chance to build a network any other way.'

David's been 'away' considerably longer than three years, and he doesn't see himself returning to the UK as his family are now all in Strasbourg. I wondered why he chose English theatre and not French, if he was looking for a way of creating new cultural ties. 'I don't want to play Molière in the way it's been played for four hundred years,' he replied. For him, what we have in British theatre is unique and dynamic and constantly moving forward, whereas he experiences French theatre as a much more static repetition. FEATS was a way for him to keep in touch with British culture, and yes, a reimagining of Molière might not keep you in touch with much more than Molière.

David talked about the sociability of being involved in theatre, about widening his network, about it being a leveller, and how you learn things beyond the immediate words on the page, like problem solving and how to work within constraints. We discussed the feelings that performing gave him, and as he described getting something absolutely right and that flash of 'yeah, I've got it', he demonstrated with a gesture, of people in the palm of his hand. Throughout our conversation, David was modest and thoughtful but for that second, in the middle of a busy bar, he was transported, and I got a glimpse of who he would be onstage. I asked David why he thought people in his situation chose amateur theatre and not, for instance, a sports team. 'We do it at school, it's part of our education system, then maybe at university. It's part of us.' The same is true of sports, of course, but with fewer options – you're either in the team or out. Everything he touched on was what I was coming to see as true about amateur theatre. That it allows us to develop unique talents and gives us unique opportunities. That it is a social community. And also, that amateur theatre is uniquely British; that to be British is to have it imbued in our psyche somewhere and somehow. That theatre is in our cultural bones. You might not be involved with it personally, but that's irrelevant. It's still there, still part of the skeleton.

All the time we were chatting, David was introducing me to people as they swooped past our leaning post. I talked to Andy from the English Comedy Club in Brussels, who 'opened my big mouth and ended up stage-managing'; he reckoned that am-dram helped him make Brussels his home, gave him a friendship group in what he describes as a 'vibrant, thriving scene'. I spoke to Wendy who talked about community spirit, and the fantastic feeling of seeing 'something happening that people enjoy and knowing you played a role in it'. Like Andy, she was another backstage person, not in it for the applause.

Then old-timer Dermot, who called it 'a wonderfully human business'.

There are no prizes for guessing that *The Hunchback Variations*, the thing I'd been most dreading, turned out to be my favourite. I watched Quasimodo, played in English with a French accent by a German actor, muttering to himself as he pulled random objects from a box onstage – a pot, a bell, a fork, stones, some cling film – with a sense of timing some professionals would weep for, and decided I wanted to talk to that actor, to know why *he* does it. I think I already knew the answer, really. That despite his eye being glued shut and his hair made into a matted carpet and fake warts on his face and a dirty sackcloth costume, and despite there being many other different, simpler ways to get a high, there is actually nothing like the hit of applause, of laughter. That feeling, as David had it, of 'yeah, I've got it'.

So the next evening, I cornered actor Harald Djuerkin in the theatre bar, and asked how he felt. 'Amazing!' he replied. 'Nothing comparable!' Harald, whose English is better than mine, is an unassuming and charming man, and a member of the English-speaking Hamburg Players, founded in 1965. 'There's a small community of English-speaking theatre in Hamburg,' he said. 'I went to the University Players and was cast in the Scottish Play.' I smiled; there was absolutely no way he was going to utter the word Macbeth here, it's a theatrical superstition that it brings bad luck. I liked that it had travelled. 'I got a tiny role and I thought oh, I really like that.' Harald's second play in English was Terry Pratchett's

Wyrd Sisters, and he was in that when the director of *The Hunchback Variations* spotted him and his fellow cast member, Martin John Mills. It's a satisfying creative flow from one to the other, from *Wyrd Sisters* to *The Hunchback Variations*, both bound up with twisty playful language, both delightfully ridiculous. *Hunchback* is an absurdist play about Chekhov and stage directions, and Harald and I marvelled at performing it in front of this particular FEATS audience, people who really know their theatre. This play was perfect for them, they picked up every tiny nuance, every laugh that Harald and Martin wrung out of it. Harald described getting 'absolute joy' from an audience's laughter – it was that damn word again. Bloody joy, trailing after me from theatre to theatre, actor to actor. But joy is only one part of Harald's experience. He also sees it as 'a constant learning process', both about a play, and about oneself. 'I'm actually a very shy person, not that outgoing. I'm a different person from doing this. I've got more secure, definitely. You go onstage in a costume like this, you could be very vulnerable.' His skill was such that he could sit with that vulnerability and push the moment as far as he could.

I asked Harald if he'd have liked to act professionally, and his answer dispelled another myth around the amateur experience. Actually, it doesn't just dispel the myth, it crumples it into a ball and boots it out the window. There is a perception, lurking around, that people do amateur theatre because they couldn't hack it professionally. That they're all secretly hankering after fame and that this option is second best. But that is far from how amateur theatre people see what they do. This is absolutely not a sop, a stopgap, a consolation prize. Harald told me about a professional actor friend who was humiliated by a director. 'I'm so happy I'm involved in amateur theatre. I can do it just for fun, and nobody can take the piss out of me. You don't *have* to be out there. We have this community, people come and say afterwards "thank you", and that's enough.' The way he sold it, the idea of being an amateur was infinitely more appealing. 'It's not your job,' he said, underlining his point. 'We do it for fun.'

I asked Harald if he went to the theatre a lot, and when he said 'not really', just as David had, I understood something else, too. Both of these responses were another stamp of approval for amateur dramatics. Being part of amateur theatre is not a question of experiencing theatre in any which way you can, soaking it up like a greedy eater mops up the gravy. It's not a matter of 'I'll live, eat, breathe the theatre', but 'I'll live, eat, breathe THIS theatre'. They were interested in the doing, the participating, the creating, not the consuming.

Everywhere I went on this trip, I met amateur theatre people with an extraordinary knowledge of plays and theatre. Having that repository of completely specific information might feel, at first glance, totally useless in your everyday life. When are you ever in a situation where someone yells 'The captain's unconscious, we need someone who's played Ophelia to fly this plane!'? But in having expansive libraries, amateur theatre people get a lot more besides. Knowing who was writing what and when gives you an understanding of theatre history, a timeline of playwrights and changing tastes and mores. And also, a history of Britain itself. Our theatrical canon can spread the whole story out for you, if you want. Where there are gaps and omissions – where are the women? where are the black writers? – you learn from that too. About where the power and agency lies. About what's not written, and why. I was constantly on the back foot, and constantly appreciating the dexterity and intellect that amateur theatre had stimulated in people. This massive collection in the amateur theatrical mind feels like a huge untapped resource. Like, they could really *do* something with it . . . if they weren't too busy putting on a show.

I'd gone to FEATS to celebrate some Britishness, and what did I leave with? Had I marched off home in a plastic Union Jack bowler hat singing 'Jerusalem'? No. Had I found a kind of national identity I could embrace? Did this festival celebrate Britishness in a way I could get behind? Could I be proud to be British if it was about theatre being in my bones? It felt like all I was coming home with were more questions. But there was one thing that was very clear: how easy people found it to participate. Without overanalysing, they'd enriched their lives in really good ways. Nobody was fretting about the deep significance of anything, nobody was getting hyperbolic or meaningful, they'd just joined in, and got on with the show. It was almost tangible, that bubbling kinship. That these people were celebrating a part of British culture, its theatre, its language, was incidental. It was me who was getting kind of giddy with the romanticism of it all. 'Theatre breeds friendship,' someone told me, and maybe it was that, or maybe it was the beer. Or maybe – and this feels like ancient tectonic plates shifting – it was about finding a way to feel 'home'. It seemed like a door was opening.

CHAPTER 12

Take to the Stage

I am sitting at my desk writing one afternoon when a stream of WhatsApp messages starts to ping through on my phone, a rolling collection of voice memos. I listen to the first one. It's short and recitative, a man's deep voice with a slight Brummie tinge, my absolute favourite kind.

'*Ciel et enfer. Ciel et enfer*,' the voice says. 'Meaning: heaven and hell.'

I listen to the next message.

'*Je m'en foutisme. Je m'en foutisme*. Meaning: I don't care.'

It's Sean, from the *Variation* cast. It seems he's not just a knitting pattern model, but also a linguistic expert. He is carefully pronouncing all the French words in the play, and providing translations, I presume to help other members of the cast who are less sure. The voice memos roll on. The next few are just strings of words.

'*Saint Germaine. Marguerite Coutier. Almonde. Et le Bain. Grand Duke August.*'

'*Théâtre du Casino municipal.*'

Then, '*Non, chérie. C'est une habitude abominable. Je te demande pardon,*' he said, then translated it for us. 'Meaning: no, dear, it's a terrible habit, I do beg your pardon.' I'm not sure what terrible habit that referred to, probably smoking. But blimey, I think, I'd much rather be called '*chérie*' than 'dear'. 'Calm down, *chérie*' sounds marginally more acceptable.

'*Qu'est-ce qui si amusement*?' he went on. Meaning: what's so funny?' Then, '*Fabergé. Marquis de Beaux Prix. Pompadour. Balenciaga.*' Oooh, I recognise that word. '*Detouqueville. Pâté en croute. Vol au vent.*' I recognise those words too; *Balenciaga* and *vol au vent* really lent themselves to Sean's French-Brummie accent. I play all the voice memos again.

Then I get an email, from Alison, the director. A couple of weeks had passed since I'd been to a rehearsal. 'It's getting there, but we are still on the hunt for Ron,' she writes. 'You wouldn't think it would be so hard to find a 26ish year old to do a main part. But fingers crossed, somebody will put their head above the parapet.' I thought they'd have found Ron by now. I'm a bit concerned. Time is ticking on, and a significant point in the rehearsal process is being reached: the production is moving onto the stage.

For the first few weeks, this Ron-less cast had been doing all their rehearsing in the Harlequin room. The playing space had been marked out on the floor, but it isn't the same as being on the actual stage. The sense of projection and scope just aren't comparable. The stage was occupied by *Absent*

Friends, the Ayckbourn production that had opened Highbury's seventy-seventh season, and it's impossible to rehearse one play on another play's set. Once *Absent Friends* came down, the stage crew and cast worked together to remove their set, at a strike party, traditionally held on the Sunday morning after the Saturday last-night party. These are tender affairs. Walls are lowered slowly to the ground, props are quietly put away, people tiptoe around, voices are subdued, and a lot of coffee is required. As soon as one set is struck, the crew start bringing in the next, and once the stage is OK to walk on – in our case, when the rostra have been laid out, bolted down and covered with a safe and solid floor – the director gets the all-clear. Alison has been told they'd get the stage the following Wednesday, and I want to be there. Even if there is still no Ron.

I want, too, to get the whole production experience. I'm not just there for the onstage glory, I want to meet the back-stage crew who will be building the set ready for 'my' cast. So I pitch up on that Wednesday morning, work-party day, and offer my services. What can I do? Give me a job. Which end of a screwdriver is which?

Mum comes with me – or rather, I go with Mum, as she's working as usual in the Costume Department. We go up there first, and she introduces me to everyone, again. I'm immediately given the important job of putting the kettle on and making coffee, for everyone else. I've brought my own coffee in with me, in a flask, like a ridiculous snob. I might as well have yelled 'I live in LONDON, you know, have you heard of

FLAT WHITES?' I distribute mugs and ignore everyone wincing at how strong I've made it. ('It's how we do things in LONDON.') Fizzing with too much caffeine, everyone gets on with their tasks. Doreen sits at the sewing machine, putting a new zip in a taffeta ballgown the exact purple and rustle of my favourite Quality Street. Another woman is pulling costumes off a huge rail and hanging them ready for Alison to inspect, to see if they'll be good enough for Rose. Another woman is unwrapping cream leather elbow-length gloves from a bag of donations – 'They're gorgeous!' I exclaim. 'We've got hundreds of pairs of gloves,' comes the unimpressed reply, as she puts them into a huge plastic box marked Gloves, 'but we're bound to use them.' Someone else is grubbing around looking for a clown's hat needed for a hire, and another hat for an unseasonal Edwardian garden party. Mum starts ironing a heap of white cotton things, which looks to me like some kind of punishment. Everyone is busy round the huge table. This is one of those areas you can't mechanise or automate, it needs people. Specifically, it seems, it needs women. There is one man helping with the men's costumes, and Mum has made sure he got his coffee exactly how he likes it. But apart from him, this is a female domain.

Downstairs, on the stage and in the workshops, the gender split is reversed. Here, it is all male, apart from one woman. 'This is my harem,' says Christine, looking up from her job of screwing a plywood top to the rostra. The half-dozen men pay no heed, busy with various tasks. I would definitely require my own harem to be more attentive.

The *Absent Friends* set came down on Sunday, today is Wednesday, and they've cracked on apace, in those few days. The rostra are all laid out, creating a playing space set on the slant, exactly as Malcolm had shown in his design in the production meeting. I remind myself that the audience is in the Mediterranean. Right at the back of the stage, plywood is being cut into shape for Christine to screw down. Everything so far is on the horizontal, but two men, Les and Cos, are putting up the first flat. The space is going from 2D to 3. Les is holding the ladder, with Cos at the top of it drilling a hole to fix a hinge, and I grab the flat from the other side to stop it wobbling. I'm not really helping much, but I feel busy, and the men smile at me encouragingly. She's doing her best, bless her. With that done, I wander over to another guy, Rob, who is filling in a difficult corner between the rostra and the proscenium arch. I'm looking for conversation and connection, looking to fit in down here because I hadn't felt like I did up with the women in Costume. This is more me, even though I'm not a retired man in a branded fleece, nor a woman looking for a harem. Not right now.

'You can help me,' Rob says. 'I'm making a template so I can fill this gap.' Within five minutes I am sawing, drilling and screwing. Only once did he have to show me how to draw a straight line with the handle of a saw (why did I not know that? Oh yeah, it's because I never saw things) and only once does he have to point out that I have the drill on reverse. I feel like an apprentice on my first day, only I'm fifty-seven and go 'ooof' when I stand up. As we work, Rob and I chat. He used to work at the Albany Empire, in Deptford, he says. So did I! I reply; we work out that he was there three years before me, maybe two. A time gap that would have felt unbridgeable in our youth has shrunk to the length of a stride as we have aged. I am looking for connections, I find them everywhere I go, and they weird me out.

We chat, and I saw and screw things, and drill in reverse. There is a clatter across the stage, and I look up and see some huge flats being brought in through the access doors that open onto the driveway at the side of the theatre. These doors are as tall as a house, and as wide. From a trolley outside, someone is feeding the long flats in to Phil, who stacks them. Or maybe it was Richard, or Steve. Another piece of the set, a massive arched doorway, is manhandled through. (Gendered language feels very appropriate, here.) 'It's heavy,' says Malcolm, 'it used to be on the *Crossroads* set, this did.' I am baffled on two counts. How did a piece of notoriously flimsy *Crossroads* scenery come to be so heavy? And how did it come to be here? The low autumn sun streams in through the open doors, dust motes fly high, men lift and carry and move stuff in. There is a kind of romance to it all.

We have a brief break, in the theatre's cafe. I am given some coffee that tastes like mushroom water but I drink it because I want to fit in (and I'd left my flask in Costume, upstairs). To mask my lack of eagerness for the coffee, I enthuse too much about the excellent and classy selection of biscuits, the really thick chocolatey coating, to nobody in particular. I chat to Cos and Les, both of whom are from London, so we swap postcodes, we talk Ealing, Acton, Green Lanes. Les is a retired biochemist who found himself in Birmingham because it had a good calligraphy course. 'Come for the calligraphy, stay for the am-dram,' I say, to no response. 'It's a good catch-phrase . . .' I tail off. I agree, this is not my best material.

After coffee, I go and talk to Tony in the workshop – Tony Huggins, the one who'd worked at *Spitting Images*, as Steve had called it. Because everyone had told me how brilliant he was, about how he could do anything, anything at all, in my mind Tony had taken on the proportions of a colossus. I am expecting a giant of a man, and instead find someone slight, quiet and humble, now approaching his seventieth birthday. He runs me through his story, about how he joined Birmingham Rep in 1971, about working for Central TV. We share some of our memories of *Spitting Image*, the washing machine he'd had to make for a Dot Cotton sketch. (The name 'Dot Cotton' took both of us quite a while to find. Him: 'The one who smoked a lot.' Me: Wendy Richards? Pat Butcher? That ginger girl who yelled 'Riiickeeeeee'?) We talk about finding stuff in skips. What's your favourite thing you had to make for a show? I ask him. 'I made a car,' he says, 'Greased Lightning. I only binned it two weeks ago. I kept the wheels though.' He describes a ship he'd built for *Treasure Island* at the Rep, about how the stage had parted and the ship appeared from below, through the gap, and how he'd sneak into the back of the theatre some days, at the matinee, to watch it rise up, because it looked so amazing. As he talks about it, I can see that he is mentally reliving the sense of pleasure, just briefly, almost a smile of pride on his lips. What brought you to Highbury, once you'd retired? I ask. 'My wife was in that play . . . you know . . . there's an old lady in it –' *Ladykillers*? I suggest, before he's even finished his sentence. 'Yes!' he says, as amazed and impressed with me as I am. Do you watch the plays here? I ask him. 'Sometimes I'll watch the rehearsal,' he says. But for Tony, the play is not the thing, this theatre is, as it had been with Harald and David at FEATS. 'It's in the blood,' he says. 'Under my skin.' When he goes, he tells me, he's leaving his own workshop to Highbury. 'If there's anything they'd want.'

When I return to the stage, the huge *Crossroads* door is already fixed in place and I have to walk through it. *Crossroads*, man! This is my culture, my people. Of course I walk through it.

At the end of the morning, I go to collect Mum and bump into Alison on her way out of Costume. She has a pile of shirts under one arm, and is clutching a polystyrene head, the kind used to keep wigs on. She isn't normally here on a Wednesday morning, but is using her holiday entitlement to find costumes. That's what happens when you're in the midst of it. We talk about the 'no Ron situation,' and while she's doing a good impression of being calm on the surface, there is a slight ripple in her voice. 'The play's close to cancelling,' she tells me. 'We've got one week to find him.' As far as I know, no play has ever been pulled in Highbury's long history. So there is also the portentous Hand of History, wagging a stern finger at Alison.

An extra pressure. We stand there discussing gender-switching the role. You can't just apply it halfway down the road, Alison says, and she's right. You can't suddenly rejig the whole of a cast to fit a new plan. Plus, it would still mean casting, with one month to go, a charismatic young *woman* with a dancer's build. It's a huge part to take on, regardless of who does it. Gender-switching the role wouldn't solve the problem, it would just shift that problem over to a woman . . . (and if that scenario sounds familiar, please take a moment to fill in your own political analysis).

It feels like I am in a play-within-a-play. The Ron-less situation has all the ingredients: there is a bonded central group, they are in jeopardy, there is brinkmanship, and there is trouble. I could step back from it all, as an observer, and see what a great 'journey' this makes, for me, for writing this book. I could put myself and my plot requirements right at the centre of it. Without this uncertainty, things would run smoothly, and being able to report 'tra-la-la, everything went well' would not exactly make for an interesting process. Hurrah for me! This is the drama that I really need. This is what I am here for. In one week, I think, when Ron is cast, we'd all go 'Phew! We found someone right at the last minute! That was hair-raising! Everyone, carry on.'

Only hang on, maybe we wouldn't. Maybe this won't end like it does in plays. Maybe this will end in disaster, with no Ron, and therefore no play, and all this work for nothing. Not my work, *their* work. People will feel humiliated and disappointed. And they are working hard, they've committed to this *as if it mattered.* I stop for a moment. Everyone has welcomed me here, tolerated my stupid coffee habits and my sitting in corners scribbling notes and turning up randomly when I feel like it. Everyone has been open, respectful and warm. I feel a bit selfish and absorbed in my own agenda. And then I realise. It does matter. They matter, to me. The cast, the crew, everyone. It's under my skin, too. I've slid away from questioning everything and standing aside and not quite feeling connected, to being invested. I've moved beyond the whole selfish idea that this 'will we, won't we' is providing a good plot point for my book. 'Won't we' would be a terrible outcome for everyone, including me. It is time to stop treating this like a fun plot point, time to stop being cavalier.

When I arrive back at the theatre that evening for the first rehearsal on set, things have moved on since the morning. I am pleased to see that the *Crossroads* arch isn't just standing on its own now, it has walls attached to it. There is a cast member I haven't met yet – Rob, one of the two difficult-to-find men – and I introduce myself to him. I'm writing a book about amateur theatre, I say, offering my hand. 'Ah, but this isn't amateur theatre,' he replies. 'It's unpaid, non-professional theatre.' But it is amateur, I say, whatever word you choose. 'No,' he insists. 'Amateur says twee church-hall theatre. This is as good as any professional theatre.' OK, we'll have to agree to disagree, I say. I am not giving an inch here, I will not be amateursplained. I stalk proudly away, then nearly fall off the edge of the stage as I go. I hope he didn't notice. I sit in the front row of the auditorium, in the Mediterranean, and conspicuously make notes, a little crossly. Then rehearsals start, and I see that he is really very good. Damn it.

Because we – yes, it is 'we' now – are on the stage for the first time, things slow down, everything seems new for the cast, like we're back to the early days. They are tentative again; the blocking all feels slightly off. It's different pretending to go down steps to actually going down them. Nothing was quite where they have imagined it, everyone needs to lengthen their stride to cover the distance, and having the clear height above them, right up into the flies, affects how they work, too. They can uncurl. The actors' understanding of the play has moved forward since I was last here. They are talking about subtle nuance now, about power dynamics. Their French pronunciation is pretty spot on, thanks to Sean and his voice memos. Kurt and Fiona are practically off the book, and when Maura is not onstage, she sits behind Alison and me, further up the auditorium, learning hers in a low, distracting mutter. But they are tired; working without a Ron is getting more difficult. After one section, Alison stops the rehearsal and asks Louise if Rose is going to show 'overwhelming emotion', as per the stage directions. 'I will,' Louise replies. 'I'll work up to it.' By 9.30 a bunch of fading actors, a couple of whom had come here straight from work, are getting their notes from Alison. I'm exhausted too.

Louise and I chat as we walk to our cars. She is fed up, acting opposite nobody.

'It's really frustrating. I'm holding back, obviously. I feel like I can't give everything to this role, not yet. Normally I'd be off the book by now but there's something stopping me'.

Still, I think, one week to go and we'll have our Ron. We definitely will. Then Louise can give it everything. One week.

The days tick slowly past, and I get no word. There is a constant little niggle in my head, which will be nothing compared to what Alison and the cast are going through. I wait as patiently as I can, but I become more antsy. Show yourself, Ron, I think. You're really annoying me now, given how much I hate people being late. I do a lot of pacing.

The day comes when the decision about the play's future is going to be made. I leave it as late as I can before I email Alison. I don't want to bug her. 'Any news?' I enquire tentatively. I really did not want the play to be cancelled now. 'I was just about to email you!' Alison replies. 'I think we have a Ron. We're going through his sections tonight with Louise. I think he's going to be fine.' I am so relieved, I do a little whoop. *Variation on a Theme* is on. Everything is going to be fine. Now, it is all systems go.

I am very keen to meet our Ron as soon as possible, anxious that he is going to be all right. He'll be nervous, I think, and I want to be part of the welcome committee. Mum is coming to the rehearsal too; we'd had a phone conversation about it. 'Would you mind,' she'd asked, 'if I prompted for this play?' Being the prompt is surely one of the least rewarding roles, sitting on a hard chair hidden at the side of the stage, not letting your attention slide for a second. The cast had wanted to get the prompt into rehearsals early so they'd become familiar with what was a pause and what was the actor drying, to get a feel for the rhythm and pacing. I was surprised at

Mum's question. Why would I mind? 'I don't want to tread on your toes.' She knew that I wanted to be Jenny, the writer, and not Jenny, Hazel's daughter. I was touched. But I'd been cavalierly stomping all over her toes without a care. I'd been scrutinising the place where she has put so much of her life, generally pronouncing on where it got things *wrong* and where it got things *right*, swanning in and out like some diva. Mum didn't intend to, but she had reminded me: where were my manners?

The first thing Mum does when we arrive at rehearsal is start introducing me to people. Mum, I hiss, leave it. In the green room, everyone is talking about 'the Baggies' and I politely beg their pardon and ask, what are the Baggies? That was foolish. They turn and look at me as one, and I can see the accusation in their eyes: 'FAKE BRUMMIE'. I might as well have said, 'What's a peaky blinder?' 'It's West Bromwich Albion,' someone replies, and not-amateur-Rob explains that they got the name because men used to go round the pitch collecting money after the game, in big bags. 'Ron' hasn't appeared in the green room yet. His real name is Jim.

I wander up to Costume, and there is Jim, having a fitting. Two women of probably treble his age are fussing over his braces and his trouser belt and all that gubbins, and he is joining in breezily. OK, I think in that brief second, he's comfortable here, and that is reassuring. This is not a young man who is nervous about the prospect of doing the part. He is ready to take it on. I'd been projecting – it is me who is feeling nervous. Where the hell have you been all this time, Ron? I want to know. What kept you?

Down on set, I watch him closely. In his first scene, he is already off the book. He has a pencil for Louise to use, he knows her stage directions as well as his own, he takes his prompt gracefully. Everything is going beautifully. Then, mid-scene, the phone in his pocket pings. He ignores it, they carry on. Then it pings again. This bugs me, but he couldn't give a damn. Ah, the young, I think, amazing brains, terrible phone etiquette. Physically, he doesn't look like the ballet dancer I've been envisaging, but he has the confidence, and that counts for a lot. He is staring down the lens with ease, saying 'yeah, I'm a dancer', and it is convincing. And with Jim's appearance, something else has happened. Now she has someone to act against, Louise has started to come alive onstage. In turn, so has Kim as Fiona, her daughter. And Sean as Kurt. This is turning into a play; there is connection, and eye contact, and actual feeling. I have some feelings too – relief, pleasure, anticipation. This place is so full of feelings.

The rehearsal carries on. Sitting in the front row of the auditorium, following the script closely, Mum gives a prompt to Louise/Rose. 'I was leaving a pause,' Louise says. 'Good golly,' says Mum, 'how many more of them?' I think about her reviews from 1955, and realise that nothing has changed.

Making the most of a scene she isn't in, Louise goes to the green room to make coffee for everyone. It will be drunk on the go, there is no interval in a rehearsal, time is precious, especially now. I join her, wanting to ask what had brought her to Highbury.

'I'd done A-level drama at school but I knew I didn't have enough talent to make it professionally. You've got to be realistic. So I did media studies and politics at De Montfort, and my original ambition was to write for the *NME*.'

We divert into a happy conversation about our favourite *NME* writers from the old days. Louise is younger than me, so our references don't always collide but we fling names around – David Quantick, Barbara Ellen, Steve Sutherland – like we are trying to hit a target. She came out of university determined to be a journalist, and after a placement at a local paper, was told she could have a job if she lost her nose ring. 'I was all nose rings, and DMs and floral dresses and lacy leggings in those days.' I knew that look well. She wrote music and film reviews, then went to the *Birmingham Mail* where she met her husband. 'He's one in a million,' she says. Three kids later, she was working in a more 'regular' job but felt something was missing. 'What have you always harboured a desire to do?' her husband asked. 'I want to act,' she said, repeating it later to a colleague at work. She'd used the secret code: her colleague was directing at Highbury, Louise auditioned for Chekhov's *The Anniversary*, and six years later, she's an active member both here and in a musical theatre group. 'The demands on actors are lighter in musical theatre. I like it better here. This is the real deal.'

We are called back to the stage, Louise is needed again, and it is time for me to go home. As we walk back into the theatre, I see Mum, standing at the front of the auditorium, her prompt script resting on the stage in front of her. She is prompting, and also reading in for Maura, who is on holiday. She is acting the part properly, not just reading aloud, and her voice is strong and full of character. She is absolutely focused, the cast are looking to her, and I can see the light bouncing around between these actors at work. The sounds of the play, the actors' voices, Alison's interjections and Mum's prompts fade out as I close the stage door behind me.

CHAPTER 13

The Play's the Thing

Jez Butterworth is the nearest thing theatre has to a rock god. He's our Bono, without (as far as I know) the tax avoidance. He certainly presented himself like an old-school rock god at the Amateur Theatre Festival, dressed in black jeans and clumpy boots, all beardy and big man striding onstage to huge applause. I half expected him to come to the front, stretch his arms up and yell, 'Hello, Ealing, are you ready to rock?' But Jez Butterworth is not a rock god, he's that most unlikely hero – a writer. He's the exact opposite of the stereotypical writer, the lonely figure with a vitamin D deficiency who sits quietly in corners scribbling in a very particular notebook with a very particular pen. To the writers among us, it's simultaneously slightly thrilling ('this is hallowed territory!') and despairing ('I'll never achieve this') that one of our own was the festival's star turn. All he's done is write some plays, told some stories – and actually, not that many. But nonetheless, as the audience response showed, his work has extraordinary impact; when *Jerusalem* and then *The Ferryman* hit the West End, people scrabbled for tickets to see his work as if it were, well, *Hamilton*. Right from the early days of *Mojo*, Butterworth has written plays you have to see. All of this tells us how crucial writers are to theatre. That sounds so obvious. Of *course* there's no theatre without plays. But in so many spheres, the writer is invisible to the audience. On-screen writing credits, for instance, often whizz past at an unreadable pace. 'However, the writer has always been at the centre of the work of the amateur theatre in this country,' Simon Callow said, at that same festival. It's something that's not always fully valued or acknowledged. And I'm pausing here, imagining all writers everywhere shrugging and muttering 'ain't that the truth'.

'I always think, in America they have an actors' theatre,' playwright David Eldridge told me, 'in Europe they have a directors' theatre, and here we have a writers' theatre.' Words have always been our currency – and it was a good choice. It's easier to pass down a theatre script than a director's vision, or an actor's craft. So what does this mean for amateur theatre?

It's easy to picture the Lord Chamberlain as an eighteenth-century old bore in a spluttering lather about the nation's morality, but a bit shocking to realise that this censoring role continued right up to the progressive and swinging 1968. (And it's handy, but not accurate, to envisage the work of censorship being in the hands of one single dreadful man, but by the 1960s it was an entire office of them.) Even then, homosexuality was absolutely to be avoided, with lesbians only slightly less terrifying than gay men. It was 'sexual plain-speaking' that angered the censors in the early 1960s, explains Nicholas de Jongh in his book *Politics, Prudery and Perversions*, all in the name of 'good taste' and 'public decency'. There is something rather salacious about reading banned words and actions from plays, you can almost hear the heavy breathing and, I'll admit, even recording the words here feels a bit transgressive. For instance, this list from censor Charles Heriot, relating to the RSC's production of Jean Genet's *The Screens* in 1963, as reported by de Jongh:

'The author seems preoccupied with anal eroticism,' Heriot wrote . . . before banning the play's roll-call of profanaties: 'fucking, pissing, farting, screwing, crap, shit, b'Jesus, unbutton my fly, bugger off, bullshit'. 'Forbid all farting' he then instructed, as well as 'up my arse . . . a spot of sperm . . . it was my pair of balls. Other-wise recommend for licence.'

The thought of Charles Heriot getting himself all damp and sweaty as he hammered the typewriter keys for 'up my arse' is a lively one, as is an image of his colleague Roland Hill. At a rehearsal of a censored play, where trouser flies were being buttoned, Hill was 'pleased to see that . . . this potentially unseemly business was conducted with relative decorum', de Jongh writes. You'd really have to be focusing very hard on an actor's flies to see that level of fine detail, which tells us less about the moral danger inherent in buttons and more about Roland Hill.

Then, finally, Britain stopped censoring theatre. On 26 September 1968, the Lord Chamberlain's Office was stripped of that role, and you might imagine that from this point we drifted into halcyon years where people were free to write what they wanted how they wanted, and when they wanted. They could at last articulate the nation's actual thoughts instead of the government-sanctioned ones and, as a result, they got carried around the place on golden pillows. And actually, post Lord Chamberlain, things were freer. It was now mostly down to private individuals to Take Great Exception and attempt to get stuff banned. Those of us who are old enough will remember Mary Whitehouse, a perpetually furious Mother Teresa-meets-*That's Life* woman, who was like a prototype Caroline Aherne character. She campaigned against anything she saw as contributing to a more 'permissive' society. In 1982, she was so incensed by the idea of a brief male rape scene in the National's production of *Romans in Britain* she took out an unsuccessful private prosecution against director Michael Bogdanov. The boggling thing is: she never even saw the play. How could she sully her eyes with it? Context and production values didn't matter, it was just the very idea.

Today, outside the odd Whitehousian blip, it's still not as simple as picking a play and putting it on, willy-nilly. There are restrictions about who gets to put on which plays and where, and some people see this as a different form of censorship, less to do with public decency, and more to do with money. The arguments revolve around licensing. No play can be performed in any public circumstance without a licence, which is issued by the rights holder – publishers like Samuel French Ltd, formed in the mid nineteenth century, and the relative newcomer at thirty years old, Nick Hern Books. Licences cost money, for the very good reason that writers need to be paid when people perform their work. (That doesn't mean your nan can't put on a show in her front room, but it does mean she can't sell tickets.) But licences don't always get granted, and that's where the feelings of censorship start. 'Rights holders prevent amateur companies from performing work if a professional company is even considering a production in the future and withhold rights for new work until all possible professional usage has been exploited,' wrote Tom Williams, the president of Chesil Theatre, Winchester, in a letter to *Sardines* magazine. His use of the words 'prevent' and 'withhold' is revealing. The suggestion is that some kind of hierarchy is being operated, entirely and unjustly at the expense of amateurs. Is this censorship, under a different guise?

Tamara von Werthern, performing rights manager of Nick Hern Books, is very clear that it's not. She does, however, understand the frustrations and feels them too, when she can't issue a licence.

'There are lots of reasons why restrictions exist, and they are quite complimentary, if you think about it. There's really high-quality amateur theatre out there. And it's quite difficult for a small professional theatre company to create enough interest and excitement around their production if there are amateur productions happening in the same place, who usually offer the tickets cheaper, where you can still have a good night out at the theatre, and you might know someone in the cast.'

Tamara is adamant that the writer, the work and the life of the work are at the heart of all her decision-making. Her passion for amateur theatre certainly doesn't feel like 'prevention' and 'withholding', as the *Sardines* letter suggested.

Tamara describes companies like Nick Hern Books as 'trying to keep the channels clear so there aren't any clashes between professional productions and amateur productions. It's a more supportive role, like a midwife.' In this crowded maternity ward we have the amateur theatre-makers, the writers (along with their agents and producers), the professional producers, and Tamara in a wipe-down apron. I presume it is the writer actually giving birth, but I'm not sure who is up at the head end, and who is down the business end watching the baby crown. Let's tiptoe away from this birthing image before it all gets too . . . amniotic.

Some writers, Tamara tells me, are very keen to present their babies to the amateur world. And 'if the writer is confident that that's what they want, then they can persuade other people'. It sounds like lots of juggling, and personal choice. 'You're finding the balance. You're trying to do what's right to all parties.' Tamara was kindly talking to me in a hectic week for her, as *Pressure* by David Haig and Nina Raine's *Consent* had just been released for licence to the amateur world. She tells me about the democratic process that determines who gets a play first.

'It's just about how quick you are off the mark. Do you have a slot for it? Can you make space for it soon? Everyone has to plan. And everyone wants the amateur premiere, but it depends on who plans it quickest, and then we can confirm who has the premiere once we have had all the applications through. We're not doing a qualitative judgement like "we think the amateur premiere should go to this theatre company". I think there is a misunderstanding by some amateur theatre companies, if they apply for something and they are rejected, that it is somehow because of the quality of their application. It never is.'

This ongoing, proactive process as described by Tamara is so full of commitment to amateur players that describing it in any kind of 'preventative' way is pretty chippy – to be fair, normally a stance I'm at home with. To look at the flip side, I asked Carole Coyne, who has been the rights officer on behalf of South London Theatre since 2005, about her experience. She has to get a lot of rights – this busy and successful theatre puts on twenty productions a year. Being in London determines their drive to be cutting-edge and is an asset in terms of membership and audience (both of which they have in abundance) but brings its own set of problems. There is so much professional theatre in London, there's more chance of competition, so rights will be restricted. 'There are times when we see a theatre not much further out doing a play,' Carole told me. 'Yasmina Reza is a case in point. On the whole, we're not allowed to do Reza, because we're a London theatre. Bromley can do them, a few miles down the road,' she said, her tone souring slightly at the mention of Bromley. Did she feel like they were being blocked? 'Oh, I *know* we're blocked. It's a deliberate thing. But I'm used to it.' I wondered if she blamed the author, or the licensing company. 'There's usually a mystery agent in between Samuel French, or Nick Hern Books, and the author,' Carole replied. That intrigued me. It felt so damn theatrical, a mystery figure lurking in dark corners, wearing a fedora. (Fedoras are an essential detail for mystery people.) 'And sometimes,' Carole went on, 'I think it might be the author themselves.' This was a stage direction I hadn't anticipated. First she'd introduced a shady George Galloway type, and now I was picturing authors answering the phone in fake voices, pretending they were out. 'There's nothing you can do about it,' Carole said, matter-of-factly. 'But most of them we get. Most of them.'

Now we have the words 'prevent', 'withhold', 'blocked' and 'mystery' to describe how it feels from the theatre company's side. But by Tamara's compelling account, that's not how things really are, and Debbie McLean, head of licensing at Samuel French, agreed. 'Lots of authors and their agents see how valuable the amateur market can be and have worked closely with us over the years to have their works available and licensed to the amateur market.' 'Valuable amateur market' – is that how it feels to actual, living, breathing, playwrights? I wondered. I needed to ask a couple.

April de Angelis leapt right to the heart of it. 'One of the first things is that it's kind of an artery,' she said of amateur theatre, 'that goes into you both artistically and financially.' *Playhouse Creatures*, which April wrote back in 1993, is a case in point. It was the first all-women play she wrote, and as a lot of amateur theatre groups have a lot more women than men, it's become quite an amateur staple.

'My agent once said to me, "You know, your play is the most requested play at this agency for amateur players" – and I was just completely overwhelmed with joy. It's a radical play about women and theatre and sexual politics – and it's great that loads of women are taking it up. Amateur theatre has given that play a new life, given it a sense of significance and given me a sense of significance as a writer.'

That letter from Tom Williams in *Sardines* magazine had also mentioned money: 'Amateur theatre is the true backbone of theatre in the country. In many areas it is the only theatre available. Just think of the income that many of our leading playwrights get from royalties paid by amateur theatre.' I asked what it meant financially for April, in a tough artistic climate.

'Sometimes it's the amateur theatre, and colleges, that keep you going as a writer. People buying the book to perform the play, that's also income. I don't think I could've survived without the amateur.'

'The amateur sector has played, and continues to play, a significant, if hidden role in this interwoven texture of playwright support,' is how academics Helen Nicholson, Nadine Holdsworth and Jane Milling describe it in their book *The*

Ecologies of Amateur Theatre. And income can go hand-in-hand with self-belief.

'There's nothing like a cheque from your agent to make you feel like you're a writer,' April said. For someone whose work is seen in big repertory theatres, the West End and the National, alongside all the regular amateur productions, it's hard to imagine that might be a problem for April. You don't still need that confirmation of status, do you? 'I do! It's really real – look, you wrote that thing and somebody paid for it! I often meet people who say, "Oh, I had the pleasure of doing *Playhouse Creatures*." You might be getting one professional production of a particular play every three years, but you're getting six amateur productions. It's amazing.'

Tamara described that as 'a real affirmation that your script works. What you've written speaks to people from the page enough for them to fall in love with it, pick it up and put it on.' April's experience with amateur theatres has meant that the amateur, that 'valuable marketplace' as Debbie McLean put it, is in her mind when she's writing. 'Because it is a market. To write, you have to be able to sell things.' It might be counterintuitive to the creative process to see it that way, but it's an unaffordable luxury not to. You could spend your life travelling round amateur productions of *Playhouse Creatures*, I said, when you're really old. 'I'm so going to do that,' April replied. 'I'm about a year away.' Amateur theatres love writers, I added, by way of temptation, describing the reception I'd seen Jez Butterworth get. 'You just need a beard,' April replied, and with perfect timing, her eye on that marketplace, 'which I can grow.'

Bearded David Eldridge was one step ahead. I asked him how he felt about amateurs producing his work, and his instant response was that it is 'amazing, something I never get in the way of'. He described the intimate process of being involved in the first, professional production of a play, being part of that team and then, 'I really do like letting it go out in the world, and other people doing it.' Did he imagine when he started out that there would be this other wing to his work? 'I hoped there would. One of the things I really get out of amateur productions is when a group of people are doing a play, they really want to do it, it's in their spare time, therefore there's something about the spirit of the play that always seems to come through.'

David told me about an amateur production he'd been to, of his play, *Embezzled*. 'There was a brilliant moment during the third act where Doreen gets a bowl of jellied eels poured over her head, and they did it with these bits of polystyrene that they'd painted, and they all started to corpse onstage, and the audience started to corpse as well. The whole show stopped for two minutes because we're all crying with laughter at these ridiculous polystyrene eels. And I so enjoyed that evening, it was fantastic because they were all giving it some welly and they cared about it a lot. For me, there's a bit of magic in that. I can't necessarily give you a rational explanation for it.'

I asked him about having a financial lifeline via amateurs and he agreed readily with April, remembering a time when he'd had a lot of noise and success, and then things went very quiet for a year, leaving him wondering what he was going to do next. We talked about the divide in professional theatre between people who come from affluence and nest eggs, and those from backgrounds like his, without those cushions. It's a divide that is currently getting wider. For David, sometimes even getting a modest royalty of £150 has made a difference – psychologically, emotionally but also practically. 'But the thing that enchants me most about amateurs is just that the play is being done, that someone has come across the play somehow. That always tickles me pink, just the thought of it.'

Amateur theatre is not just great for established play-wrights. It can also be a career starter. 'New writing from amongst the amateur theatre membership is a dynamic element of theatre-making activity with multiple modes of encouragement for fledgling writers through competitions, play readings and amateur production,' explains *The Ecologies of Amateur Theatre*. And Simon Callow echoed that, speaking about Questors Theatre from their main stage. 'The writer has always been at the centre of the work of the amateur theatre in this country. This very theatre has a magnificent record of creating new work. *Rosencrantz* had its first success here. It's one of a huge number of plays generated by the amateur theatre.'

When I'd visited People's Theatre in Newcastle, Tony Childs was proud of playwright Alison Carr, and how their theatre had played its part in her career. Alison joined the People's Theatre in 2004, 'because they run the People's Play Award, and I thought you had to be a member to enter it'.

She had been writing plays since leaving university, then had her first professional production of a half-hour play. Next she wanted to get something on in her home-town. She missed the People Play Award deadline in 2004, but once she'd taken the scary step of turning up she decided to stay, and hung around doing different things. When it came up again two years later, she went in for it, and won. Her play, *My Mam Was An Ice-Cream Blonde*, was given a week's run, in the region where she lived. It was a good platform for her.

'I genuinely felt like I'd arrived, not realising it would take many years and I'm still trying to arrive. I remember the first night, it felt so exciting going into the theatre and watching my play onstage. I remember rehearsals, everyone enjoying it and really, when it's amateur theatre and it's people's free time they're devoting for no pay, it has to be fun or what is the point?'

Alison got the chance to feel like a star for the week, she got great reviews, and it was followed by work for New Writing North, and the Old Vic's 24 Hour Plays. Being part of that resulted in her securing an agent, and she's had two more plays produced by People's Theatre since, one commissioned for their centenary celebrations, and then a promenade play for the RSC Open Stages in 2012. 'It had to have a big cast, and in professional theatre you often don't get the chance to have a big cast. It was a great experience.'

And now amateur theatre was coming back into her career, from another direction. The rights to *Iris*, her first commission for Newcastle's Live Theatre, had just become available, and the play was getting its amateur premiere at People's Theatre in autumn 2019. Another perfect circle.

'And I'm still a member of People's. I perform sometimes in shows, and that helps me understand what it's like on the other side of it. You can't be a slave to it, but it's good having an awareness. And the community here at People's, the support is insane. I always know that if they can people will turn out for stuff. Friends for life. I'm so glad I accidentally joined too early.'

Alongside the financial lifeline, having your work repeatedly chosen and put on does something else – it creates a 'national repertoire', something which holds a lot of meaning. It's not about just one play by one playwright being repeated over and over until we've all seen it. It's not just about Shakespeare or the classics. It's about the whole collected body of theatre writing; how things come to be known and established, what becomes the bedrock, who our key writers are, who we choose to represent us. This is not about one-off trends, or a kind of theatrical Eurovision. It's much more lasting and sustained. It's our canon, and it has to be an organic, growing thing. Batons are passed on, new writers come through, some stay and others go; the landscape changes its gender, its race, its subjects and objects over time. We hope. Not always quickly enough, and not all gaps get noticed or filled. But responsibility for that canon does not lie solely in professional theatre. 'Amateur theatre has been a dynamic shaper of the national repertoire alongside subsidised and commercial theatrical venues,' said that 2013 report, *Our*

Creative Talent. And 'amateur theatre production remains a key, if largely unrecognised component of the repetition and reproduction of plays. It also supports playwrights as part of a process of forming the national repertoire,' write Helen Nicholson et al. 'Some of the works and playwrights that we now consider canonical have achieved that status in part because of their production and support within the amateur sector.'

Greg Giesekam writes about play selection in, *Luvvies and rude mechanicals?,* his work on amateur theatre in Scotland.

> Scots writers such as James Bridie, Joe Corrie, James Scotland and Harry Glass have long been a staple of the amateur movement, and there is the expected popularity of figures such as Wilde, Coward and Ayckbourn. But there is evidence here of a considerable number of groups attempting to broaden their repertoire in quite adventurous ways. The work is not perhaps as hidebound as popular myth ... might suggest.

As an example, Giesekam cites Tony Roper's popular play *The Steamie,* which has turned into a 'banker' for many clubs and, from that, become part of Scotland's national repertoire. It's reasonable to say, then, that amateur theatre has played a key role in a national Scottish theatre. 'The contribution that amateur groups and community theatre projects make to the national theatre of Scotland should be recognised,' Giesekam writes. And note, he uses 'make' in the present tense. This has been replicated in Irish theatre history, too, where playwrights who are now considered some of the finest in the world – Sean O'Casey, for instance – first found their voices on the amateur stage. Amateur theatre is responsible for such a lot that is hidden beneath the surface. You could describe it as a backbone, in fact.

Being 'canonical' might sound weighty, but it doesn't necessarily mean being heavy, difficult or unpopular, as responses to *The Steamie* prove. But 'popular' can be a difficult word for some people, almost as bad as 'broad appeal'. Culture often seems to be ranked: the fewer people who like something, the more important it is and the more seriously we take it. If absolutely nobody liked your work, or only three people could afford to go to it, that would be the best result. Serious drama is ranked higher than comedy. Opera is ranked highest of all (except for light opera, which plummets down the ranking again. But I agree with that, light opera is terrible). There are countless plays, usually comedies, that are deemed trivial or silly, and it's a double whammy if they concern themselves with women or domestic issues. And OK, I admit it, I too hate some popular things. Make me watch *Mrs Brown's Boys* if you really want to punish me.

But plays march on with no regard to intellectual snobbery. And some of them have been elevated to 'national repertoire' status because of the way the amateur theatre, players and audiences, have taken them to their heart. Hurrah for amateurs. Tim Firth's *Calendar Girls* is a prime example. It's a particularly British story of adversity overcome with fun and discreet nudity that has been taken to the bosom (pun intended) of the amateur sector. 'Partly because it's fun to take your kit off,' Helen Nicholson said when I spoke to her. 'It's the vicar's wife's chance not to be seen as the vicar's wife.' *Calendar Girls* didn't start in amateur theatre, but that's where it most fully and joyfully lives now, and Firth knew that was a possibility.

> Part of the reason I came up with the idea of writing it for the theatre was to potentially release it to the amateur market. I'd watched companies around me report the paucity of plays for women . . . it was a chance to write a group comedy, where I'm happiest. A group comedy for women.

After its release for amateurs, *Calendar Girls* became the most produced play in the UK, recording 666 productions in its original eighteen-month period. That is no surprise. Much of its appeal lies in its ability to appear entirely superficial, but not be. It's a play that sensitively explores issues around ageing, death, loss and friendship. And there's more in its favour; it features lots of older women, its tone is irreverent without being explicit, there is personal salvation, reinvention, and there are buns. Baking and breasts – two British obsessions.

Becoming part of the national repertoire via repeated amateur production is a vital source of income for writers. And it keeps putting their work in front of people, keeps it alive and breathing. One other thing amateur theatre does for writers is take on the second production of *new* work, something the professional theatre is reluctant to do, after that immediate commission. (The process is this: new work is commissioned in the professional theatre, but very often, after that first run, the new play won't be put on by another professional company for a long time. Maybe because it's had all the splash it's going to get for now, nobody wants the second outing, second casting, and so on. The 'shine' has gone.) This is the amateurs' chance. They can swoop in and give a new play its second outing. They're getting something pretty contemporary that hasn't been done to death. It's a win for them.

People often make assumptions about am-dram based on misconceptions that it's all 'old plays by old people'. And sure, we love our history, we celebrate it, and the fact that Shakespeare is a perennial favourite is a testament, not a failing. But alongside all the classics, amateur theatre is packed with modern people, addressing modern ideas. Some of it is even political. South London Theatre actively seeks to be at the cutting edge. At Highbury, Rob, one of the *Variation* cast, told me that his most rewarding role had been as a serial killer in *Frozen* by Bryony Lavery. People's Theatre Studio opened with a production of Jez Butterworth's *The River*. I saw Sarah Kane's work at FEATS, and Polly Stenham's *That Face* at Questors. It's not only work that is expected, and it's not always produced in ways you might expect, especially if you are still stuck on thinking that the amateur stage is one eternally repeated production of *No Sex Please, We're British*. That thought, in itself, is a nightmare.

There's one final surprising statistic. We're familiar with the gender split of around 60/40 women/men on the amateur stage. British Theatre Repertoire did a survey in 2013 and reported that of the fifty-eight new plays presented by amateurs in their surveyed theatres, 42 per cent were written by women. That is a much higher proportion than in the professional theatre. Another statistic: in 2018, Nick Hern Books published sixty-three plays by women, and thirty-two by men, which is astonishing, brilliant and worth celebrating. I asked Tamara von Werthern what she put that down to. 'If we didn't have the amateur community clamouring for good female roles,' she replied, 'there is no doubt the landscape would be different.' The plays of note would all be male. Change is not just in the air, it's already happening, in our amateur theatres. We have amateur women to thank for that.

CHAPTER 14

Champagne and Olives

If you look for it, you can find am-dram everywhere. In city offices, on trading and factory floors. In church halls, scout huts, doctors, surgeries, bank vaults and barns. On ships and in planes, in armies and among air crews. Clinging on to the cliff edges of the country, and at the heart of urban sprawls, in suburbs, schools, colleges and prisons. We know – from Noel Rands's stories and from the participants at FEATS – that theatre-making doesn't stay at home when we travel abroad. Wherever British people go in the world, they have taken amateur theatre with them, for all sorts of reasons: as part of the process of making full lives as immigrants, for leisure, to create social links – or as a cultural imposition. (There is a lot of written material on how Shakespeare was used as a colonial tool in acts of imperialism. I'm assuming that not one single reader is falling off his/her chair at that.) One place where Brits have certainly gathered in great numbers, nearly a quarter of a million of them, and a good half at pensionable age, is the south coast of Spain. It stands to reason, then, that there would be English-speaking amateur theatre there, if you looked for it.

So I looked, and found it on the Costa del Sol. And found myself watching it on a Wednesday evening towards the end of summer, in the clubhouse of El Paraiso Golf Club. This was my first visit to the 'Costa del Golf', the name it's given itself, written on large blue signs along the highway, next to the billboards for Ricky Martin and 'classy' property developments. 'Not even ironically?' a friend asked before I went. Not even ironically, I replied. I'm not anti-golf – some of my best friends are golfers – but it's still shorthand for a whole set of social attitudes and aspirations and a love of pastel-coloured sweaters. Unless you're Scottish, golf seems to run the full gamut of political persuasion from UKIP to Tory. It would take quite a lot to shift that set of stereotypes.

I had come to the clubhouse for a rehearsed reading of *Champagne and Olives*, a new play by June Rendle. The title made me think back to Unity Theatre and their success with *Winkles and Champagne*, though I suspected the two plays might have a different . . . thrust. If I hadn't expected to be visiting a Spanish golf club when I started writing about amateur theatre, I hadn't quite expected June either. She was in her late eighties, a little older than my mother, and if your mental picture of the English pensioner in Malaga is all elastic waistbands and comfy sandals from the back of the *Sunday Express* magazine, which I confess mine was, then it needs to move fifty miles along the coast, and be a bit more upmarket. June is in the Judi Dench, Sheila Hancock mould; she pitched up looking striking and stylish with twinkling eyes, glamorously cropped white-blond hair, and a slash of lipstick. She is the kind of woman who I could easily imagine as a fashion icon on the streets of New York, or a delightfully sardonic judge on *RuPaul's Drag Race*.

Earlier that day, I'd met June at my hotel. We needed a quiet spot to talk. I wanted to know how she came to be a keen member of Marbella's International Theatre Studio (ITS), one of two English amateur dramatic groups on this bit of the coast. (I liked the 'Studio' bit, it's intense, very theatre, very black polo neck.) We found an empty seating area that seemed perfect, and settled in. But the minute we started talking, people began pulling up metal shutters and dragging furniture around. Coffee was being ground nearby at an exceptional volume. When two men arrived with drills and ladders and started pulling ceiling tiles down next to us, it felt like we were in a bad farce. Like consummate professionals, we ploughed on, and within five minutes, had made a connection. Of course, this seemed to be happening to me everywhere. June told me she'd started off in Walsall, 'in the Midlands', she added, an unnecessary detail for me. I know Walsall, I'm from Sutton Coldfield. 'Oooh, Sutton Coldfield,' she said, putting on her poshest tones, which is how people who know the area always react. I'm not actually posh, I always deflect. I'm from Burbigub.

The next connection: June had acted at Highbury Little Theatre, in the sixties. That felt like an amazing coincidence. 'I was in *The Skin of Our Teeth*,' she said, 'and *Peer Gynt*,' which she pronounced with a bit of a Norwegian twist, like some people say 'pizza' with an Italian accent, or 'rucksack' in a German one. You'll know Mollie Randall, John English, Dicky Bird, I said, and 'Yes,' she said, 'I knew all those names.' I could feel myself trying to restrict my verbal exclamation marks, trying not to squeak excitedly. You'd have known my mum and dad, I said, almost holding my breath. I said their names, Hazel Landreth, Philip Landreth, in an encouraging tone. Go on, please remember, go on. But there wasn't the same flicker of recognition. Oh. No matter. It was enough for now that we could draw a line between her life and mine, where I'd never have imagined a line to be. In the moment, it felt spooky. But I don't want to go all 'oooh it was fate' because that is a slippery slope and before I knew it I'd be at a psychic show putting my hand up enthusiastically when the medium asked 'Does anyone here know a woman?'

June hadn't intended to be an amateur actor, she'd intended to be a professional one. 'I was offered a scholarship to RADA at the age of sixteen but rejected it,' she told me. Her father didn't approve, and he was a forceful man. 'Acting was one step up from prostitution, in those days,' she said. I asked if she regretted not going, expecting that pat, polite answer about living a rich and full life and blah de blah. But I'd underestimated June. 'I wouldn't have met my husband,' she said, 'but still –' and here she added emphatic arm gestures – 'I regret it to this day.' Instead of RADA and London, June trained at night school in Walsall, working

225

through her bronze, silver and gold medals with a teacher called Fanny Mason.

'She had a very Victorian style, no suggestion of Method or Stanislavsky. The acting degree examination took place in a theatre, with a panel of three judges, who joined me onstage at the end to congratulate me on the highest marks ever achieved, and said I was qualified for the West End. I'm still waiting for that.'

Maybe someone will read this and cast June in a West End production. Maybe the same person who is going to cast Barbara as a Scottish granny in *EastEnders*.

When June married, thoughts of the professional theatre were put aside – 'That's just how it was then.' The expectations were the same for June as they were for Miss Millie Crompton from Port Sunlight, who got her silver tea service when she left to marry. Instead, June acted as an amateur wherever she and her husband lived, in Walsall, then over to Berkshire. She even performed in front of the Queen Mother at the opening night of the Abbey Theatre in St Albans in 1968. 'The lights went up and I could see, in the front row, this big pink outfit . . .' and here June, with her expressive hands, described an enormous dandelion explosion, or the floof of a powder puff. 'It was her! She was the best actress out of all of us, really. After the play, we were introduced, and someone asked if she wanted to come to our after-show drinks. She said she'd love to, but she had all these security men. Totally convincing. Really.'

Once her children were growing up, June did start getting some professional TV work, and her CV includes this gem:

'In Birmingham she was on the permanent staff of *Lunch Box*, a daily television magazine programme, with Noele Gordon.' Noele Gordon off *Crossroads*! Here we are again!

When June and her husband first came to Marbella, it was for holidays, two weeks at a time, 'not long enough to commit to anything in the theatre'. Then they settled here full time in 2005, and June kept working creatively. She became 'Director of the Theatre of the Air' for Talk Radio Europe, the English-speaking radio station in Marbella, which broadcast her three-act play *The Girls at the Spanish Golf Club* from which *Champagne and Olives* has been adapted. In its original form, it was a cast of eight women and a variety of accents, which is June's expertise. 'Give me any accent, any dialect, I can do it,' she declared, and we'd cycled through a few in our chat, including Brummie and Norwegian. Now, she directed, produced and wrote. Do you still act, June? 'I played the lead in *Three Tall Women* by Edward Albee last month for ITS, to a standing ovation. So I think you can still call me an actress.' She was so damn classy. I was looking forward to the evening more and more.

At 7 p.m. I was strolling from my hotel on the hill down to El Paraiso Golf Club. On both sides of the quiet road, nature had been bullied into submission. On my left were rows of fancy gated villas, with golf buggies parked in their driveways beside large cars which all looked the same to me. Everything was planted in regimental form, and I knew that if I had a ruler, I'd be able to confirm that they were all exactly the same distance apart. Even the hibiscuses rambled politely. To my right was the golf course, the edge of which butted up to the road. From my hotel window it had looked like a film set. Paths neat as ribbon, grass flat and uniform as cloth. The only things that were not absolutely identikit were the huge date palms dotted around. Thick solid trunks like pillars, and almost-neon orange fruits exploding like fireworks from underneath the palm fronds, bobbing on the evening breeze. As I walked, a golf buggy pulled up on the course, a woman determinedly jumped out and grabbed a club from her bag. She marched over and surveyed a golf ball lying in the grass. She ignored me, surveyed the target, surveyed the ball. It all looked quite furious. She took a stance, wiggled a bit and hit the ball. Tink. It was such a tinny little noise. I wanted something meaty, with heft. Golf is so disappointing.

I was minding my own business as I dawdled along when a car pulled up beside me. Aye aye, I thought, here comes trouble, I'm being kerb-crawled. The door popped open, and I was getting ready to yell FUCK YOU, YOU SORDID LITTLE MAN, but sometimes it's a good thing I'm old and my reactions are slow. 'Do you want a lift, Jenny? You're going the wrong way.' It was Miles, June's son. 'How did you know I was here, Miles? Do you have me microchipped?' I joked, hopping in. 'I saw you take the wrong road,' he replied, doing a U-turn and heading off in the opposite direction. We drove through the golf-club gates less than a minute later.

The clubhouse looked very typically Spanish, a low square building with arched gateways and towers, painted in a flat ochre yellow, all the signs in tile work. At the main door, there was a small welcome committee – Diane King, the president of ITS, and her brother were greeting everyone as they went in. The guests, mostly couples, mostly middle-aged, were drinking vodka and Cokes or gin and tonics in glasses the size of goldfish bowls; I didn't think I'd have the upper-body strength to lift one to my mouth. We made small talk, about seeing Chekhov in Cyprus, about the food served in exclusive boarding schools, and about a borzoi dog who only answered to orders in French, even though its owners weren't French.

The clubhouse was exactly like a room in a nice traditional pub. The shine of a nylon-rich patterned carpet, a fake fireplace with fake flowers in it. Down one wall was a set of green-painted boards, a roll of honour to past golf captains, their names recorded in fancy gold calligraphy. The only concession to the location was air con, already humming noisily. There was a tiny stage, set with a wingback chair and a telescope. Diane King had saved me a seat next to her in the front row. I listened to the accents around me. At FEATS, I thought, it was mostly English-speaking but with a variety of European accents flying around. Here, the accents were Northern, or Midlands, or 'I'm from Peterborough,' said the woman further up the row, whose name I didn't quite catch when she offered it. Cordelia like King Lear's daughter? I asked, the kind of horribly pretentious thing I say that makes me such a hit at parties. 'No, Delia like Delia Smith the cook,' she replied, 'though I can't cook.' Delia's thing was singing, not acting; she was a member of the CAP (Charity and Pleasure) Singers.

'We're a mix of ages,' she said, 'fifty-five to eighty-six.' She and her husband Karl, who did a lot of the scenery for ITS, had lived here for twenty-one years. Before that, it had been India, and East Germany in 1990 just after the Wall came down. 'I learned an awful lot about politics in those five years,' she told me. 'They were an eye-opener.' Now they were retired, and her social life was 'very, very hectic'. The rest of her family was in the UK, and it dawned on me: when you throw your lot in with your partner, you make a deal – if there's no other family around, you have to build one. Sure, amateur theatre creates community everywhere – that has been a recurring theme. But maybe when you move away it's just that bit more important, because it's community, or nothing? I thought that might not be quite the thing to say to someone I'd just met, it might feel more of a confrontation than a question. I'd already had looks when I'd called people expats (it's gauche, they prefer 'residents') and I hadn't dared broach the words 'immigrant' or 'Brexit'. I decided to leave that thought until I knew them better.

The eighty chairs in the venue had filled, and it was time to start. Diane stood up, stepped onto the stage and bam, it was like seeing Christmas lights go on. She went from conversational to broadcast mode without taking a breath – it was impressive. She welcomed everyone and introduced the first play of the night – *The Window*. Miles, playing the lead character Tremayne, took the stage in a silk dressing gown and cravat. (Cravats are the male equivalent of turbans – only people in amateur theatre wear them, to indicate a certain type of character. I don't think I've ever seen a cravat in real life.) The premise of the play was that Tremayne, who was blind, paid another man, Ken, to spy through the telescope on a woman who lived across the way, and report back. So far, so uncomfortable. Things got pretty heated because this woman had men visiting her every night. 'There's a man,' Ken said, his eye to the telescope, 'they're making love.' 'Describe it, Ken, describe it,' pleaded Tremayne. The audience laughed, we were all nervous. Oh God no, please *don't* describe it, Ken, I thought. Fortunately, Ken moved on, and I became increasingly perplexed. Why would anyone choose this play? What do we learn from it about the human condition? Nothing good. Were we entertained? I don't know about other people, but peeping Toms as a theme mostly make me anxious. It wasn't helping that the audience had very poor volume control. 'He's sweating buckets,' someone said loudly. 'It's that cardi,' her companion answered, in her outdoor voice. Diane kept me fed with titbits of gossip. 'His wife is a professional actress,' she said, pointing to Ken. Why does everyone keep talking? I thought.

In the interval, I went outside and stared across the golf course. A friend texted me 'Where are you?' 'I'm in a golf club in Marbella,' I texted back. 'What the hell are you doing there?' she asked. 'Thinking about starting a class war,' I replied.

After a short break, it was time for *Champagne and Olives*. June came onstage to introduce it; she looked terrifically glamorous. Long dangly earrings, a fashionably draped subtle dress and a fabulous sense of timing. Six women walked through the audience from the women's changing area, traipsed across the stage and disappeared behind the meagre screen. 'She's got very good legs,' Diane said, not very sotto voce, of one of them. 'And good arms?' I ventured, feeling that I should try and join in. 'That's what golf does for you,' Diane replied. One of the cast came back on the stage, dressed in an old-fashioned maid's outfit, a black dress and a white cloth hat perched on her head. Her job was to fill in directions for the audience, where required. She set the scene, telling us that the action takes place in a golf club, then told us a joke. (I knew it was a joke, by the tone of her voice.) 'Are there any Spanish people in the club? Yes, but not enough to spoil it.' Everyone laughed. I didn't get it. Are Spanish people notorious golf-club spoilers? I have no idea. The other actors came on and sat in a row. 'She was on the ships,' Diane said, pointing at the woman on the end chair, and as the play went on, Diane gave me a running commentary as if I were either hard of hearing or not terribly bright. Jokes rolled round the audience, and, again, I didn't always get them, so Diane was probably right. 'This is all very much a piss-take,' Diane loud-whispered. 'June's very good.'

And it was good – June's play was funny, insightful, and the characters were well developed. It was very site-specific, so I didn't always get her observations about a particular kind of person in Marbella, but I admire a community that can stand a bit of gentle mocking; there's an assurance to it I'm not sure I possess. *Champagne and Olives* tells the story of a group of golfing lady chums who get lured into the confidence of a wealthy American who, in an unsurprising twist, ends up swindling them. In forty minutes, I learned a lot about the people here. About their hierarchies, their attitude to money, their gated developments and their priorities. One plot point revolved around the wealthy American impressing the golfing friends because she had a lilac Rolls. To my mind, it was a jibe about the shallow nature of materialism, and money not buying taste, but I couldn't say with certainty that is how the audience saw it.

The play ended, there was loud applause (which I joined enthusiastically) and Diane bounded up onstage again. She did her thank yous, then said, 'And thanks to our guest, Jenny Lau . . . Lay . . . Lausss . . .' LANDRETH, I said loudly, my face flaming. 'Jenny Landreth,' said Diane, indicating me, there in the front row. I inclined my head politely in her direction, wishing I could be ejected into space. I don't like being pointed out.

Audience members crowded round June at the bar. 'Is this based on a true story?' someone asked. 'Yes,' she replied. 'There was a group of men who got ripped off, I just changed it from men to women.' 'This area is totally ripe for scams,' someone said, looking directly at me. Maybe he had seen my texts about class war. 'People see a lot of wealthy people living together and they want some of it. We have to be very, very careful.' I pretended to care, there was a lot of amateur drama going on in my 'sympathetic and concerned' face. I congratulated Miles on his performance as Tremayne; I knew he'd studied drama at university, like I had, so I talked to him about the feelings Hilary Jennings, of Southside Players, had planted as a seed in me – about squashing a performance instinct down over the years, only for it to spill out at some point later, about how it can lay dormant and then just burst forth. Don't you want, do you think, don't you just . . . I tried to package my enthusiasm into a manageable slab. 'I'd like to do more,' he said guardedly. I could sense he was resisting *his* instinct, to back away. I'd been too flamboyant with my feelings, too gaudy. My arms had gone all extravagant gesture, and it was too much, I know. I just wasn't used to so much gin in one drink . . .

Then Carmel joined us, the woman 'on the ships'. Earlier, someone had described her to me as 'the fairy dust you sprinkle on a dull event' and that really fitted. She told me how she'd found ITS. She'd run a bar, and did a bit of stand-up comedy – the hen party, stag party, twenty-first birthday kind of thing – and it had taken off quite well. Then her mum died.

'There was nothing to keep me here, so I went to sea on the *QE2*, I was what they called a shoppy. [Someone who works in the ship shops.] Towards the end, I was producing, directing, presenting and hosting all the cruise shows. When the flag came down, I went to Miami and qualified as an art auctioneer. That was the same thing, every day I was three hours with a mic, the centre of attention.'

Did it feel inevitable, I asked, that you'd always do something related to performance? 'I'm a Leo,' she replied, 'I love showing off.' Astrology! I hadn't even considered that up to now. Maybe it's the answer to everything. (It isn't.)

Eventually, Carmel 'swallowed the anchor and came home to Marbella', and when an old friend said 'there's a part here with your name on it' she accepted it. 'Here' was ITS. 'I did this part and I've never looked back. I played a character called Marcia who was terrified of thunderstorms so I spent the whole play screaming in cupboards. At the end of the day, you get the applause, you get more bums on seats, people come up and say "you were fabulous" . . . of course it's being stroked but I absolutely love it. I've seen people actually falling off their chairs with laughter, people were hysterical during *Dirty Dusting*.' I told Carmel I'd look that one up, but I knew I wouldn't. I had a fair idea of what it would entail. 'Then in *Three Tall Women* – we were worried it would be too heavy. But the feedback we got was fantastic. My monologue was about being shagged by the stable boy, and yeah, they loved it. My boss was in one night, but you just forget everything, and give it your best shot.'

On my way back to the hotel, I was thinking about community. For there to be insiders, there are, by necessity, outsiders. Every person here had been so welcoming, greeting me with a beaming smile, tolerating my questions. But I felt distanced from this lifestyle on the Costa del Golf. As I walked, I tuned out of my thoughts and into the noises. I heard a small Spanish owl. And then it started to rain, and I blessed the relief it brought on this clammy night. Underneath the sound of falling water, as I listened more closely, I heard a hiss, and then I realised: it wasn't rain I could feel, it was a sprinkler. They were watering the golf course. I chuckled to myself. No, I thought, this is not my community. I'll stay a happy outsider.

Back in England, I phoned my mum. 'Do you remember a June Rendle at Highbury?' I asked, and she replied, politely and unconvincingly, 'I'm sure that name rings a bell.' Actually, I was relieved. I was glad that neither of them could really remember the other. I think I'd have felt sad if Mum could remember June, but June couldn't remember my mum. That would have been unbalanced, and not like the spirit of community, of amateur theatre, at all.

CHAPTER 15

The Plough and the Stars

Ireland has its own Costa del Golf, only they don't call it that. I was driving along it on a grey day in early December, south out of Dublin. The wind was strong, and I was gripping the wheel of my tiny rental car to stop it from being buffeted across the motorway lanes; it was raining so hard I was holding my breath as I overtook lorries and their spray swarmed over the car like an unfriendly ghost, making me temporarily, terrifyingly, unable to see a thing. I wanted to go home. This was a country and western song waiting to happen.

I was headed to the All Ireland One Act Drama Finals, being held in the village of Kilmuckridge, and I had some idea of what to expect. The rain, obviously. Everyone knows that. And I'd already been to FEATS, so I understood how competition in amateur theatre might look and how adjudication works. A few days before the trip, I'd had a conversation about rural amateurs with James Pidgeon, who has a foot in the professional camp, as artistic director of Shoreditch Town Hall, and in the amateur, as a keen performer. Perched on uncomfortable mock-industrial stools in a Clapham coffee bar, James told me about how he started in drama. The first part of his story, doing school plays, was common; the second, doing plays with Young Farmers, I was surprised by. I associated Young Farmers with drinking and shagging and 'trying to find a wife', not with theatre. Clearly, this is my bad; as I've previously established, I am a hostage to stereotypes. But I've learned in writing this book how persistent and present am-dram is in all sorts of unexpected communities, and if you can find it in Midland Bank and the Shredded Wheat factory, why not with young farmers?

'One of the biggest things about am-dram in Young Farmers,' James explained, 'is that it addresses a huge amount of isolation issues. Somerset is now identified as one of the most deprived counties, because of its rural isolation, particularly for its young people. Young Farmers, with their twice-a-week panto rehearsals, is a way of addressing that.'

There are clearly two Somersets; the one I'm more familiar with is magazine-spread Somerset, which is all home-made cheese and sourdough starters and second homes for rock-star models from Primrose Hill who have babies and then design their own range of organic baby clothes which they get made by a woman in the village and sell in London at £50 for a pair of gender-neutral leggings for the under-twos. It wasn't that Somerset James was referring to. The Young Farmers run drama competitions which have local rounds, then regional and national ones. Performing arts are a big part of their 'offer' to young people. James wanted to give me a sense of scale.

'There must be thirty-five to forty clubs in Devon alone. My dad is still president of his local Young Farmers club. It has 150 members, it's big. And it's very clear with Young Farmers, it's all about embracing anyone, you don't have to be a farmer, or engage with farming issues.' I wondered, driving along to Kilmuckridge, if rural isolation is what brought people to amateur theatre here, too.

That night, the sky was as dark as I've seen. Where there *was* light, they had really gone for it. I'd drive a while in the pitch-black, and then come across a small house almost entirely covered in Christmas lights. Black black black black AAAAAAAARRGGGGHHHH MY EYES. The searing glare positively thrummed against the darkness, making me squint. I imagined planes travelling peacefully far above, their pilots suddenly recoiling with a 'Jeeeezus, what the . . .' at the flare from a luminous garden Santa, seen miles away up in space. Still, they were cheery. If you're going to do light pollution, fuck being tasteful.

Within twenty seconds of arriving at the hotel rendezvous, I'd met someone friendly. 'Everyone in Ireland is so friendly' – that and the rain, these are the expectations. I clambered aboard a minibus that was the festival shuttle bus to the venue and said hello to the three women waiting for us to depart. I was warmly greeted in response. 'Hi, I'm Sally,' said the woman I sat next to, and by the time we'd been driven the all-of-two hundred yards, I knew that Sally was the director of a play in this weekend's competition, and that she was 'obsessed with theatre. Ob. Sessed. I'm passionate about it. I think about little else.' We got out at the Memorial Hall, built by locals in the 1950s originally as a dance hall, and refurbished in 2011, and I could see people inside, milling about in the tiny foyer. I went in to see if I could spot Michael Johnston, director of the festival. 'I've got a beard,' he'd told me on the phone earlier, 'and I'll be in a tux.' Oh blimey, I'd said, looking down at my jeans and jumper, I haven't brought anything smart. Is everyone going to be dressed up, Michael? 'Just the committee,' he'd replied, to my relief. 'We want to make a good impression.' There he was, exactly as described; we said hello and he sorted out my ticket for the evening. People handed out paper wristbands and programmes, there were more bearded men in tuxes swanning around, and women looking very fancy for their evening of amateur theatre, some in long gowns and matching jewellery, a look I couldn't muster if my life depended on it.

From the foyer I went down a long, shabby corridor, everything was narrow and cramped, and I was wondering where the actual theatre was, expecting a room that matched these surroundings; at the end another man in a tux was handing out free bottles of water. I took one, turned right and walked into the auditorium, where my expectations were confounded. I would never have guessed from the unassuming front of this building and these scuffed, tatty corridors that there would be a large, well-appointed theatre at the back, with rows of tiered seating to my right, and more seats on the flat (the stalls, in effect) to my left. The stage was big, and stylishly set for the first play. I'd known that a drama competition had run here for over fifty years, I just hadn't expected the space to be so great – this is a small village, remember. You have an amazing theatre, I said to Michael. 'Believe it or not, bigger theatres are scattered round the country,' he replied. Once this weekend was over, all the tiered seating would be taken out, and this 'theatre' would turn back into being a village hall. 'That's the festivals for you,' Michael said. 'You get to go to little places. You came to Kilmuckridge. Places you'd have no reason to be. Rossmore, a little village in Cork, you'd never be there, it's in the middle of absolutely nowhere . . . There's dozens of these little places dotted around the country.'

In a letter to the *Irish Independent* newspaper, Dr Fiona Brennan had helpfully and succinctly laid out the history of amateur theatre in Ireland. In the 1930s, she wrote, Ireland had been fully immersed in a craze for Hollywood, and across the country, parish halls had throbbed to the sounds of the quick step, foxtrot and other such non-Irish dance tunes.

> In the ultra-conservative Ireland of its day these social activities were viewed with absolute abhorrence by both the de Valera Government and Roman Catholic church and castigated as evil influences on Ireland's moral well-being. When the Church enforced a Lenten ban on such activities, people turned to the stage and amateur drama.

That Lenten ban on laughing and dancing meant an unprecedented rise in the creation of drama groups across

Ireland – because drama, of course, only ever means 'serious', they're notably *never* jolly, nobody *ever* laughs or makes any physical contact with another human . . . And with that rise came the founding of competitive festivals. Some traditions from this time are still observed. 'It could never run in Easter week,' Michael told me, 'and still to this day Easter dictates when everything is finished.' The misery of Lent is so ingrained in me, I'd no idea that it might actually have done something good, like creating a healthy amateur theatre scene in Ireland. The Church had been important at the very start of this amateur story, and it was still dictating things here, now. The Amateur Drama Council of Ireland was founded in 1952, and the first All Ireland Amateur Drama Festival was held in 1953. 'It grew and grew and grew and it's a terrific organisation now.'

The auditorium at Kilmuckridge started filling up; I slotted myself into a corner in the stalls. Michael had told me it was going to be sold out when I'd rung a while back, to enquire about tickets. 'There's a waiting list,' he'd said, 'but I'm sure we'll sort you something, if you're coming all this way.' I'd thought then that he was being hyperbolic, trying to big up the event; I could see now that he was not. Sally sat next to me; she was up and down in her seat, waving and greeting people as she spotted them coming in. You seem to know everyone, I said. 'It's our drama family,' someone further down our row chipped in. 'You'll hear that a lot.' 'We take it very seriously,' said Sally, very seriously. Michael agreed. 'We're all friends offstage, we're all in it together but when you're on the stage and the lights come on, you're out to win at all costs.' 'See him?' Sally pointed to a guy manoeuvring into his seat ahead of us. 'He bought a car with twenty thousand kilometres on the clock. Two years later, it had seventy thousand kilometres on the clock, from him driving round the country going to see amateur theatre.' And then, 'That guy?' She turned to someone else. 'He once drove for four hours, watched *A Long Day's Journey Into Night*, then drove home again.' *A Long Day's Journey* seemed such an appropriate play for the anecdote, I wondered afterwards if she was taking the piss. Sally turned to greet the man behind us. 'Hi, Pat, this is Jenny.' Pat and I shook hands. I asked him if he was an actor. 'I try,' he replied. 'I try.'

I wondered, to Michael, if James's comments about drama addressing rural isolation were relevant here. 'When you move inland, into the centre of the country, or up to the likes of Leitrim, and Tipperary, they are absolutely rural areas, and there is very little to do in those places. For the winter months, the drama is a thing that goes on. If you're putting a three-act play out on the circuit, you really need to get started as the time changes, around October.' The way he said 'as the time changes' underlined how deeply the seasons affect these communities. It's something that's easier to forget in a big city where it never truly gets dark. During long winter evenings in a small place, the only other social hub might be the local pub; doing plays gives people options. 'This gets you over the winter. You wouldn't believe how quick January goes, you're busy getting everything ready, your lighting, your set, the sound, it's a busy, busy month. The hours just wrinkle away. When you know your first performance is in Kilmuckridge on 23 February, that sharpens things. The days are long before you know it.' I wondered if Michael knew just what an evocative picture he was painting.

The auditorium was rammed, people were standing in the aisles and the adjudicator had taken her seat – the MC's cue to come on and give his welcome speech, which included thanking all the volunteers, and a plea I'd heard elsewhere, that they needed to get more young people involved. Then he gave out the Mass times for the morning. That *was* unexpected. The only events I've ever been to where they gave out Mass times, were other Masses. I thought perhaps it might be an indicator of the evening's tone, that maybe this audience would be a no-sex, no-swearing kind of 'drama family', that the plays we were about to see would be, if not religious, then safe and old-fashioned.

I was wrong. The first play was about a man who suspected his girlfriend of infidelity, so he cooked up her beloved dog and fed it her in a retaliatory stew (entirely justifiably, in my opinion). There was muttering around the audience as they guessed what the denouement was before it came. I was more used, by now, to amateur audience's lack of volume control. Some of them seem to think the term 'theatrical whisper' applies to them and not to the actors onstage.

After the first play, we were invited to stay in our seats while the next one set up, and as I flicked through my programme, I noticed that every group was marked as either 'Open' or 'Confined'. Sally explained it to me. 'The original intent was that Confined would mean the rural groups, and Open would be the city groups. It's like football, there's lower and higher leagues.' Michael expounded further. 'The theory was that if you were in Wexford and you went about producing a play, you might have four or five people and you'd pick your best. But if you're in a little village – and Kilmuckridge would be an ideal example – your actors would be limited. It's to compare like with like.'

These groups are all working the 'circuit', which is quite the thing. Michael attempted to make it simple for me. 'The one-act circuit takes place from mid-October, with the finals – where we are now – in the first weekend of December. It isn't so intense because they're shorter plays, and that suits a lot of people because of all the work and effort that goes into it. But the three-act circuit now, that will start at the end of February until the end of March, and there's thirty-seven festivals, scattered right across the country.' Groups can enter eight festivals out of that circuit of thirty-seven; if they get three wins, they have a place at the finals. 'It's a huge achievement for a small community,' Sally told me, and there is no underestimating the sincerity, passion and hard work she, and many others, put into this. 'I'm sitting here now,' she said, 'but I'm thinking about *Juno and the Paycock*, which we're putting on in January. It's on my mind the whole time.' So many people in the room were clearly as committed to theatre as she is, demonstrated by the distances they drive, and the rapt attention they paid for the entire long evening. Make no mistake: it really matters. How will it feel if you win this final? I asked Sally. 'Like winning an Oscar,' she replied. 'You've no idea.'

As this was the finals, each play had already been performed at various festivals, and adjudicated each time. What happens in that process, Sally said, is that you 'learn, learn, learn. And by the end of the circuit, the play will be better.' Michael agreed. 'Every year the standard creeps up and up. Everybody will tell you that.' Sally had already seen all this weekend's plays, while doing the circuit with her group, the Coolgreany Amateur Dramatic Society, who were performing the following night. She'd started the group when she realised how much she wanted theatre in her life. 'I've always loved theatre. But you know, with kids, and the expense, and living in the country . . .' The time hadn't been right, then suddenly it was. The Coolgreany 'mission state-ment' records how they'd begun, in September 2009, by looking for members at the school gates, in the shop, and among friends and neighbours. 'We wanted to have some fun. We wanted to play. We wanted to build self-esteem and entertain our village. We like to think we've succeeded on all counts.' It reminded me of my conversation with Hilary Jennings. 'I think,' she'd said, 'that if you had a village produc-tion, you could find a place for everybody, and anybody.' Why is it so successful? I asked Sally. 'There's very few creative pastimes that are also sociable,' she said. 'We're adults, playing. It's playing.' People from the village of Coolgreany had found their way to play. What had happened to *my* desire to play, and did I want it back? My time at Highbury, watching *Variation on a Theme* come together, had certainly stirred some of those feelings. It had reminded me, actually, of cold-water swimming; of times when I'd felt uncertainty on a winter's morning, at the side of an unheated outdoor pool. I'd dip my toe in, then out, then in, then out, knowing that by prolonging getting in, all I was doing was stretching out the bad bit. Out of . . . fear? Just get in, quickly, without thinking, I'd often say to myself, at the side of the icy lido. I knew that I was dandling here, too, at the edges of amateur theatre, when I could see everyone else splashing around having a lovely time. So what is it, then, that's stopping me from leaping in and joining them? What on earth have I got to lose?

I asked Sally if the fantastic standard of the night was typical. 'It's because we're amateurs. We don't have to pay anyone. And rehearsing over time brings so much more to a play. So does experience.' 'You'll be blown away by the standard,' Michael had said when I'd first rung him, and I was. 'You take our festival now. Kilmuckridge, every February, comes alive with drama. And unless you're part of it, you don't realise how good it is. People think it's just locals having a hop around onstage, and it's not. The minute they hear the word "amateur" it's "ah, that wouldn't be worth going to see, it's only amateurs". But an awful lot of actors, people like Liam Neeson, Brendan Gleeson, Gabriel Byrne, they all started out in am-dram and moved on. They got the bug.'

Fiona Brennan's letter in the newspaper had mentioned famous names too. 'The amateur movement caught the imagination of ambitious young writers, producers and players,' she wrote, 'some of whom sought professional careers and succeeded.' 'We're a little nation,' Michael continued, 'with a huge diaspora across the world but we seem to punch well above our weight. We tend to do things and really get into them.'

I asked him if he knew the numbers involved in amateur theatre in Ireland, and he cited an RTE programme, which had reported that after the Catholic Church and the Gaelic Athletic Association, am-dram has the biggest member base. 'Now that was a big statement to make. It is a huge organisation. If you take it that every little village in the country has groups, they mightn't go out on the circuit, but they put on plays during the year . . . There could be eight or nine hundred groups.'

For Michael, a key part of all of this is the 'team player' element; when a group is out on the circuit with their play, nobody cares who earns what, they're just doing drama. 'You can have big influential people, and you can have people on their uppers, and they can travel around and be best of friends. It breaks down social barriers.'

I ended my conversation with him by asking him how he'd first got involved. 'Marie was the reason,' he said. Marie was his late wife, she'd been passionate about am-dram, Michael had accompanied her and got hooked. Marie had been killed in 2012 by a drunk driver. The whole world arrived in

Kilmuckridge for her funeral. 'It was really then that you see what the words "drama family" means, because people came from Kerry, from Donegal, from the four corners to pay their respects. The solidarity shown to us – that's when being a member of a drama group really comes into its own. The support we got. I can't speak highly enough of it. It really is a wonderful organisation to be part of.'

It was even darker when I drove back to my B&B that night, the Christmas lights long turned off. I lay in bed eating a family pack of Tayto's, thinking about everything Michael and Sally had said. I thought about drama families and community, about the importance of amateur theatre in Ireland, and its roots out from the Church. It felt like Michael and Sally had been secretly charged with writing a concise manifesto for amateur theatre, and they were drip-feeding it to me. Every point they'd made had underlined something or been a distillation of what I'd learned from other amateurs. It all came together, in this one place.

CHAPTER 16

First Night

I'm going to the final dress rehearsal of *Variation on a Theme* tonight, so I've pitched up at Mum's, and she has found something she wants to show me. She's left it at the top of the stairs, and though I haven't seen it for years, when I go up to fetch it, I recognise it immediately. I carefully carry down a metal box, about the size of a child's lunch box, hard-wearing and solid enough to accompany a man being sent out to work in unforgiving and dangerous circumstances. While being onstage can sometimes feel like that, this particular box had never withstood more than the tumultuous blows of the amateur actor. Mum has dug out Dad's theatrical make-up box for me.

The box is a dry hammered blue metal, with a thin handle. Its intended purpose was as some kind of toolbox, I assume, and of course, inside it are the tools of Dad's amateur trade. I'm not sure he'd have handled his dental tools with anything like this care. In the right-hand corner on the top of the box is a label, made with a Dymo label maker. *P. J. Landreth*.

I would have made that label, because it was my Dymo, I'd got it for Christmas and nobody else was allowed to touch it. This Dymo was a thing of wonder; a clunky bit of plastic that was our equivalent of modern technology. Imagine, I could make labels for anything in the world I wanted to label, anything at all. Wow. Mine was a mustardy beige; there was a flat wheel on the top with the alphabet and numbers 0–9 on it. You needed to buy tape, which was only available in limited colours (black, red, blue) and was very, very expensive and precious; I was never profligate with it. You'd feed the tape through, click the wheel round until it was on the right letter, then press the trigger handle really hard. And so on, letter by letter. Gradually your label would appear out of the spout of the machine, and only then would you know if you'd pressed each letter hard enough and spelled everything right. I'd concentrate intently, my tongue sticking out of my mouth (my dad had the same habit). If I made a spelling mistake, I'd feel sick at the waste of tape. The label was then ready to be stuck onto books, records, pieces of furniture, anyone who stood still long enough, make-up boxes like this one, for all eternity. Yes, all eternity. These labels have a longer shelf life than nuclear waste. After each of my father's initials, I had put a sturdy full stop, clearly delivered with some force. Those full stops from the past; they'll outlast us all.

I gently place the box on the dining-room table, like a bomb I have to diffuse, and Mum and I stand looking at it for a moment. I think, for a second, about leaving it untouched. On the shelf underneath my mum's tiny TV there are videos of my father in plays from the early eighties that I have yet to watch; it's OK to let some things lie. But curiosity wins. The front of the box is closed with a latch, held in place by a hair-grip. I pull the hairgrip out and the whole front panel folds down, providing a sort of apron. The first thing I notice is the smell. It is the smell of greasepaint, which is absolutely distinct. Sweet and floury, it is instantly reminiscent of sweaty dressing rooms, and bright lights and concentration and thick cloying colours pulling across tender skin. In the large section at the bottom of the box are two metal canisters of Leichner Blending Powder, their red-and-yellow lids declaring, in sixties film-poster font, that one was No. 116 'Brownish' and the other 'Neutral'. There is a pair of glasses, with no glass. 'He always wore those onstage,' Mum says, lifting them out tenderly. Above that is a drawer, which I pull open slowly. Inside is a segmented section full of treasure. There are some make-up tubes, Leichner 'Spot-Lite Klear', in various shades, No. 20 White, No. 44 Brownish Tan, and make-up sticks that are as moist and ready as if he'd used them yesterday. A comb. Mum, I say, we could get his DNA from this make-up box. 'If we ever needed to,' she replies. There is a small tin of Meloids, liquorice throat sweets, with instructions, 'shake the Meloids from this orifice as required', printed in one corner, a small arrow pointing to a hole where the sweets would be dispensed. I think how nobody uses the word 'orifice' in advertising any more. I try it, shaking some regular black nibs onto my palm, each as small as a mouse poo. In between the tubes of make-up is a big button, presumably for emergencies, and two costume rings, gaudy as any pretend king would need. 'I think these rings were from *A Man for All Seasons*,' Mum says. In the lid compartment, Dad had stored the thinner sticks of solid make-up, some pristine, some half used, some mere stubs with squeezed ends. Oranges, reds and blues, blacks and whites. There's a small jar, on its side, of now-hardened spirit gum that would have been used to stick on a moustache. And an old, calcified, elastic band, set in shape. The mirror in the lid is cracked, and there's an ancient wodge of tissue paper holding it in place. Mum and I pore over the box, picking up each tube, turning it over in our hands. We have him there, for just a minute. Mum carefully refolds the tissue paper in the lid and we take another long look before I shut the box again.

There is a bit of theatrical mythology that the final dress rehearsal is always bad. More – it is actually better that it's bad, it bodes well for the first night. The first dress rehearsal needs to be good, so everyone knows they can do this, and the last one needs to be bad, so they don't take it for granted. Then everyone and everything is heightened for the first night, running on the adrenaline of terror that actual people are paying money to see the horrendous cock-ups from the terrible final dress. That is just the way it works. It's all about pushing on and up to the light. Sometimes I think doing theatre is like deep-sea diving.

According to this theory, we should have been pleased that the last dress for *Variation* was terrible. 'We do this for fun we do this for fun we do this for fun,' Alison is chanting quietly in the green room as I arrive. How's your alcohol intake? I ask. 'I don't dare start,' she replies, and I understand; it's not a good idea to drink and dive. 'Everyone to the green room please!' she yells out of the door, and while we wait for the cast to assemble, Alison and I chat about Connie Grainger, who had directed the first thing Alison had been in here. Connie, who'd been a friend of my parents, was a formidable Highbury character, famous for her sayings. 'Adapt, adopt and improve' had been one of her favourite mantras. 'Adapt, adopt and improve!' she would pronounce, at the end of a rehearsal for whatever she was directing. It's a phrase that's perfectly suited to the world of amateur theatre, where there is never any money, never the right actor for the parts (or in this case, they pitched up very late) and nothing is ever quite how it should be. If you can't learn to work with what you have, if you can't pretend that a cheap plastic stage vase is finest china, if you can't accept that a 49-year-old grandad is perfect to play the young male lead, the amateur theatre is not the place for you. Connie was right, you have to adapt, adopt and improve. 'It was *Under Milk Wood*,' Alison says. 'I still love that piece. Me, your sister Maddie and Ros Jones had to sing a Welsh song at one point and we were round the back, in the scene dock.' In those days, the scene dock was under the stage, so the idea, I presume, was that their voices could float up through the boards to the audience. 'And we got it wrong. We were singing, and we got it wrong. So, of course we stopped, and then started again from the beginning. Connie was furious. But we didn't know. Nobody had told us that we should just keep going.' And Connie was terrifying. 'She was,' Alison says.

We make firm eye contact, puff our cheeks and blow out, glad to be away from that time.

The cast assembles in the green room. It is the first time I've seen them in costume, and of course, clothes breathe life into the characters. Just don't look too closely, you might see the wear and tear. Alison gives a pep talk. 'Go for it tonight,' she says, 'with as much energy as you've got. We want pace, and punch. Hazel [my mum] will prompt you, take it. Carry on. If you're going to come on, come on. If you're going to make a move, make it. Let's be confident. Come on!' She is unwittingly repeating another popular Connie Grainger phrase, 'punch and pace, bags of attack'. Ros Jones had told me that she and Rob still often quoted that one, with Connie's particular tone and phrasing, 'when we've watched a slow, dreary play'. Alison's speech should have been galvanising, but the atmosphere in the room doesn't shift. Nothing and nobody rise to match her gusto. The cast are flat, tired and worried. There simply hasn't been enough time to rehearse properly; the people might have gelled – in adversity, perhaps – but the words haven't. Nothing has stuck, and the uncertainty that generates makes everything, even the bits that had felt stable before, slide away like mud down a mountain. Nobody is making eye contact, certainly not with me. I suspect there is a bit of 'oh fuck, things aren't going well, and there's a bloody writer in the room'. But I feel like an insider, part of it all, not an observer. I feel hyped up and jumpy; I want to find some magic Connie phrase so that I can snap them into confidence. I wish I could fix it, it's a natural instinct.

There is quite a lot of pacing, from me as well as them. 'Love your outfit,' I say to Kim, who is wearing what might have once been a fashionable bathing cover-up. 'I think it's made of towels,' she says. 'We used to wear a lot of things made from towels,' I reply.

I watch the first half sitting beside Alison in the auditorium. It is not great, and everyone knows it. There are whole scenes where the voice I hear most often is Mum's, prompting calmly and clearly. It's only the dress rehearsal, I say to myself, constantly. I start to pay close attention to what I can feel from the actors, and mostly, it is anxiety rolling off the stage. My feelings of resentment towards the play itself for being so stupidly difficult are growing; I start to hate its nonsense sentences, so damn wordy and inconsequential. I *knew* I was right, at the start, when I'd muttered to myself about some plays deserving to remain unperformed. But feeling right does't help. Fucking Rattigan. He can take the full rap for this from me. Nobody really believes in their performance, the cast are underselling the lines they do remember. The body language is all crossed arms and downcast eyes. It is possibly the most stressful thing I've ever been to, and I've visited Disneyland Paris with my in-laws. Still, I want to be useful, I want to have something worthwhile to say. I can't remain silent, that would be too revealing. So at the end of the first act, I give Alison the only helpful note I can muster. 'You need the rosé wine to be in a clear bottle,' I tell her. 'Rosé wine is never served in dark green glass.' Look at me and all my contributions to this play.

I decide to spend the second half of the dress rehearsal in the green room, a good vantage point for actor-watching. The play is being relayed on a small monitor in the corner, which feels a bit like watching CCTV in a newsagent's you know is about to be robbed. As the second half starts, Sean, playing Kurt, is sitting in there in his tux. Sean has been a reassuring figure in this cast since that very first rehearsal, when he'd already got his accent sorted and had clearly done some work on who Kurt was, knowing that they shared a birthday. It was Sean who I'd listened to declaiming French words on WhatsApp. Sean has stage presence too; the minute he strides on, exuding confidence, it spills out into the auditorium, and the audience (even at rehearsals, when it is just me and Alison) can relax. For someone playing a Nazi, that is quite a feat. He's been involved in amateur theatre for only five or six years, he tells me, starting off in his local church amateur group after he retired from marketing management. (I am momentarily disappointed – not a knitting pattern model or linguistics expert, then.) In one of his first roles, his brother got cast as his son, which sounds problematic. 'Psychologically very damaging.' Then he came to Highbury, where 'I said I'd never do panto, never sing onstage, and never do drag'. I'm confident I know the punchline to this one. 'And I did them all last year.' Yep, I am ahead of him. What do you get from it? 'There's great camaraderie. This is something we've all worked on together, and it's an achievement.' It is, I say, but underneath, I'm wondering how we'll rescue that sense of achievement from this fucking Rattigan.

Jim comes in, our late-arriving Ron. 'Look,' he says, showing me some photos on the noticeboard. 'That's me. And there. And there.' Pinned up there are three versions of Jim in the youth theatre, which is how he'd got started in this place, thirteen years ago. We sit and talk, about plays, writing, words, acting. He is full of it, everything all ahead of him, this creative life. I think, with training Jim could be a really good professional actor, but I don't say that, not tonight. It's not the right time. And it would feel like I was saying 'there's something better than this for you', and through everything I've seen and all the people I've spoken to, I am not now convinced that is true. Then Kim blows in, and for her, the sooner she can be a professional, the better. 'I physically can't *not* be onstage,' she declares, in a dramatic teenage fashion I am familiar with from home. 'Without the theatre I would literally go mad.' That sounds like addiction, I tentatively suggest, adding an uplift to the end of my sentence, to make it clear I'm being flip. 'An addiction, and a therapy,' she replies. 'I feel things very deeply. Theatre is the place I can get my emotions out.' I think you might actually be a nightmare, I dare to joke. 'I am!' she responds gleefully. She has her drama school auditions ahead of her, and I so much want her to make it. Jim, too, as a writer, actor, whatever. I really want it to work for these young people.

This is what happens when you go to amateur theatre. You start caring about young people who are not your own. Ridiculous.

The final dress is finished; it is 11 p.m. by the time Alison comes into the green room to give her last set of notes before the first night. I have consistently been amazed by how hard these people work; tonight, everyone is drained. 'Actually, you might not believe it, but you were great tonight,' she says. No one believes it. I don't. She gives a few final pointers about stagecraft and folding your arms and looking upstage too much; all of their gestures, given how things had gone, are clearly psychological indicators – the actors are failing to mask their desire to be anywhere but onstage. She ends with 'we've had worse dress rehearsals'. 'Have you really?' mutters my mum, sitting beside me. I nudge her harshly in the ribs.

The next night, Monday, is supposed to be the night off between final dress and first night. A night to relax, to let everything filter through your mind, to remember things like 'do I still have a family?' and how it feels to go home straight from work and put your PJs on. This Monday night, though, the cast decide to meet at the theatre and run lines. We all pitch up. The atmosphere is full of dread; we're a bit beyond small talk. There's no way that a couple of hours is going to transform much. Fucking Rattigan. But we split up to find separate spaces to work – some in the green room, some onstage – and start running tricky bits, over and over. I'm on the stage with Rob, who has a couple of pages with Rose that are proving a stumbling block. At last, I'm the lead! We go over and over it. Rob's working hard to overcome the psychological barrier he's put up around this scene. 'I've never got it right = I never will.' We work on. We go over it again. When he gets it right,

Rob is really good, and when he gets it wrong, he's really giving himself a hard time. I'm aware enough to know that saying 'it's the fucking *playwright's* fault' won't help much. The utter frustration is visceral, when you feel you'll *never* get it, when you want to punch yourself or something, when you want to furiously throw your script to the back of the auditorium, but watch it instead flop feebly two metres away and you have to walk over, pick it up again and keep going. Everything's a fucking metaphor. Just keep going. Keep pushing on.

We leave the theatre at midnight. They all have to get up for work in the morning, but what about *me*? I've got a busy life too, you know.

It's Tuesday night, and I am back at Highbury, this time as a member of the audience for the first night. I'm with my sister Ruth, and I'm milling around almost as if I'm an ordinary person. You would not guess from looking at me that I am shitting it for the cast backstage. Smile and nod – that was another one of Connie Grainger's phrases. Smile and nod.

I said before that there are two experiences of being at the theatre – either you're part of the play, or you're in the audience. I'd like to finesse that slightly. There are three experiences of being at the theatre. You're part of the play, or you're part of the audience, or you're watching an amateur production, in which case you are somewhere in the middle. On this first night, that's certainly where I am. In that third, middle spot. It is *not* relaxing.

It isn't just because I've come to care about all of these people as individuals, although that does have me sweating before the opening music even starts. I am also feeling strongly what I'd learned from my conversation with Helen Nicholson. That there is something about seeing an amateur production, wherever it is played out, that is quantifiably different. It's a live interaction. 'There is a very special relationship between the audience and the performer onstage,' Helen had said, 'so the atmosphere in the room can create a really good night out,' even if what you're seeing is not to your taste. And as we surely know by now, this Rattigan is absolutely not to my taste. 'There's a thing that happens in an amateur audience, and that is that people talk to each other. "Why am I here, what am I doing?" You rarely see that in professional theatre.'

On this particular night, I want to do more than talk to the audience. I want to stand onstage before the play starts and give them a small lecture about the complicated circumstances. Or stand in the foyer as they filter in, wearing a sandwich board on which I will have written: 'These performers have only had two weeks' (I'll have underlined that, to stress it, or added some exclamation marks) 'to get to grips with this complex and wordy play.' I want the audience to understand that what they are about to see has not had time to be polished. What I do instead is have a gin and tonic, about half the size of a Marbella one.

At the final bell, I take my seat next to Ruth. We look at our programme, and I go through the cast list with her, telling her what I know about everyone. Double ontology works best, of course, when things are going well. That was unlikely tonight. 'Sean was a marketing manager. Louise does PR, she used to be a journalist,' I tell Ruth. 'Rob, he works at a shop in Sutton – he's really good. Kim's at school, the same year as Jo, they're both equally obsessed with Shakespeare.' 'Young people are weird,' Ruth, a drama teacher for thirty years, says. I know, I say.

Our seats are smack bang in the middle of the auditorium. I can see and hear the reactions of everyone around me. There are a couple right in front of me who are loudly not enjoying it, and it's like he wants me to feel his displeasure. He's almost becoming part of the performance, loudly squirming and wincing. She is constantly nudging him uncomfortably. He is almost certainly asking Helen's question, 'why am I here?', only not in a rhetorical way. And yet, he returns after the interval. One of the biggest leaps I've made in my adult life is not returning after an interval, if I'm not having a good time. It is utterly liberating, and I commend it. But this unhappy man is clearly not as evolved as me. Having him in my line of vision is an abject lesson in how much other people's lack of enjoyment can affect you, if you are alive to it. Having been so distracted by it tonight, I would like to pledge that I'll always behave well in a theatre audience, but it's an unrealistic goal.

Tonight is not a good show. There is no prettying that up. I wish for the sake of this book that it wasn't this way, but actually, in this moment, I'm far beyond thinking about my own narrative and much more concerned with theirs. The performance creaks and groans and flails along, and from my seat I will them through it with every fibre of my being, leaning forward tensely the whole time. I want it to be over so badly. Actors not knowing their lines is anxiety-inducing at the best of times – I witnessed a distinguished actor absolutely destroy the last half an hour of a seven-hour-long play in the West End, because it seemed as though she had no idea what she was supposed to say next. We'd put in six and a half hours before she appeared, a commitment I don't readily make, then the whole lot was brought crashing down. She was a reminder of the fragility of the process. But maybe it was double ontology that saw us through the *Variation* first night, in a way it wouldn't have done on a professional stage. Because apart from me, taut as a tightrope, and the loudly groaning man in front of me, the rest of the audience politely watch, appreciate all the effort and hard work onstage, and applaud loudly at the end. My God, I am grateful to them.

The night is long. The gin barely stretches me to the interval. I had promised to buy the cast a drink at the end, but I am relieved when none of them come through to the bar. They all just want to go home. We all just want to go home.

CHAPTER 17

The Theory of Everything

Why do people do amateur theatre? That question has been answered anecdotally in all sorts of ways by all sorts of people I met while writing this book. There are as many answers as there are kinds of theatre and kinds of participants. I want to see if personal stories are reflected in theory. To see if there are 'official' reasons for what people have expressed instinctively. It is time to mine for meaning beyond 'my dad was in *The Browning Version*', to step back, and ask on a broader level: who are the amateur theatricals, why do they do it, what are the barriers to inclusion, and where does it all sit in our cultural landscape? Something more rooted in data and academic study. I want to see if I can find, in theoretical research, some of the answers to questions I've asked myself along the way.

We know already that there is buoyancy in the statistics, but rubber ducks are buoyant. The numbers might have told us that more people than we thought do amateur theatre, but not 'why', on any meaningful level. April de Angelis referred to amateur theatre as something that 'draws people who are utterly committed to it', and made a wider, more political point about its purpose.

'I was just reading Timothy Snyder, who writes about totalitarianism, and tyranny, and the ten things you do to prevent totalitarianism. And he said, "Join some kind of group," and I thought, he means amateur dramatics. Any community organisation that does things together is a strike against tyranny.'

I laughed, delighted to consider amateur theatre as a radical political force, as sticking it to the man. It's so *not* what people imagine.

When I asked Helen Nicholson for her thoughts on 'why', she began with an important observation. 'There's not one amateur theatre,' she said. 'There are so many different sorts and they fulfil very different functions in different places, have different roles.' Helen had started her work on *The Ecologies of Amateur Theatre* resistant to carrying out research in cities, because the preconception is that cutting edge or new work is city-based, whereas suburban am-dram is quite often denigrated. 'There's a very different sort of amateur theatre if you're in a theatre in Devon than there is if you're in one of the big amateur theatres in London. So we started in suburbs, towns, garden cities, villages, seaside towns, and of course, what you get is a whole range.'

Outside of the metropolis, Helen found some local amateur theatres that might only do two shows a year, putting on maybe a panto and a whodunnit in a village hall or community centre, with an audience of friends and family. Companies that might fulfil – create? – the stereotype of what an amateur theatre company is. But as Helen pointed out, that stereotype is not the whole story of amateur theatre. (And my response is: even if it was, SO WHAT? Does that theatre have no value in itself? And, lo, I find myself circling back to the earlier argument about old people.)

Stereotypes cause other problems in amateur theatre; you could call them 'barriers to collaboration'. One that Helen defined is the perception of amateur theatre as middle class, but in her view, participation is more of a spectrum, there can be a good class mix; in towns and villages, it's often *not* the middle class who participate.

'One of the most moving experiences I had was in a bungalow, in a suburban house outside London, watching a group of plumbers and electricians rehearsing *Journey's End* in a conservatory. To see them taking that play really seriously in that context was very moving. When Arts Councilly people talk about "hard to reach" groups, the least likely to access the arts are white, middle-aged working-class men, and there they were.'

Michael Boyd, former artistic director of the Royal Shakespeare Company, agreed that it's a cliché to say it's all middle class. For him, it goes along with the received idea that the amateur theatre is culturally twenty-five years behind professional theatre. 'In some areas I would say it's ahead of professional theatre, for instance in its relationship with its audience. It has certainly been ahead in its relationship to docudrama and factual, reported reality shows. The catalyst might be a professional artist from outside, but the appetite and the energy for the project has come from the community.'

So we can dismiss the class perception. 'But it is predominantly white,' Helen said. 'We found two things. Firstly, it tends to thrive in towns and villages, where the demographic is not as culturally mixed. Secondly, a lot of people join am-dram by word of mouth, and that revealed the segregation of society more broadly.'

If the continuation of amateur theatre is reliant on personal relationships and introductions, and no one is including or inviting black and minority ethnic people, nothing will change. And for theatre communities to diversify meaningfully, it takes more than one BAME person being a role model or exemplar, because that's an impossible ask of any individual. To be clear: one black person does not diversity make. And it's not the responsibility of black people to invite more black people – that is not inclusion. It's so infuriating when the answer is always that it's the responsibility of the excluded group. My other love, swimming, is a comparable example. The engagement with swimming in black communities has a much lower take-up. It's not that black people *can't* swim (as per that racist trope), it's that they often *don't*, for social, cultural and financial reasons. You look at a group of swimmers – they are disproportionately white, because of those historical exclusions of BAME communities. What then happens is that assumptions and leaps of understanding are made, some of which, but not all, are racist. You look at a group of amateur actors – it's the same. Every time a person 'reads' that situation and decrees that black people don't swim, or don't do amateur theatre, for *reasons*, it perpetuates the status quo. Instead, we need to change that situation, by outreach, by role models (plural), by shifting the parameters of how things are organised, who we talk to, and how.

It might come down to simple, and obvious, maths in the end, though. There is more integration in more mixed communities; diverse amateur theatre exists in diverse communities. That is reflected in the *Our Creative Talent* statistics, which show that of the 5.9 million arts participants, 97,100 are BAME, which translates to 2 per cent of average group participation. In London that goes up to 10 per cent, while the North-East is the least diverse, at 0.3 per cent. 'It's not amateur theatre that's gatekeeping, I think it's society that is divided,' Helen Nicholson said, though she added that she felt it 'shifting and changing. It's a social shift that needs to generate a cultural shift.' But it's a long haul.

To find out how it feels to be part of the shift Helen described, I asked actor Raagni Sharma about her amateur experience. 'I love am-dram,' she said. 'I'll fly the flag for it.' She found it by chance when she was unwell, full of anxiety and depression, spending weeks on end in her bedroom with the curtains closed and not in school. 'One of the doctors asked, "So what do you like to do? What could help you leave the house?" I told him I like to act but I don't know anything I could do, and he said, "Why don't you do amateur dramatics?" I looked online, and I saw that Belmont Theatre

had auditions for *Rebecca*, and thought, that sounds interesting. And I got the part of the second Mrs de Winter and
it helped me so much, that play, it got me into acting professionally now. It saved me, at that point. I could be a different
person, and that contrast was a real joy for me. A light in a
very dark time.'

Raagni went off to university to do biology, still holding
on to her desire to act, and once she'd graduated, auditioned
for an amateur production of *Proof*. She got the role of
Catherine, played by Gwyneth Paltrow in the film, and won a
local 'best actress' award. 'It was a great role, and it was generally very well received,' she said. But one critic's reaction upset
her, and when she told me about it, I could see that it was
still painful.

The play had got a fantastic review, including this great
mention for Raagni: 'Raagni, taking on the central character
of the play, performed her role with strength and intelligence
– her timing and reactions were excellent and she certainly
held my attention throughout.' So far so good. But then came
this: 'there was an imbalance between the two sisters which
was unhelpful given that the crux of the play was about the
genes we inherit from our parents.' The 'imbalance' the
reviewer was referring to is the colour of the two actors' skin.
One sister was white, and Raagni is a woman of colour. The
reviewer continued down this road. 'Yes, I understand the
problems of casting in amateur theatre which can be limiting
and yes, I understand the need to give everyone an opportunity
based on talent – but nonetheless, [it was] distracting.'

If it was difficult for me, and perhaps you, to read that, imagine how it felt for Raagni. It was all very Quentin Letts. Her casting, her ethnicity, had become a problem, her race, a distraction. The reviewer was happy to believe the characters were in Chicago, Raagni pointed out, she was happy to believe all sorts of things – but Raagni's skin colour was something she could not get over. 'I remember being so sad. The fact she wrote about it being "limiting". To me that read that they cast an Asian actress because they couldn't find a better white actress, whereas in the professional world, of course they'd have found someone better.'

'All groups consider themselves open and inclusive,' *Our Creative Talent* states. But that 'consider themselves' is doing a lot of obfuscating and could be described as disingenuous. If my neighbour says something racist, but 'considers herself' not racist, that doesn't mean she's not racist. And while Raagni is really happy to 'fly the flag' for amateur drama, because it gave her roles and experience she was unlikely to get in professional theatre, this example makes it clear that 'barriers to collaboration' exist both on the stage and off it. If we're asking why amateur theatre isn't more diverse, the answer, in Raagni's experience, lies with that review more than with her onstage experience. The theatres were happy to cast her, for her talent. The reviewer found her race a 'distraction'. That is not acceptable.

Michael Boyd agreed that there is a lot of work to be done on diversity in the amateur world. 'In the professional world, I think it's moving quite well now. Amateur theatre, though, probably is still pretty white.' Under Michael's guidance, the RSC put on a major festival of amateur theatre around the time of the Olympics, and the fact that one of our biggest artistic institutions chose to collaborate with amateur theatre was a fantastic seal of approval. I asked him why they'd decided to do it. First, he put it into context. 'One question I was asking myself was how can the RSC be a national theatre, from a small market town in Warwickshire, and also, how can it be a community theatre.' Historically, the RSC had held residencies, for instance in Newcastle, but it was felt that was beginning to run out of steam and specialness. 'Where we could potentially cover the whole nation was through our Education Department. They were the part of the RSC that, day in, day out, was dealing with the real nation, a complete cross-section of all income groups, all ethnicities, everything, including those who were perhaps culturally, as a community, slightly antipathetic towards theatre.'

Michael and his team concentrated on working with schools, those 'with a high proportion of free school meals. That was the way we identified them.' It was important for him that the RSC moved away from the sharp-elbowed, 4x4-driving 'filtered nation' who'd always be front of the queue to buy tickets. The world of privilege. His priorities lay with the 93 per cent who don't go to private school.

'We were reaching, for instance, some members of the Islamic communities in Birmingham. It's not in their habit, but they'd come to see their kids. These were kids who were getting no encouragement, and possibly discouragement from their parents, but they were getting much more buy-in from their parents thereafter, and it was great. Then we started discussing the idea of a community project that, at a time of celebrating what Britishness or Englishness might mean in 2012, was addressing head-on the tremendous strength of the amateur theatre movement.'

It was so good to hear Michael use the words 'tremendous strength'. Another seal of approval. What he said also raised the question of whether amateur theatre is intrinsically part of 'Britishness', and answered with what I heard as a resounding 'yes'. It was a question that other people had found harder to answer; I'd found it tricky myself, when I'd travelled to FEATS and to Marbella. Often, and certainly currently, notions of national identity, of Englishness and Britishness, are brandished most aggressively by members of the right and the far right, with their rallying cries and their racism and their in-your-face insistence about what being 'truly' English means. As I've said before, I feel no allegiance to the flag of St George, perhaps because those people claim such angry ownership of it; I'm much more interested in definitions of Englishness and Britishness that are inclusive, progressive and fluid. But finding it difficult to define what our national identity might *be* doesn't stop us from deciding what it might *contain*. The Olympic opening ceremony, those glorious few hours, had set out to show what Britishness might include: everything from black cabs to the NHS, from a literary heritage and James Bond, to 'grit and determination' and industry, and our incredible pop culture. And now, the RSC was adding amateur theatre to the list. Of course, nobody is consciously doing am-dram because 'it's part of my national identity'. It's not an overt motivation. But it is part of it, whether people realise it or not. The RSC was formalising that.

Then came the next part of the RSC's process. They hired Ian Wainwright to travel the country, make the contacts within the amateur world and see what kind of a body of work was out there. According to Michael, he was amazed. 'There were amateur groups working in the armed forces and with veterans from the forces. There were groups associated maybe with a shop they worked in, a business they worked in, as well as youth groups and the more traditional middle-class neighbourhood amateur theatres.'

The RSC had found what I'd found: amateurs, everywhere. They decided to hold a major festival of work from all over Britain; it was a tremendous success, the quality of the work was extremely high and the legacy has lived on. Now, amateurs grab the chance to work with the RSC whenever they offer workshops and courses and space. That the beloved RSC take them seriously counts for an awful lot.

I asked Michael if he felt amateurs learned from professionals; he was clear it was a two-way street. Firstly, our old friend double ontology. That conspiratorial relationship between amateur actor and audience is 'an ambition for complicity' which makes for good theatre. 'And there was a direct energy and a kind of entrepreneurial shrewdness on the part of the amateur companies, because of course they're working with no subsidy whatsoever, that we could learn from.' What professionals could offer amateurs was more obvious. '"Here's a really up-to-date lighting board, this is how it works."' And the discipline of a rehearsal room when you're being paid money. You really do turn up and you really do work hard while you're there and you maintain an intensity of focus that is sustained.'

I haven't seen evidence that amateurs don't work hard, I said, a touch defensively. He was prosaic. 'People have lives, they sometimes don't turn up.' And I remembered my immediate experience with *Variation on a Theme*, remembered that sometimes shows are difficult to cast and have to go off half cocked, and I quietly concurred.

We have this thriving amateur culture as the backbone to our country, and we accept that it is part of our national identity. But asking people *why* amateur theatre has come to be our 'thing' had proved to be a conversation-stopper in the past, and I initially thought it had stopped Michael, too. But it turned out he has an enviable skill of not speaking until he's thought about the answer, and then when he does speak, he does it in beautiful sentences not peppered with all the ums and ers and likes and stumbles that trip other people (me) up. After a silence, he replied, 'You could argue that there have been two major cultural moments in the life of the country that did serious damage to received popular, shared culture. One was the Reformation, with its sweeping away of the rituals surrounding the Catholic Church, the liturgy, the behaviours and sometimes even the quasi-dramatic. Songs, images, festival days. And the other being the Industrial Revolution, which uprooted people and put them in an urban context, separated from a daily, monthly, annual reality that would remind them of these rituals.'

Michael Johnston had reminded me of this in Kilmuckridge, where a sense of seasonal ritual was still alive. 'Possibly local theatre has picked up some of the slack left by that,' Boyd continued. 'It's provided an avenue for self-expression. I think finding a space for communal, shared expression is intrinsic to being human. A sharing of stories.'

Creating space and telling stories – that's what we're doing, in all of this. Amateur theatre is where we come to quench our need. The need for call and response, for communicating together, for ritual and community. The idea that it's part of a historic timeline is humbling and compelling magic.

I asked the same question – why is amateur theatre our thing? – of Helen Nicholson. Where Michael cited the Reformation and the Industrial Revolution, she saw it as coming from the Restoration. 'When Italy did opera,' she said, 'Britain did theatre, quite bawdy theatre often.' We do love being bawdy – be it saucy postcards, *Carry On* or burlesque. (I say 'we', I'm somewhat less of a fan.) Being a theatre academic, Helen is obviously aware of all the antecedents to the Restoration, all the mystery plays and the guilds, and so on. But she is not convinced it's a straightforward, linear development. 'I think there are moments of theatrical invention. And habit. Once it's there it perpetuates.' It becomes tradition through repetition; and what we choose to repeat reveals something about who we are. But all the things you find in theatre – can you not find them in football too? What is it about theatre that is particular? 'In theatre, there are multiple jobs to do. Lighting, costume, that sense of a shared endeavour towards something that is imagined, and fictional. That relationship between the multiple craft skills is really significant.'

Does the amateur theatre exist because it's 'tradition'? I asked Lucy Neal. Do we keep joining in just because it's there? She told me about taking a Spanish artist to the grand hall of Battersea Arts Centre on the day of a bazaar. 'It was thumping. Gorgeous. I was asking her if she'd noticed differences, in terms of civic life. "I think you have, in Britain, many, many more civic charities and groupings and clubs," and as she said that, we walked into a physical manifestation of what she was talking about. So, I think some of the amateur life does come from that. Civic engagement. People step out of their door and join in with something. It is how British society knits itself, in the layers of gatherings.'

There's also what Lucy called 'deadline magic'. The pressure of time, working towards a set deadline, creates an energy and buzz that is very particular to theatre. Everyone is focused on it. 'To keep coming back to rehearsal, learning your lines, being nervous – it's fun. Whatever adversities and challenges you're facing in your life, fun is going to help you stay connected to the energy of other people.' And to think, people describe it simply as 'putting on a play' . . .

'The theatre is about being somebody else. I might be acting, or in the lighting box; either place gives me a different sort of identity,' Helen said. That doesn't stop once you leave the theatre; you carry around the idea that you also have a creative identity. It's how you're seen – and being 'seen' has a power not to be underestimated. 'It comes back to the process of making and making-do.' The craft process creates community and creates sociability and that is a really important part of it.'

For James Pidgeon, there's a level of risk in theatre. 'I think you either have it or you don't, in your blood, to embrace that.' This physical metaphor feels appropriate for such a physical activity. 'It fascinates me why people do land on something cultural,' he said. 'It extends beyond sport because of the inclusivity and accessibility of it.' *Why* do they though? I persisted annoyingly. 'I don't think there's one answer. We are a creative nation, and this is how our creativity shows itself.'

There's also a cross-generational aspect. Theatre brings people together from across ages – where else, for instance, would a 26-year-old Jim, playing Ron in *Variation on a Theme*, have worked with my 87-year-old mother? It's like an apprenticeship: layers of expertise passed on from generation to generation that give people a sense of identity and belonging. They might have different perspectives, but are united because all the focus is on the play. It's possible to be in the same room as someone who voted Brexit, in other words, and not want to push them off a cliff. Get to know them as people, not as collections of beliefs or ideas. Finding shared purpose has driven humans since ... well, since they flooded out of churches to watch Bible stories brought to life. Since they sat round fires and watched John play a captured boar. Since forever.

Lucy Neal told me a story about her great-great-aunt, Mary Neal, whose work was in revitalising English folk songs so working-class girls could understand their heritage. She had a falling-out with Cecil Sharp, and he accused her, publicly, of being an amateur. 'She stood tall. "YES! I am an amateur! I am an amateur in the truest sense of the word!" Because to be amateur is to be part of this proud tradition of what our cultural inheritance is. And it is that we are people and we learn from each other and we exchange our songs, and our singing and dancing comes from love of the world, the universe we are in. Our feet stamping on the earth is how we say I am here. I am taking part. I am connected. These are my songs, these are my people.'

Amateur theatre is our collective feet, stamping on stages, using words that we've passed down and down, until the pages they're written on have become tattered with use.

Let's end on money. Greg Giesekam writes in *Luvvies and rude mechanicals?* that 'it should be acknowledged that many amateur groups make a substantial contribution to their local communities', and he means, I think, artistically, socially *and* financially. Alongside the more abstract notions of 'place-making', this is one aspect that is definable. We can count cash. 'The annual turnover of amateur societies [in Scotland] is approximately £6.8 million,' which is not a sum to be trifled with. Local money pours out, local money pours in. Ticket income is spent on hiring halls, and making costumes, and buying set-building materials, and licensing plays, and replacing bulbs and roofs, and renting chairs and stocking bars. The better condition a hall is kept in, the more it can accrue from hire. There's knock-on gain for all sorts of local businesses. The amateur theatre sector may have been maligned and sidelined, Amber Massie-Blomfield said, 'But people are increasingly aware of a) the scale of it, how many millions of people are involved, and b) the economics of it. The size of budgets lots of amateur theatres have. In cold economic terms it is undervalued.'

'Arts and culture have a key role in regenerating communities,' stated the *Our Creative Talent* report, using off-putting phrases like 'urban capital development' and 'strategic regeneration initiatives'. 'Embedded in grass roots, voluntary arts has a deeper, fundamental role to play,' not least in 'creating demand for facilities'. I could hear the cash registers ringing once again. But I also feel a great big 'oh fuck off' when money is invoked, even when it is me doing the invoking. Because money changes how we view creativity. As Helen Nicholson, Nadine Holdsworth and Jane Milling write, in an article called 'Theatre, Performance and the Amateur Turn' published in the *Contemporary Theatre Review*, 'the creative economy means creativity is valued when it's operationalised for explicitly economic benefits and outcomes. Amateur creativity is not valued in this rubric, except as a training ground for future employment.' And amateurs clearly *should* be valued, in financial terms alone. The fact that they make money is significant!

Helen rounded it off succinctly. 'All the cultural values can go to hell,' she said, with the kind of bluntness I love. The whys and the wherefores, the digging into national and personal identity, can ultimately all bog off. Because, she said, 'when you think about the hundreds of thousands of people who, year in, year out, put on amateur productions without any government support, and no cultural recognition, they manage to do it and create a sense of purpose for themselves, a sense of identity, of joy. And without professionals going in to transform and empower them. That seems to be a really important thing.' She is right. Let's not lose sight, amid all the rhetoric and the cash-counting and the theorising, that this is a joyful thing we're doing. Just being busy, being human.

CHAPTER 18

Final Curtain Call

Two weeks later, I am back at Highbury for the last night of *Variation on a Theme* and I am anxious. The first-night performance had been . . . not great. There's no other way to butter them parsnips but committing it to print still feels like a harsh judgement. Every night since then, while I have sat on my sofa at home worrying, the actors have kept getting back onstage and kept doing the work. As someone who's more likely to change her name and move county than face doing something difficult, I am full of admiration for them. Getting up and going again is one thing. Doing that, in front of people who have paid money to see you do it, is not a situation I would have handled with any grace.

Tonight, I am watching the play from back where I started hundreds of years ago. I am up in the sound and lighting box, this time perched on a chair behind a guy called Andrew, who's operating the show single-handedly. Things have moved on. This time, I accessed the box via a conventional door, rather than up a ladder through a hole in the floor, and neither Andrew nor I smoke throughout the play, as my dad would have done. And it all has less of a Professor Branestawm/Heath Robinson feel than it used to have 'in my day', if you'll excuse me going all Werther's Originals. Now, there is slick black technology, sliders that move smoothly and quietly, and discreet columns of lights from monitors flickering up and down in the corner. The production noises, those distinctive and satisfyingly meaty clicks of the Revox buttons you pressed firmly as you came to a sound cue, have been replaced by the subtle click of a mouse. Where I was once the most modern thing in here, now I am the least. The need for watchful silence, however, is the same as it ever was.

In the box, Andrew leans forward, presses a button and speaks smoothly into a mic, making the announcements to front of house. 'Ladies and gentlemen, tonight's performance will begin in five minutes.' I settle in, do my final bits of shuffling round, and watch as the last of the audience file in. My anxiety rises. I breathe out slowly. The ushers close the doors to the auditorium, Andrew waits for his cue to start from the stage manager, then brings the house lights down, the opening music up and, for the last time, we begin.

As Andrew is sitting in front of me, my view of the stage is obscured by his back, bowed over the equipment; his focus is intense as he follows the book. A memory: tracing the lines on a script with my finger as the actors said them, eyes constantly flicking up to the stage, down to the page, on alert for a highlighted section that told me to cue something, hit something, start something. You hear a play so differently when you're tracking it line by line, cutting it into tiny chunks of concentration. You don't really 'watch' a play, when you're working on it, but it still goes in; you get an instinct for when the pace is right. You know when there's a long speech, or a tricky bit coming up that requires every bit of your attention. You know when there's a page or two where you can take a breath. You know if things are going well or badly, and you know what a nightmare it is when actors skip pages, come to cues too early or too late, or fail to come on at all. If that happens, it requires instant decision-making from you, maybe even some reparative action that you hope will convey a message to the cast onstage – here, it's this bit now. Obviously, that's not something exclusive to amateur theatre, the 'missing out two pages and hoping the crew will catch on pretty quickly' thing. We've all seen things on the professional stage where it's clear an actor has entirely skipped a speech, or someone's forgotten it's their turn to speak, and an uneasy silence falls, other actors trying to say 'it's you now' with their widened eyes or purposeful glares. Remember my experience of watching the venerable actor on the West End stage? That night, the audience could feel – or at least I could – the tension of the cast around her, silently asking each other: Who is going to pick up this dropped ball? Who is going to dig us out of this? And their nerves transferred to us, the audience, suddenly aware how quickly the contract we'd made could fall apart. Everything onstage, good and bad, requires the response of a technical crew offstage; sitting here on this last night of the play makes me remember that backstage work is *work*. This part of a performance is as important as what you're watching, and it's often sorely overlooked. I remember too what Hilary Jennings said, how 'amateur theatre is so bonding because it's one of the few times in life where everybody involved has adrenaline'. Up in this sound box, my adrenaline certainly flows. I am pumped with it, and now I have to sit still and be quiet.

Tonight is also Bonfire Night; the first half of the play is punctuated by the distant whiz-bangs of fireworks, and my attention keeps flitting off and out into the cold Sutton night. These things happen. It matters less that I am distracted, and more that the cast are not. We are coming to the end of something – this immediate experience, and my journey. More than anything, I want the landing to be smooth.

In the two weeks that I've been at home on the sofa, something has shifted. I could feel it when I went into the green room beforehand and the cast were ad-libbing in character. A good sign. A backstage crew member came in waving a piece of paper. 'You got a review,' he said, and it got handed round, everybody reading it silently, tensely scanning for their own mention, then relaxing and sharing snippets out loud, with smiles. When it was pinned on the blue felt noticeboard, I wandered casually over to look at it, don't mind me, and I was relieved to see it was good, every actor was praised, as well as the set. Readers were being urged to go. I was delighted.

Around me, the cast were starting to be nostalgic already. 'I'll miss it,' said Sean, a bit ruefully, 'the people.'

The play starts, and onstage the shift is more obvious. If I say 'the magic has happened' it would suggest that things have come together by the wave of a wand, rather than by relentless hard work and determination. But the *play* has happened. They've got there. The cast are relaxed, and when that happens, things can go beyond words on a page. They can live. A look, a gesture, a smile, some fun even. All the angst and uncertainty has disappeared, and once the lines start to flow, there is something entirely different being created up there. It has become what it should have been at the start, if the pieces had slotted into place more smoothly. We can see their talent at last, feed off their energy. It feels conversational and spontaneous, and yes, it is a paradox that more time and rehearsal can make it feel like that. And with all of this, the play itself unfolds in front of me. The skill of Rattigan is revealed, his variations on a theme. Once I stop worrying about whether they know the lines, I start to hear them properly. I start to get what he meant. The relationships between characters are unfolding, the dynamics; the flirtations and the frustrations become evident. It becomes a story, confidently told. And I think: perhaps I took all my concerns out on the writer. Really, I should have known better.

Because the cast are relaxed and having fun, the audience are too; they've given us permission; it translates from the stage across to the auditorium. Of course, most of this audience have no idea of how bumpy the flight has been. They've got on the plane for the last leg of the journey, they don't need to know about the storms we've flown through. They just see what is happening now, on this particular night. But while this audience can be in the moment, I carry the story. I know that this really has been a process, a flight that has taken off later than its allotted time. But for tonight, I am able to forget about the miles they've travelled and just enjoy flying. I'm still tense though, up in the sound box. There is no let-up on that until the final curtain falls.

I am the first to leave the post-show party, which is exactly as it should be. I've been an observer all along, and they've tolerated me even when things were really difficult. For this bit of it, the cast really don't need observing. It's hard to relax when there's a sober person in the corner with her notebook, mysteriously jotting things down, and anyway, what would I have jotted? 'Jim drinks a cider'? 'Sean is a Martini man'? (Sean is *absolutely* a Martini man, I would put money on it. I'd also put money on the bar not serving Martinis.) And perhaps it is a good job I leave when I do, because as I head to the car park, I start to feel a bit emotional. Following this play through from familiarisation to tonight, the last night, hasn't gone exactly as I'd thought it would. I haven't, for instance, been required to step into a role, stunning everyone with my talent. ('Who'd have thought it? She looks so ordinary.') I'm sure it hasn't gone as Highbury had hoped either, when they agreed that I could follow them. I know from conversations with Mum that she felt caught in the middle, wanting to protect her beloved theatre from the cruel pen of the truth-seeking writer, her daughter. Highbury had wanted to show me their best, and what I saw, what I've recorded, was a more bloody, painful journey. I witnessed some failing before the final success. Letting someone record that is brave, from any company's perspective, and I am really grateful. But actually, in the travails, I think I learned more. How people really strive, in every detail, over long, long hours. How to get up, when you've been pushed down. Resilience, grit and determination. The phoenix! (Here I go again, with the theatrics). But whatever I'd hoped for, I hadn't expected what I feel now, as I go home. I hadn't expected to care so damn much. I'd forgotten how bonding it all was, and how that bonding really grabs you, even if you're just an observer, even if you're resolutely determined that it won't happen. I thought, what an absolute privilege it has been, to take part with these people. The way they had allowed me to wander in and snoop around, to ask my questions, to sit and watch them as they tried and tried again, worked and worked. Telling them they were wrong about the word 'amateur' and the colour of the wine bottle; poking my nose right into the minutiae of their lives, making notes on every detail. I think how impressive they are, in their openness, their inclusion, their absolute dedication. To a stupid, neglected play! To performing in a small local theatre! To all of this. It is a good job I didn't stay. I might have given an embarrassing, impromptu speech, and I might have cried.

The Highbury experience has reminded me of everything I'd had when I was growing up there. It has reminded me viscerally of my dad. Though he is never forgotten – I still see him sometimes, randomly, on the street, wearing the pale blue-lined jacket he was particularly fond of – it has brought him roaringly back to life, the very smell of him. He pervades everything again, like he did when he was alive. He is right beside me. It reminds me, too, of the bonds I formed years ago, particularly with three of the people from that *Sutton Coldfield News* photo from August 1980: Adrian Middleton, Mike Agnew and Michael Browne, now Sherwin (his professional stage name). I think I will test those bonds, see if they stretched this far, from 1980 to now. So I make contact with them. When I meet Michael Sherwin, the only one of us working as an actor, he and I fall into it straight off. 'You look the same!' we say simultaneously, as he comes out of a West End stage door after his matinee. He takes me to the Ivy, round the corner, where he is a member and I am not, we have a cup of tea together, and reminisce. He remembers being dragged along to Highbury's youth theatre, and how 'someone said "let's do some impro" and I legged it'. We've all felt that about impro, most of us just from an audience perspective. Michael stayed at Highbury until he went to Birmingham Drama School, but had still gone back there, like I had, in his school summer holidays. 'The best play I ever did was with your dad,' he says. 'Your dad was brilliant.' I smile, a bit chuffed – Dad would've liked that compliment. I text my sister on my way home from our meeting. 'I met Michael Browne!' 'Can he stride yet?' she texts back, remembering how we used to tease him. 'He can,' I reply.

I meet Mike Agnew for a lunchtime pint after he'd given a class in musical theatre at a drama school nearby, and we too are straight back to our teenage years. He's now dating someone we were at school with. Mike had been the one I'd first got drunk with, on pints of whisky in Highbury bar lock-ins. 'In some ways Highbury was like church,' he says. 'My religion was theatre.' It's a feeling I've already expressed and it's funny to have it presented back to me. Mike had gone to Guildford Drama School, and on to a career behind the camera, as a well-respected TV light entertainment director. As we drink, sitting on a pub bench on a busy London street, I recall our first whisky hangovers, they seem a million miles away, and at the same time, right there within reach.

I speak to Adrian Middleton via Facebook. He describes his life now as 'a glorious state of semi-retirement', in a 'rural idyll' on Dartmoor with his husband Pat. My timing, contacting him, was bang on. 'Funnily enough,' he says, 'we've got involved with the local am-dram society. Last year we wrote the songs and I directed a musical about assisted dying called *Killing Elsa*.' I remember his prodigious piano-playing skills, how I'd watch him, with a tiny regret that I chose *The Flintstones* over my own piano lessons. 'The writer had heard that we both used to work in the theatre and that we were musicians. Originally he just wanted advice about the script which turned into writing the songs followed closely by the director pulling out and me reluctantly taking on that role too.' These sound like familiar am-dram tactics – find someone's skillset and exploit them fully. 'As it happens it was great fun and a great success locally and sold out every night.' We have to end our conversation when Ade needs to go and water his greenhouse, something I would not have predicted, decades ago.

I tested the bonds, and they stretched exactly far enough. We recognised each other, we reminisced. There was fondness, but no pretence that we should all put on a show, just like the old days, because we'd all moved on. But the foundations were solid, and that was all the reassurance I needed. It had meant something, to us all. I wasn't making that bit up.

When I'd gone to Questors and spoken to the artistic director, Alex Marker, I'd asked him a big question: what is Questors' future? His answer usefully painted a very complete picture of where *all* amateur theatre stands, and where it could potentially go, hitting points others have made to me along the way, and wrapping everything up neatly.

'The professional theatre scene has grown; it shows that theatre is very much alive. Participants have an infinitely wider choice of what they can do on a Saturday night, so amateur theatre is facing greater competition. But I think there is hope.' (Hurrah! I certainly don't want to end feeling pessimistic.) 'The digital revolution runs the risk of making us more isolated, removes us from the process of actually making something. Yet there has been an explosion in festivals, craft groups, baking and making; people seeking "live" rather than purely online experiences. Drama is about contact. Its fundamental strength is that it is local, it is of the community and it is participatory. Engaging with the moods, hopes and concerns of those who make up your local community – this is, perhaps, where amateur theatre can take its next cue from. At a time when arts funding is dwindling, drama is gradually evaporating from the curricula and councils are having to cut all but essential local services, amateur theatre is ideally placed as an activity to bring people together.'

In offering a vision for his own theatre, Alex expressed so much hope and potential that his words could become a future manifesto for all of them.

All the questions I've asked about myself throughout this process: am I going to fit in here? am I going to find myself? what will this bring me? All the memories that have come trickling back, from being accidentally whipped onstage, to the glory of my dad's laugh. In the end, it's not about these questions, or these memories. It's about the amateur theatricals, all of them. It's about the sheer bloody hard work from every single cast member of *Variation on a Theme*. It's about Barbara Hughes, who reminded me that amateur theatre can be a healing space, and Mic Wright, who shared that it can save a life. About Hilary Jennings, who showed that it can be a place of community, to find your people, whatever role you choose to take; Raagni Sharma, for whom it gave opportunity, self-confidence and experience; Hannah Maxwell and Brenda Gilhooley, showing that it can be a gateway to expressing yourself how you choose. About Noel Rands, who took it wherever he went, and the people at FEATS, who still do. It's about Rob and Ros Jones, who showed that it can bring enduring love alongside all the pleasure, and Michael Johnston in Kilmuckridge, for whom it proved, in adversity, that it can be as good as any family. It's about the wonderful Josephine Hinde, who reminded me to take care of our memories, and that the simple act of listening can be immeasurable.

We can count the contributions that amateur theatre makes to its communities, we can count the money, we can count the plays and the players. We can eulogise about 'place-making' and storytelling, and what performance gives you, in life and work. We can talk academically about the national repertoire, fret about national identity, and worry for the future of younger generations, in a country that doesn't value the humanities because they are hard to monetise.

But one word has rung through all of this: joy. It has been repeated by everyone I've met. We can't quantify joy, and we can't force it. It's just there, going about its business. If we don't value amateur theatre, then we don't value joy. If something brings you joy, it's adding immensely to your experience of being human, and why on earth should that remain hidden, or demeaned, or devalued? Celebrate it. Yell it. Make plays about it.

I'll come back to Simon Callow one last time.

'In the amateur theatre, love is all you need. All the same requirements apply to the professional theatre as to the amateur. But you're doing it for love. You don't have to make a living out of it, you're not putting yourself up again and again to be knocked down. You have a great and golden opportunity, you have time, you have facilities, you have numbers on your side. You have the opportunity, as you always have done, to show a much more civilised side of theatre, which is based simply on love.'

Love and joy. These essential human things, absolutely abounding in amateur theatre. If you're in it, you already know that. And if you're not? Well, I'm not sure what you're waiting for. Break a leg.

My dad in Henrik Ibsen's *The Doll's House* at Highbury in 1981, which was to be one of his last performances.

Epilogue

I am on the phone to my mum, same as we are every Monday and Friday at 6 p.m., a ritual established at a time when calls got cheaper at 6 p.m. 'What are you doing tonight?' she asks me. Going to the theatre, I reply, to see *Equus*, I've never seen it. 'Never seen it?' she says, in disbelief. 'Did you not see me in *Equus*? I played the mother. Ward Young was my husband.' I probably wasn't allowed to when you were in it, I say to her. 'I suppose not,' she says. 'It is a bit . . .' Don't tell me, I say, I want it to be a surprise. 'Oh, it will be,' she says. 'I hope you enjoy it.'

I sit in the theatre that night, watching this very well-known play that I've managed to miss my whole life, even the Daniel Radcliffe production. (Or maybe *especially* the Daniel Radcliffe production.) About halfway through the first act, I am struck with a feeling of utter pointlessness. I realise: I absolutely do not give a shit about this production, this evening. One thing *has* snared my attention: I'm amused to see that the height differential between my mum and Ward

Young (she very short, he very tall) is the same between the actors playing those roles in this cast. In tonight's 'mother' I can see my mum in her younger years, and I enjoy that little memory connection. But apart from that – I feel nowt. I've become so immersed in the world of amateur theatre that there is something missing from this professional production. I am missing that feeling of engagement. There is not even a single ontology. I don't care about anyone in the cast, or the fancy staging, and I'm not invested in the story. I simply am not bringing myself to it, and it isn't bringing anything to me. The only thing I keep doing is thinking about how Highbury would have staged it when Mum was in it. Tonight, the 'horses' are played by a group of beautiful young people, and all they make me think is 'well, Highbury would have found that a bugger to cast'. I think: I've changed. Amateur theatre has changed me. And: this is not a bad thing.

A few months later – one day after I've handed in the first draft of this book so possibly looking a bit bug-eyed and hunched – I go back to Highbury to talk about what I've learned about amateur theatre while writing about it, at a Little Theatre Guild conference. The place is packed with people from theatres all over the country, I am doing my talk in that same room upstairs, the Upper Foyer, where I'd nearly expired from heat on the familiarisation day. Mum comes with me to the talk, she introduces me to people. In the theatre foyer, Les, who I'd met at the work party, has an exhibition of his calligraphy.

At the end of the day, after my talk, I feel my conclusion land. I realise something. There have been months of writing and thinking about amateur theatre, questioning what I feel about it, and what I want from it. 'Are you going to end up coming back to amateur theatre?' Hilary Jennings had asked me. I'd compared it to cold-water swimming, wondering why I was dandling on the edge, and not throwing myself in. And when the answer suddenly bubbles to the surface, it is so blindingly obvious it's almost embarrassing.

It would be so *neat* to report that I've joined an amateur group and I'm back onstage, that south London is ringing to the sound of applause for my magnificence. But neat isn't true.

What *is* true is that I have, actually, found my role. Much like a play, it needed time to emerge, and much like an audience, I needed it to end before I could really see it in its entirety. My role is this one. I'm an observer, scribbling notes in a carefully chosen notebook, then writing this book. (You see? Embarrassingly obvious.) Writing is my role. And it's the perfect one for me. It just took a lot of years, and this process, for me to see it.

Acknowledgements

There were a few people who kept me going writing this book. Firstly, and particularly, I owe big thanks to Wendy Lee and Jackie O'Farrell, for being early readers and fantastic supporters in every way. Thank you to John O'Farrell, Sheetal Sharma, Dayna Winer, Martin Pople, Tara Duffy, Lee Randal, Nina Davies, Justin Lewis, Alistair Petrie, Caitlin Finnegan Vaughan, my three sisters and my book club ladies. Thank you to all the people at Highbury who were welcoming and supportive, particularly Alison Cahill, the cast and crew of *Variation on a Theme* and Sandy Haynes.

Thanks to David Simpkin, Sally Stevens, Hilary Jennings, Tony Childs, Jane at amdram.co.uk, Lucy Neal, the V&A Theatre Archives, Richard Humphry, Noel Rands, Brian Hocken and Josephine Hinde, June Rendle and Miles Rendle in Marbella, Rob and Ros Jones, Michael Johnston in Kilmuckridge, and everyone who gave me their time and attention. It's much appreciated. Along the way, I had many offers of amateurs wanting to share their experiences with me, and

I'm grateful to them for that, though I've only been able to include a tiny selection.

Thank you so much to my agent, Becky Thomas – you are ace. Always there. And my editor Poppy Hampson – you're ace too.

And a massive thank you to Charlie and Izzy Jo. My beloved two.

The presence of my dad absolutely rang out through the process of writing this book; it was a complete pleasure for me, and an unexpected bonus. Thanks mostly, though, go to my mum. This book is for her.

Bibliography

Books

Simon Callow, *Charles Dickens and the Great Theatre of the World*, 2012, Harper Press

Colin Chambers, *The Story of Unity Theatre*, 1989, Lawrence & Wishart

Michael Dobson, *Shakespeare and Amateur Performance*, 2011, Cambridge University Press

John English and Mollie Randall, *Theatre Arts Centre, A Beginning*, 1947, Highbury Little Theatre

Gwenan Evans and others, *A Few Drops of Water: The Story of the Questors Theatre 1929–1989*, 1989, Mattock Press

Greg Giesekam, *Luvvies and rude mechanicals?: Amateur and community theatre in Scotland*, 2000, Scottish Arts Council

Michael Green, *The Art of Coarse Acting*, 1964, Arrow Books

Nicholas de Jongh, *Politics, Prudery and Perversions*, 2000, Methuen

Amber Massie-Blomfield, *Twenty Theatres to See Before You Die*, 2018, Penned in the Margins

Helen Nicholson, Nadine Holdsworth and Jane Milling, *The Ecologies of Amateur Theatre*, 2018, Palgrave Macmillan

Allardyce Nicoll, *British Drama* (revised edn), 1978, Harrap

Sybil Rosenfeld, *Temples of Thespis*, 1978, Society for Theatre Research

George Taylor, *History of the Amateur Theatre*, 1976, Venton

Reg Tolley, *Memories of a Highbury Ham*, 2005, Highbury Theatre Centre

Dumayne Warne, *Fifty Years of Amateur Theatre*, 1949, NODA

Richard Webb, *Mrs D, The Life of Anne Damer*, 2013, Brewin Books

John N. Young, *A Century of Service*, 1999, NODA

Other publications

E. Martin Browne, 'The British Drama League', *Educational Theatre Journal*, October 1953, Vol. 5, No. 3

David Coates, 'A Whistle Stop Tour of Amateur Theatricals in Nineteenth Century Britain', 2017 lecture, Society for Theatre Research

Fiona Dodd, Andrew Graves and Karen Taws, *Our Creative Talent*, 2013 report for Department for Culture, Media and Sports, and Arts Council England

Rose Fenton, *The Work of Visiting Arts in Iran in the Field of Performing Arts 2001-2005*, 2006, Visiting Arts

Evelyn Howe, 'Amateur Theatre in Georgian England', *History Today*, September 1970, Vol. 20, Issue 9

Dan Rebellato interview with Sarah Kane: www.danrebellato.co.uk

Edwin R. Schoell, 'The Amateur Theatre in Great Britain', *Educational Theatre Journal*, May 1963, Vol. 15, No. 2

Carol Seagrove, *History of the British Theatre Association and Library*, 1994, MA thesis for Loughborough University

Index

penguin.co.uk/vintage